Contention and Democracy in Europe, 1650–2000

Contention and Democracy in Europe, 1650–2000, analyzes relationships between democratization, de-democratization, and contentious politics. Building on recent theoretical innovations, *Contention and Democracy* uses a sustained comparison of French and British histories since 1650 as a springboard for more general comparisons across Europe. It goes on to demonstrate that democratization occurred as a result of struggles during which (as in 19th-century Britain and France) few, if any, of the participants were self-consciously trying to create democratic institutions. Favorable circumstances for democratization, it shows, vary from era to era and region to region as functions of previous history, international environments, available models of political organization, and predominant patterns of social relations. Many reversals – substantial phases of de-democratization – occurred in the European experiences surveyed.

Charles Tilly is Joseph L. Buttenwieser Professor of Social Science at Columbia University. He has previously taught at the University of Delaware, Harvard University, the University of Toronto, the University of Michigan, and the New School for Social Research. He is a member of the National Academy of Sciences, the American Academy of Arts and Sciences, and the American Philosophical Society. Among his many books are three recently published by Cambridge University Press: *Dynamics of Contention* (with Doug McAdam and Sidney Tarrow), *Silence and Voice in the Study of Contentious Politics* (with Ronald Aminzade and others), and *The Politics of Collective Violence*.

To my grandchildren
May they inhabit – and promote – a more democratic world

Cambridge Studies in Contentious Politics

Editors

Doug McAdam   *Stanford University and Center for Advanced Study in the Behavioral Sciences*
Sidney Tarrow   *Cornell University*
Charles Tilly   *Columbia University*

Ronald Aminzade et al., *Silence and Voice in the Study of Contentious Politics*
Jack A. Goldstone, editor, *States, Parties, and Social Movements*
Doug McAdam, Sidney Tarrow, and Charles Tilly, *Dynamics of Contention*
Charles Tilly, *The Politics of Collective Violence*

Contention and Democracy in Europe, 1650–2000

CHARLES TILLY
Columbia University

CAMBRIDGE
UNIVERSITY PRESS

PUBLISHED BY THE PRESS SYNDICATE OF THE UNIVERSITY OF CAMBRIDGE
The Pitt Building, Trumpington Street, Cambridge, United Kingdom

CAMBRIDGE UNIVERSITY PRESS
The Edinburgh Building, Cambridge CB2 2RU, UK
40 West 20th Street, New York, NY 10011-4211, USA
477 Williamstown Road, Port Melbourne, VIC 3207, Australia
Ruiz de Alarcón 13, 28014 Madrid, Spain
Dock House, The Waterfront, Cape Town 8001, South Africa

http://www.cambridge.org

First published 2004

Printed in the United States of America

Typeface Janson Text 10/13 pt.   *System* LʰTEX 2$_\varepsilon$ [TB]

A catalog record for this book is available from the British Library.

Library of Congress Cataloging in Publication Data

Tilly, Charles.
  Contention and democracy in Europe, 1650-2000 / Charles Tilly.
    p.   cm. – (Cambridge studies in contentious politics)
  Includes bibliographical references and index.
  ISBN 0-521-83008-7 – ISBN 0-521-53713-4 (pb.)
    1. Europe – Politics and government.   2. Democracy – Europe.   I. Title.   II. Series.

JN8.T55 2003
320.94 – dc21   2003055122

ISBN 0 521 83008 7 hardback
ISBN 0 521 53713 4 paperback

Contents

Preface

Readers blessed (or cursed) with long memories will recognize that this book enters a territory once traversed majestically by my teacher Barrington Moore, Jr. It differs from Moore's vividly inspiring *Social Origins of Dictatorship and Democracy* by concentrating on democratization and de-democratization, by resisting analyses that pass retroactively from outcome to origin, and by moving from close comparison of Britain and France to explanation of variation over Europe as a whole. Other admirers of Barrington Moore (e.g., Dietrich Rueschemeyer, Evelyne Huber, and John Stephens) have commonly followed him by concentrating on explaining long-run outcomes – why different countries ended up with different sorts of political regimes. Although this book certainly traces the impact of particular histories on contemporary politics, its claim to attention rests instead on the identification of mechanisms and processes that promote, inhibit, or reverse democratization. It concentrates on trajectories rather than origins and destinations. Still, anyone who knows Moore's work will see how his emphasis on political consequences of struggle has carried over into his one-time student's efforts.

Let it be clear that, like Barrington Moore himself, I hold no dewy-eyed vision of actually existing democracies. Except for a few revolutionary moments, I know of no European national regime, past or present, in which a small number of rich and well-connected men – I mean men – did not wield disproportionate influence over the government. In every formally democratic regime of which I am aware, stigmatized minorities have lacked protection from arbitrary governmental action. I regard my own American regime as a deeply flawed democracy that recurrently de-democratizes by excluding significant segments of its population from public politics, by inscribing social inequalities in public life, by baffling popular will, and by failing to offer equal protection to its citizens. In this book "democratic" simply means less undemocratic than most other regimes – escaping to some extent from the petty tyranny and monolithic authoritarianism that have been the two usual forms of government throughout the world over the last 5,000 years.

Let me also signal three difficulties I faced in writing this book: multiple scales, diverse literatures, and subversive explanations. My resolution of those difficulties may bother some readers. First, multiple scales. The book's analyses alternate among very different scales: the European continent as a whole over substantial periods of time, major European regions across centuries, entire countries over periods from twenty to 350 years, particular regions within the same countries (e.g., England, Ireland, and Scotland within the British Isles) during varying lengths of time, particular crises, episodes, and persons at specific points in time. At none of these levels did I assemble continuous, comprehensive evidence for all the relevant units. Once I dug into my investigation, I quickly abandoned an early plan to produce ratings of democratization for all European polities period by period from 1650 to 2000; I realized that the point was not to provide a neat, consistent explanation of a single variable but to follow a complex process across its many levels. As a consequence, the evidence presented shifts scale repeatedly, and remains incomplete at every scale.

Here is the second difficulty. The book draws on the vast and largely separate literatures of European history, democratization, and contentious politics. Specialists in those fields will most likely feel that I have slighted their favorite segments of those literatures, and thus appear to claim more originality for my observations and arguments than they deserve, not to mention avoiding objections that one analyst or another might raise against my descriptions and explanations. I regret that likelihood. But I consider the alternative – full citation and discussion of the relevant literature and its controversies – to be worse. It would produce a book twice as long and twice as dense. Writing a book about all of Europe since 1650, I have necessarily turned repeatedly to published articles, monographs, syntheses, handbooks, and encyclopedias in order to clarify events, to establish chronologies, and to identify places, events, or persons. Except when it seemed that readers would need reassurance or an opportunity to follow up some claim, however, I have cited such publications only when quoting them directly or drawing evidence from them that is not readily available elsewhere.

My decision to reduce citations and discussions of relevant literature also meant resisting the temptation to line up publicly on one side or another of existing controversies. Only practitioners of French history, for example, will easily recognize that Chapter 4 rejects much of the revisionism concerning the French Revolution and its aftermath promoted by my late friend François Furet. (The chapter even revives the idea of a bourgeois revolution, much reviled by a generation of French historians.) Since I have written extensively on European historiography, theories of contentious politics, revolutions, and democratization, readers who want to know where I stand in the big debates should have no trouble looking up my positions. Meanwhile, they will benefit from a less cluttered text in the present book.

My third difficulty concerned subversive explanations. Both common sense and the bulk of social science treat individual dispositions as the fundamental causes of social processes. Culturalists, phenomenologists, behaviorists, and methodological individualists alike converge on reconstruction of dispositions of individuals just before the point of action as the explanations of those individuals' actions, then propose to aggregate individual actions into social processes such as democratization and de-democratization. My years of complaints about the logic of explanation through individual dispositions have, alas, made almost no difference in prevailing practices. Instead of preaching, this book simply subverts prevailing practices, asking readers to consider whether its explanations provide accounts of European democratization and de-democratization superior to those currently on offer.

The book's explanations qualify as subversive in three regards: as first laid out in Tables 1.1 to 1.3, the mechanisms and processes proposed to explain democratization (1) treat dispositions chiefly as outcomes rather than causes, (2) privilege relational over environmental and cognitive mechanisms, and (3) insist that mechanisms such as brokerage operate at the same level as the social processes we are explaining rather than always moving to a more microscopic level on the model of chemical explanations for molecular processes. Even among the minority of social scientists who have developed an enthusiasm for mechanisms as explanations, these three positions qualify as subversive. In writing the book, however, I decided that since my exhortations had been doing little good, it would be better simply to go about my explanatory work and let readers judge the results, subversive or not. As a consequence, I have sometimes compared my explanations with others currently available, but have not wasted words calling attention to competing logics of explanation.

I have also suppressed the urge to expand each argument into questions of conceptualization, measurement, explanation, and theoretical elaboration.

Some of my previous work has, for instance, conceptualized and compared revolutionary processes in painstaking detail, but this book settles for a simple characterization of its revolutions. Readers who feel that I pass too quickly through those terrains can find closely related but more extensive statements in these publications:

1993   *European Revolutions, 1492–1992.* Oxford: Basil Blackwell.

1993   "Contentious Repertoires in Great Britain, 1758–1834." *Social Science History* 17: 253–280.

1995   "Democracy Is a Lake." In George Reid Andrews and Herrick Chapman, eds., *The Social Construction of Democracy.* New York: New York University Press; Basingstoke: Macmillan.

1995   "To Explain Political Processes." *American Journal of Sociology* 100: 1594–1610.

1997   "Parliamentarization of Popular Contention in Great Britain, 1758–1834." *Theory and Society* 26: 245–273.

1998   "Democracy, Social Change, and Economies in Transition." In Joan M. Nelson, Charles Tilly, and Lee Walker, eds., *Transforming Post-Communist Political Economies.* Washington: National Academy Press.

1998   "Armed Force, Regimes, Contention, and Democratization in Europe since 1650." Research Monograph 19, Center for the Study of Democracy, University of California, Irvine; available online at www.democ.uci.edu/democ.

1998   "Regimes and Contention." Columbia International Affairs On-line (CIAO) working paper, www.columbia.edu/sec/dlc/ciao/wps/sites/css.html.

1999   "Why Worry about Citizenship?" In Michael P. Hanagan and Charles Tilly, eds., *Expanding Citizenship, Reconfiguring States.* Lanham, Md.: Rowman & Littlefield.

2000   "Processes and Mechanisms of Democratization." *Sociological Theory* 18: 1–16.

2001   "Mechanisms in Political Processes." *Annual Review of Political Science* 4: 21–41.

2001   (with Doug McAdam and Sidney Tarrow), *Dynamics of Contention.* Cambridge: Cambridge University Press.

2001   "Democracy" (vol. 2), "Collective Action" (vol. 3), and "Social Class" (vol. 3). In Peter N. Stearns, ed., *Encyclopedia of European Social History*, 6 vols. New York: Scribner's.

2001   "Historical Analysis of Political Processes." In Jonathan H. Turner, ed., *Handbook of Sociological Theory*. New York: Kluwer/Plenum.
2001   "Historical Sociology." In *International Encyclopedia of the Behavioral and Social Sciences*. Amsterdam: Elsevier. Vol. 10, pp. 6753–6757.
2001   "Public Violence." In *International Encyclopedia of the Behavioral and Social Sciences*. Amsterdam: Elsevier. Vol. 24, pp. 16206–16211.
2002   "Neuere angloamerikanische Sozialgeschichte." In Günther Lottes and Joachim Eibach, eds., *Kompass der Geschichtswissenschaft*. Göttingen: Vandenhoeck & Ruprecht.
2002   "Event Catalogs as Theories." *Sociological Theory* 20: 248–254.
2002   *Stories, Identities, and Political Change*. Lanham, Md.: Rowman & Littlefield.
2003   *The Politics of Collective Violence*. Cambridge: Cambridge University Press.

Close readers will notice that I have borrowed a number of ideas and facts (e.g., the calendars of revolutionary situations in Chapters 3–5, which come from *European Revolutions*) without attribution from these publications. Again, it would have encumbered the text without profit to provide citations of all my own previous statements on the book's topics. More extensive overlap with previous publications occurs in two circumstances: (1) when I have adapted whole passages from earlier writings and (2) when I have published adaptations from the manuscript as I wrote it. As a result of one circumstance or the other, significant overlaps appear between portions of the book's text and

1992   "Cities, Bourgeois, and Revolution in France." In M'hammed Sabour, ed., *Liberté, égalité, fraternité: Bicentenaire de la grande révolution française*. Joensuu, Finland: Joensuun Yliopisto. University of Joensuu Publications in Social Sciences, 14.
1995   "Citizenship, Identity and Social History" and "The Emergence of Citizenship in France and Elsewhere." In Charles Tilly, ed., *Citizenship, Identity and Social History*. Cambridge: Cambridge University Press.
1998   "Social Movements and (All Sorts of) Other Political Interactions – Local, National, and International – Including Identities. Several Divagations from a Common Path, Beginning with British Struggles over Catholic Emancipation, 1780–1829, and Ending with Contemporary Nationalism." *Theory and Society* 27: 453–480.

2000   "Struggle, Democratization, and Political Transformation." In
         Waltraud Schelkle, Wolf-Hagen Krauth, Martin Kohli, and Georg
         Elwert, eds., *Paradigms of Social Change: Modernization, Development,
         Transformation, Evolution.* Frankfurt and New York: Campus Verlag
         and St. Martin's.

Chapter 7, furthermore, greatly expands one of my contributions to
Doug McAdam, Sidney Tarrow, and Charles Tilly, *Dynamics of Contention*
(Cambridge University Press, 2001), but also borrows text wholesale from
that section of *Dynamics*.

For suggestions, information, criticism, and advice, I am grateful to Ron
Aminzade, Wayne te Brake, Carmenza Gallo, Michael Hanagan, Sidney
Tarrow, Nicholas Toloudis, Takeshi Wada, Viviana Zelizer, two anonymous
readers for Cambridge University Press, and audiences at the Brandenburg
Academy of Sciences, Cornell University, the University of Geneva, and the
American Sociological Association. Serving on Marc Lerner's dissertation
committee (see Lerner 2003) gave me welcome access to his incomparable
knowledge of Schwyz, Zurich, and Vaud as well as his warnings against
blunders in my rendering of Swiss history, but it also put me on my mettle
not to poach a young scholar's distinctive, valuable contribution to studies
of European democratization. Stephanie Sakson contributed sure-handed
editing, and Robert Swanson crafted a lucid index. The National Science
Foundation, the Mellon Foundation, and the Center for Advanced Study
in the Behavioral Sciences jointly supported two sojourns and multiple
meetings at the center during which I formulated ideas for this book and
wrote some of the text.

New York City
May 2003

1

Contention and Democracy

Unlike its 20th-century counterparts, the *Leeds Mercury* for 30 March 1871 devoted its opening pages entirely to classified advertising, official announcements, and market reports. But by page 4, as usual, the newspaper had plunged into the day's urgent political affairs. "The result of the Paris elections," declared the *Mercury*'s editorial writer,

gives such authority to the Commune as may be assumed to flow from an illegal proceeding to condone a revolt. It is simply, however, the authority of usurpation based upon the vote of a minority, the majority abstaining from the exercise of their rights, and so far giving a colourable sanction to acts which they had not the courage to protest against or to oppose. The victory has been won, as such victories too often are won, by the unscrupulous exercise of power in the name of liberty. For the moment, the Party of Disorder, of Anarchy, of Revolution, and of Tyranny have triumphed, and it may be that with the phrases of liberty, equality, and fraternity on their lips, they will for a time hold their own by a Reign of terror which will once more and for another generation make French Republicanism a bye word and a scorn in the mouths of all men.

The *Mercury*'s editorialist intertwined three themes commonly voiced by 19th- and 20th-century commentators on France, emphatically including British and French antirevolutionaries: comparison of current struggles with the revolution of 1789, association of revolution with terror, and assertion that if a revolution occurred, it could not possibly have represented the majority will.

After much more in the same vein, the editorial pronounced a scathing but ultimately fearful judgment:

At present the Commune has no legal authority. It is neither more nor less than a revolutionary body, and as the authority of the Government has not been overthrown, its assumption cannot be recognised without danger to the lawful Government of

1

the country. There may be, and probably is, sufficient ground for demanding a reform of the municipal system of government in force in Paris, and the large towns of France. Indeed, the necessity of reform has been admitted, and unless the violence of the commune outrages public opinion, such reform must now come speedily; but the right of Paris to an autonomy, independent of the National Government, is a right which cannot be conceded. It is a claim for which there is no justification. There is too much reason to fear that it covers designs which would make property a curse instead of a blessing, by imposing the burthen of taxation upon the rich, and providing work for the poor at the cost of the State. So long as these theories remain theories France can afford to smile at them. They are the dreams of visionaries. Unfortunately the visionaries are in power in Paris, and in all probability will seek to realise their dreams, pursuing their ends blindly, and at all costs.

The editorial ended with a prediction: that the Commune would leave a legacy of "misery and distress, from which all will suffer, and none more than the poor" (*Leeds Mercury*, 30 March 1871, pp. 4–5). Thus once again, according to the *Mercury*, French people had revealed their propensity for revolutionary adventurism. Violent victories, in a self-righteous British view, could produce only long-term defeats for reason and democratic order.

What had happened? In 1848, French revolutionaries replaced their monarchy with a republic that provided work for its many unemployed and greatly expanded workers' rights, including nearly universal manhood suffrage. At the end of 1851, elected president Louis Napoleon Bonaparte (nephew of the earlier emperor) swept away the republic with a coup d'état, then created his own empire the following year. Louis Napoleon's coup initiated eighteen years of urbanization, industrialization, political consolidation, and, toward the end, liberalization with increasingly turbulent rule. War with Prussia proved his downfall. On 1 September 1870, France's commanding general Macmahon surrendered and Prussian forces took Napoleon III captive at Sedan. Three days later, a relatively peaceful revolution terminated the empire, established a republic, and formed a government of national defense in Paris. But Prussian armies continued to batter their French foes, as a determined Prussian siege of Paris began on 5 January. German artillery then pounded the city for three weeks.

Ninety thousand National Guards and regular troops under a reluctant General Trochu made a spectacularly unsuccessful attempt to break out and reach Versailles on 19 January. On 28 January, French national authorities signed an armistice turning the forts of Paris over to German occupation. But Parisians, mobilized in political clubs and connected by the National Guard's Central Committee, began to organize the city's resistance and

2

self-rule. In Paris and elsewhere, radicals agitated for pursuit of the war against Prussia as well as for more decentralized and democratic forms of government. A new national regime, led by Adolphe Thiers and based in Bordeaux, cut off National Guard stipends. It also passed ineffectual measures calling for Parisians to resume rent payments and other routine obligations.

Seeking to break Parisian resistance, Thiers ordered his forces to seize the National Guard's cannon. The army's effort to do so before dawn on 18 March called Parisians into the streets, incited the killing of two army generals in Montmartre, and precipitated what the *Leeds Mercury* was soon calling another revolution. At that point, the National Guard's Central Committee occupied the Hôtel de Ville, constituting a de facto municipal government. After city-wide elections (Sunday, 26 March) brought revolutionary leaders into office, on 28 March they declared Paris an autonomous Commune. Until government troops invaded the city and took it back street by street two months later, the Commune ruled Paris through a structure built on revolutionary committees and the neighborhood-based National Guard backed by flourishing popular associations (Gaillard 1971; Gould 1995; Greenberg 1971; Gullickson 1996; Johnson 1996; Lafargue 1997; Lissagaray 1969; Rougerie 1964).

Speaking in Free Trade Hall, Manchester, almost exactly a year after the Commune's declaration, British Conservative leader Benjamin Disraeli compared the British Reform Acts of 1832 and 1867:

Lord Grey, in his measure of 1832, which was no doubt a statesmanlike measure, committed a great and for a time it appeared an irretrievable error. By that measure he fortified the legitimate influence of the aristocracy, and accorded to the middle classes great and salutary franchises; but he not only made no provision for the representation of the working classes in the Constitution, but he absolutely abolished those ancient franchises which the working classes had peculiarly enjoyed from time immemorial. Gentlemen, that was the origin of Chartism, and of that electoral uneasiness which existed in this country more or less for 35 years. (*Times* [of London], 4 April 1872, p. 5)

Disraeli had it right. Renewing a long-term campaign in 1830, a vast mobilization of middle-class and working-class activists had created a crisis to which the British government finally responded by passing the Reform Act of 1832. The act not only excluded the great bulk of workers from voting for Parliament while effectively enfranchising many masters and merchants who had previously lacked the vote, but also increased the property requirements for suffrage in a number of boroughs where ordinary workers had previously voted in considerable numbers. The worker-based Chartist movement that surged repeatedly between 1838 and 1848 only to collapse in a year of French revolution had indeed represented those excluded by the 1832 settlement. Despite arising in the context of widespread struggles between workers and capitalists, the movement had focused not on workers' rights as such but on democratic reform, including manhood suffrage.

In practice, furthermore, the 1832 Reform Act gave electoral advantages to Liberals over their Conservative rivals. The act created 144 parliamentary seats elected by property-holding county voters, 323 seats elected by property holders in recognized urban boroughs, and four seats elected by university officers. On the whole, Liberals did better in boroughs and in county districts that included many city-based property holders. In that respect the Conservatives of 1867 could reasonably see the 1832 Reform as having underrepresented their likely supporters. If they could push through a new reform that would shift parliamentary seats from boroughs to enlarged county electorates (where landlords had a good chance of swaying votes of their tenants and workers), Conservatives could actually gain electoral power. They also had a mixed interest in the working-class franchise: a modest increase was likely to favor the Liberals by drawing in skilled workers who at that point benefited more directly from Liberal programs, but an increase large enough to enfranchise general laborers could well increase Conservative support through patronage and through divisions within the working class.

Liberals nevertheless had strong incentives to broaden both the urban electorate and its parliamentary representation. County by county and borough by borough, parliamentary representation remained the same from 1832 to 1866. Over the same period, however, rising rural property values and urban capitalization lifted many men above the property thresholds for voting. Economic expansion thus increased the county electorate by 47 percent while increasing the borough electorate by 82 percent, but the numbers of MPs per borough and per county remained unchanged. That meant the number of electors per MP rose more rapidly in the Liberals' preferred territories than in the Conservatives'. A move toward representation proportional to local population and, especially, toward increase in the number of borough seats would therefore benefit Liberals. From 1865 onward, Reform Unions and similar organizations brought middle-class radicals and working-class activists into a nationwide campaign of public meetings and marches on behalf of parliamentary reform. All this served as context for intricate parliamentary struggles during which Liberals failed to push through their leaders' reform bill in 1866 but Conservatives managed to get their own much-amended version passed in 1867.

Disraeli, who had led Parliament as it passed the 1867 Act, twitted the Liberals who long talked reform but did nothing about it. The Conservatives, he said, were more decisive:

And, gentlemen, what has been the result? In 1848 there was a French Revolution and a Republic was established. No one can have forgotten what the effect was in this country. I remember the day when not a woman could leave her house in London, and when cannon were placed on Westminster Bridge. A year ago there was another revolution in France, and a Republic was again established of the most menacing character. What happened in this country? You could not get half a dozen men to assemble in a street and grumble. Why? Because the people had got what they wanted. They were content and they were grateful. (*Times*, 4 April 1872, p. 5).

Thus France gave lessons in revolution, while Britain gave lessons in democracy. Or so went a frequent British boast.

To be sure, five years earlier many conservatives – including some full-fledged Conservative party members in Parliament – had looked at the 1867 Reform Bill as a prologue to revolution. Speaking of Disraeli, Lord Carnarvon then thundered, "If you borrow your political ethics from the ethics of the political adventurer, you may depend upon it, the whole of your representative institutions will crumble beneath your feet" (Evans 1983: 351). As enacted, the Reform Bill did almost double the electorate, allowing most male working-class householders to vote for parliamentary candidates and inaugurating a period in which both Liberals and Conservatives had to calculate the effects of their policies on workers' votes. Disraeli's final maneuvers and concessions had produced a more radical bill than even leading Liberals had advocated. In retrospect, nevertheless, the British ruling classes generally congratulated themselves on avoiding revolution by judicious enlargement of the electorate, and thus of political life as a whole. They also frequently pointed across the Channel to the bad example set by the contentious French.

To Explain Contention, Democratization, and Their Connections

However we evaluate the British self-image, comparison of French and British politics in the time of the Paris Commune does reveal impressive national differences in the forms, dynamics, and outcomes of contention. That comparison does raise questions about the foundations of democratic politics. Confluence between investigations of national differences in contentious politics and of democracy's diverse origins identifies the river this book navigates. Seen from upstream, *Contention and Democracy in Europe* concerns explanation of the various trajectories followed by contentious politics – politics in which people make concerted claims bearing on each other's interests. Seen from downstream, the same book concerns the diverse origins of democratic institutions. If the book does its work well, it will establish that the two streams, although separable for the sake of argument, eventually join so extensively as to become indistinguishable. To explain the varieties of contentious politics is also to explain a rare, contingent outcome of contentious politics: democracy.

Contrasting French and British experiences between 1825 and 1871 offer a slice of the European world this book seeks to explain. On the French side: movement from revolution to revolution through a brief, turbulent democratic experiment, the return of authoritarian government, a phase of hesitant democratization and expanding contention followed by war, disintegration of the regime, and new attempts at revolution. On the British side: vast mobilizations for religious rights and parliamentary reform capped by modest concessions to previous outsiders and tightened control over Irish dissidents, widespread but ultimately ineffectual campaigns for workers' political rights, formation of a militant nationalist movement in Ireland, and contained struggles yielding some democratization, at least in Great Britain if not in Ireland. In both French and British experiences we witness intimate interaction of popular contention and democracy-affecting changes of regime.

The 19th-century histories of France and Great Britain hardly exhaust the ranges of contentious politics and democracy. In the perspective of a 21st-century world where South Africa, Slovenia, Costa Rica, India, Canada, and Portugal all count as democracies of sorts, the experiences of France and Britain display strong resemblances and connections: similar and interacting patterns in legalization for organized workers, in policing of public order, in expansion of the franchise, in formation of popularly responsible governments, in creation of political parties, and much more. Political leaders and activists in the two countries communicated with each other repeatedly, sometimes borrowed each other's political solutions to shared problems, and even more often reacted by differentiating themselves from their cross-channel neighbors. Still, France and Britain arrived at relatively vigorous, viable democratic polities by different but continuously contentious paths, provided models of political organization that significantly influenced other countries, and accumulated histories of contention – democratic and otherwise – that have challenged generations of analysts.

To explain similarities and differences in French and British experience since 1650 constitutes a reasonable start toward more general explanations of variation within Europe as a whole. Since European polities and their immediate transplants originated most of the contemporary institutions we recognize as democratic, furthermore, any explanation that gets right the last few centuries of European involvement in contention and democracy offers some promise of helping to identify likely origins of democracy elsewhere. This book uses sustained comparison of French and British histories since 1650 or so as a springboard for more general comparisons within Europe. From there it leaps to ideas concerning the rest of the world.

Stated without definition of terms and in stark preliminary form, here are the book's guiding arguments:

1. Differing combinations of coercion, capital, and commitment in various regions promote the formation of significantly different kinds of regimes, and different directions of regime change, within those regions.
2. Trajectories of regimes within a two-dimensional space defined by (a) degree of governmental capacity and (b) extent of protected consultation significantly affect both their prospects for democracy and the character of their democracy if it arrives.
3. In the long run, increases in governmental capacity and protected consultation reinforce each other, as state expansion generates resistance, bargaining, and provisional settlements, on one side, while on the other side protected consultation encourages demands for expansion of state intervention, which in turn promote increases in capacity.
4. At the extremes, where capacity develops farther and faster than consultation, the path to democracy (if any) passes through authoritarianism; if protected consultation develops farther and faster than capacity and the regime survives, the path then passes through a risky zone of capacity building.
5. Although the organizational forms – elections, terms of office, areal representation, deliberative assemblies, and so on – adopted by democratizing regimes often emulate or adapt institutions that have strong precedents in villages, cities, regional jurisdictions, or

7

adjacent national regimes, they almost never evolve directly from those institutions.

6. Creation of citizenship – rights and obligations linking whole categories of a regime's subject population to governmental agents – is a necessary but not sufficient condition of democratization.

7. In high-capacity regimes, nondemocratic citizenship sometimes forms, and with extensive integration of citizens into regimes even reduces or inhibits democracy.

8. Nevertheless, the prior presence of citizenship, other things equal, generally facilitates democratization.

9. Both creation of citizenship and democratization depend on changes in three arenas – categorical inequality, trust networks, and public politics – as well as on interactions among those changes.

10. Regularities in democratization consist not of standard general sequences or sufficient conditions but of recurrent causal mechanisms that in varying combinations and sequences produce changes in categorical inequality, networks of trust, and public politics.

11. Under specifiable circumstances, revolution, conquest, confrontation, and colonization accelerate and concentrate some of those crucial causal mechanisms.

12. Almost all of the crucial democracy-promoting causal mechanisms involve popular contention – politically constituted actors' making of public, collective claims on other actors, including agents of government – as correlates, causes, and effects.

13. In the course of democratization, repertoires of political contention (arrays of widely available claim-making performances) shift from predominantly parochial, particular, and bifurcated interactions based largely on embedded identities to predominantly cosmopolitan, modular, and autonomous interactions based largely on detached identities.

The book's point is to pursue this line of argument by means of broad but careful historical comparisons among European national experiences between 1650 and 2000.

Having already promised – or threatened! – too much, let me retrench immediately. At best, this book does no more than make understandable and plausible the approach just sketched. It tells defensible stories about European political histories, pointing out parallels between those stories and the arguments. It neither lays out systematic evidence for the thirteen assertions in my list nor provides decisive refutations of competing explanations. It merely illustrates the sorts of causal mechanisms a more detailed set of explanations would require – showing, for example, that tactical alliances between dissident power holders and political outsiders promoted democratization under some circumstances despite the absence of explicitly democratic programs on either side of the alliance. For the most part it settles for demonstrating that democratization commonly occurred as a result of struggles during which (as in 19th-century Britain and France) few if any of the participants were self-consciously trying to create democratic institutions.

Such an approach involves high-risk wagers in theory and method. It rests on the assumption that democracy emerges contingently from political struggle in the medium run rather than being a product either of age-old character traits or of short-term constitutional innovations. Partisans of political culture, on one side, and of democratization as legal reform, on the other, have often bet against that assumption. My inquiry guesses, furthermore, that the social world's order does not reside in general laws, repeated large-scale sequences, or regular relationships among variables. We should not search for a single set of circumstances or a repeated series of events that everywhere produces democracy. Nor should we look for actors having democratic intentions, seeking to discover how and when they get chances to realize those intentions. We should look instead for robust, recurrent causal mechanisms that combine differently, with different aggregate outcomes, in different settings. (More on mechanisms in a moment.)

As a consequence, we should expect that prevailing circumstances for democratization vary significantly from era to era and region to region as functions of previous histories, international environments, available models of political organization, and predominant patterns of social relations. We should also expect to discover not one but multiple paths to democracy. If all these assumptions hold, then close comparison of historical experiences with an eye to recurrent causal mechanisms and their combinations offers the greatest promise of advancing explanations of democratization. If the assumptions are wrong, the book's review of European experiences with democratization will still provide grindable grist for other analysts' mills.

Previous analyses of democratization provide inspiration and context for this book. Since Aristotle, western thinkers have repeatedly addressed two fundamental questions. First, what connections exist between democratization and human well-being? Second, under what conditions and by what means do durable democratic regimes come into existence? In recent years, western political analysts have searched for general answers to these two questions that would simultaneously fit the experiences of long-established democracies, account for the tumultuous histories of democratization and de-democratization across the globe since World War II, and provide guidance for the promotion of durable democracy in the contemporary world. On the count of well-being, for example, students of democracy have explored the hopeful possibility that democratic regimes make war against each other less frequently than other pairs of regimes, hence that over the long run world democratization would reduce the prevalence of war across the globe (Gowa 1999). Yet most theorists rest with the assumption that democracy constitutes a good in itself, and therefore enhances human well-being simply by taking shape.

When it comes to the origins of durable democratic regimes, disagreements flourish, but an implicit agreement has emerged on the nature of the explanatory problem. On the whole, recent theorists have rejected conceptions of democratization as a gradual deposit from long-term social processes or as a set of political changes that might occur piecemeal, in different orders, through different paths. They have preferred the idea that under specifiable conditions some fairly regular and rapid process transports regimes from undemocratic into democratic territory. Most analysts have tried to specify those conditions and to identify the crucial process. As a consequence, empirical studies of democratization have alternated between cross-sectional comparisons of democratic and undemocratic regimes (asking, e.g., whether some critical level of prosperity separates the one from the other) and close examination of circumstances prevailing just before or during transitions from undemocratic to democratic regimes (asking, e.g., whether failures of military rulers to manage national crises regularly precipitate democratization).

What sorts of *explanations* do such efforts involve? We can distinguish roughly among four styles of argument in recent attempts to explain democratization and de-democratization: necessary conditions, variables, sequences, and clusters. *Necessary condition* arguments sometimes spill over into specification of *sufficient* conditions for democratization – identification of the circumstances under which a regime always democratizes. If successful, such an effort would not only establish a general law, but also indicate what conditions one would have to discover or promote on the way to producing new democratic regimes. The justly renowned synthesis of Rueschemeyer, Stephens, and Stephens (1992: 75–78), for example, makes allowance for variation among regions and periods, but still comes down to an overall formulation of necessary, and perhaps sufficient, conditions: transnational diffusion of democratic ideas and practices; a measure of national unity; an autonomous, effective state; economic growth; generation of subordinate classes by that growth; growing organizational density of civil society; and mobilization of subordinate classes on behalf of collective rights and political participation. As Ruth Berins Collier sums up the final segment of their argument:

Democracy is an outcome of the struggle between the dominant and subordinate classes and hence an outcome of the balance of class power. Democratization occurs when the democracy-demanding classes, above all the working class, are stronger than the democracy-resisting classes, who reject the demands and pressures of the former, though there is also room in this account for democratic initiatives by other classes as a co-optive response to a working-class threat. (Collier 1999: 10).

At a minimum, then, Rueschemeyer et al. stipulate necessary conditions for democratization. They come close to stipulating sufficient conditions.

Other scholars emphasize *variables* that in differing combinations can all promote democratization. In 1991, Samuel P. Huntington published *The Third Wave*. The book's ideas immediately began organizing a new round of research and theory. Speaking of the wave of democratization he saw as beginning in the 1970s, Huntington identified five explanatory variables as crucial: (1) delegitimation of authoritarian regimes through internal failures and external rejections, (2) global economic growth and its expansion of democracy-demanding populations, (3) shift of the Catholic Church toward political reform, (4) shifts in policies of external actors (notably the European Union, the United States, and Russia) toward authoritarian regimes, and (5) spiraling demonstration effects (Huntington 1991: 45–46). Rather than treating them as a set of necessary conditions for democratization, Huntington explicitly treated these variables as differing in weight for different democratizing regimes; he argued, for example, that "politics and external forces" inhibited the effects of economic growth on democratization in Czechoslovakia and East Germany (Huntington 1991: 63).

Sequence arguments repeatedly tempt analysts of democratization. Many analysts, for example, distinguish four distinct stages, each one a prerequisite of the next stage: development of preconditions, exit from authoritarianism, transition to democracy, and democratic consolidation (see, e.g., Sørensen 1998: 24–63, and, for critique, Carothers 2002). Typically, theorists treat the preconditions stage as a long-term development. They then present the next three – exit, transition, and consolidation – as outcomes of choices

11

and interactions among major political actors. Conversely, reversals (e.g., exit from fragile democracy into new authoritarianism) result from failure of conditions for the next stage combined with undemocratic choices and interactions among major political actors (see, e.g., Diamond 1999: 64–116). In an influential formulation, Juan Linz and Alfred Stepan declare:

Behaviorally, democracy becomes the only game in town when no significant political groups seriously attempt to overthrow the democratic regime or secede from the state. When this situation obtains, the behavior of the newly elected government that has emerged from the democratic transition is no longer dominated by the problem of how to avoid democratic breakdown. Attitudinally, democracy becomes the only game in town when, even in the face of severe political and economic crises, the overwhelming majority of the people believe that any further political change must emerge from within the parameters of democratic formulas. Constitutionally, democracy becomes the only game in town when all the actors in the polity become habituated to the fact that political conflict will be resolved according to the established norms and that violations of these norms are likely to be both ineffective and costly. In short, with consolidation, democracy becomes routinized and deeply internalized in social, institutional, and even psychological life, as well as in calculations for achieving success. (Linz and Stepan 1996: 5)

Linz and Stepan go on to claim that a consolidated regime breaks down only in response to new circumstances "in which the democratic regime cannot solve a set of problems, a nondemocratic alternative gains significant supporters, and former democratic regime loyalists begin to behave in a constitutionally disloyal or semiloyal manner" (Linz and Stepan 1996: 6). Consolidation, then, installs a ratchet that only exceptional force can reverse.

Cluster treatments of democratization claim that conditions, causes, and sequences of democratization vary significantly from one period, region, or type of regime to another. As a consequence, one can risk generalizations for a single cluster – for example, one of Huntington's waves – but not for democratization everywhere since the beginning of time. In a crisp example, Barbara Geddes treats recent democratization as transition from various types of authoritarian regime, then argues that the crucial processes vary depending on whether the authoritarian regime is personalist, military, single-party, or an amalgam. As she summarizes:

transitions from military rule usually begin with splits within the ruling military elite, as noted by much of the literature on Latin American transitions. In contrast, rival factions within single-party and personalist regimes have stronger incentives to cooperate with each other. Single-party regimes are quite resilient and tend to be brought down by exogenous events rather than internal splits. Personalist regimes are also relatively immune to internal splits except when calamitous economic

conditions disrupt the material underpinnings of regime loyalty. They are especially vulnerable, however, to the death of the leader and to violent overthrow.
(Geddes 1999: 122)

Geddes thereby combines necessary-condition and sequence arguments,
using sketches of strategic situations – games – entailing choices by those
who already hold pieces of power. Other cluster analysts stress variation
from region to region or period to period (e.g., Bratton and van de Walle
1997; Collier 1999; Markoff 1996b).

This book's analysis borrows especially from the necessary conditions
and clusters traditions of explanation, while generally rejecting variable and
sequence arguments. At a certain distance, it owes a great deal to Robert
Dahl's classic treatment of necessary conditions (Dahl 1998). Yet it breaks
with most current analyses of democratization in four obvious ways:

First, it denies the existence of standard sequences of change from undemocratic
to democratic regimes, insisting instead that many different paths lead to democracy because the crucial mechanisms activate in a wide variety of combinations and
orders.

Second, on similar grounds it denies that any general set of sufficient conditions
exists for democracy. (It does, however, propose some *necessary* conditions.)

Third, in contrast to the many studies that correlate transitions to democracy with
attributes of regimes at or immediately before those transitions, it denies that the
crucial causes of democratization activate immediately before or during a regime's
crossing of a well-defined boundary between undemocratic and democratic politics.
It therefore spends little effort on yes-no comparisons, concentrating instead on
time-consuming processes that promote or inhibit democratization.

Fourth, while conceding that many political regimes stay in place because people
attach other valued routines to them despite the regimes' defects, it denies that
democracy enjoys a super-stable position such that once arrived in that position a
country only de-democratizes through crisis and breakdown. Although democracy
has, indeed, become more prevalent in recent centuries, de-democratization still
occurs frequently and widely.

Again, if these principles are wrong, the book still provides well-
documented narratives of multiple European experiences. Since most general accounts of democratization in the contemporary world look back at
European democratization as a calm, orderly, and definitive process, that
contribution alone should justify the book.

What are we trying to explain? Democratization means *increases in the
breadth and equality of relations between governmental agents and members of
the government's subject population, in binding consultation of a government's
subject population with respect to governmental personnel, resources, and policy,*

13

and in protection of that population (especially minorities within it) from arbitrary action by governmental agents. In shorthand, we can speak of increases or decreases in *protected consultation*, calling high levels of protected consultation democratic. Democratization does not mean arrival at full, definitive democratic functioning, but any substantial move toward higher levels of protected consultation. De-democratization – which coming pages often describe and attempt to explain – means any substantial move away from protected consultation.

This definition stresses political processes. To political process definitions some theorists prefer *substantive* definitions emphasizing such outcomes of governmental action as equity, community, and well-being. Other theorists prefer *constitutional* definitions emphasizing representative mechanisms, courts, and laws. In recent years, most western students of democratization have opted instead for *procedural* definitions. Such definitions stem ultimately from Joseph Schumpeter's (1942) minimalist view of democracy and center on the institution of competitive elections for public office (for reviews of definitions and measures, see Collier and Levitsky 1997; Geddes 1999; Inkeles 1991; Lijphart 1999; Przeworski et al. 2000: 55–59; Vanhanen 2000). I am prepared to argue the advantages of a political process definition for historical-comparative analyses (see Tilly 2001a, 2001b, 2003a). Here, however, the choice doesn't matter much practically: over Europe since 1650, substantive, constitutional, procedural, and political process criteria produce similar classifications of actually existing governments.

Although it certainly rests on shared understandings and practices, democracy does not reduce to a state of mind, a set of laws, or a common culture. It consists of active, meaningful social relations between individuals and groups that share connections with specific governments. As we will see abundantly later on, furthermore, democracy is always relative to those specific governments: democracy sometimes prevails, for example, within households, shops, or villages that in turn form part of emphatically undemocratic systems at a larger scale. Internally undemocratic parties, unions, and associations, furthermore, sometimes participate in unquestionably democratic public politics. Although the borrowing of democratic practices (such as contested elections) across scales will figure importantly in the stories of democratization to come, this book concentrates on democracy and democratization at a national scale, at the level of states.

From the political process understanding of democratization follows a set of distinctions that recur throughout the book: among public politics, contentious politics, and citizen-agent relations. The three form an overlapping set. *Public politics* includes all externally visible interactions among constituted political actors (those having a name and standing within a given regime), including agents of government. Within public politics, *contentious politics* includes all discontinuous, collective making of claims among constituted political actors. Noncontentious politics still makes up the bulk of all political interaction, since it includes tax collection, census taking, military service, diffusion of political information, processing of government-mediated benefits, internal organizational activitity of constituted political actors, and related processes that go on most of the time without discontinuous, public, collective claim making. Although the conduct of such relatively noncontentious political activities incrementally affects democratization and de-democratization, I argue that contentious politics figures more directly and immediately in those changes.

Overlapping both contentious and noncontentious politics, *citizen-agent relations* include all interactions between subjects of a given government and established agents of that government. (Later I argue that full-fledged citizenship appears only in a limited set of political regimes, but it will save many words to call all subjects of a given regime its "citizens" and to apply the phrase "citizen-agent relations" across all regimes.) Democratization consists of a set of changes in citizen-agent relations: broadening them, equalizing them, protecting them, and subjecting them to binding consultation. Distinctions among public politics, contentious politics, and citizen-agent relations matter because democratization centers on shifts in citizen-agent relations, those shifts depend on more general alterations in public politics, and political contention causes those shifts.

How so? Crucial changes in social relations underlying democratization take place in three interacting sectors: public politics, categorical inequality, and networks of trust. In the course of democratization, the bulk of a government's subject population acquires roughly equal rights to participate in public politics, a process that in turn establishes binding, protected, relatively equal claims on a government's agents, activities, and resources. In a related process, categorical inequality declines in those areas of social life that either constitute or immediately support participation in public politics. (As distinguished from individual inequality, categorical inequality distinguishes such sets as female-male, black-white-Asian, and Muslim-Hindu-Sikh from each other.)

In addition to – and in concert with – changes in public politics and categorical inequality, certain alterations of trust networks promote democratization. A significant shift occurs in the locus of interpersonal networks on which people rely when undertaking risky long-term enterprises such as marriage, long-distance trade, membership in crafts, investment of savings, and time-consuming specialized education; such networks move from evasion of governmental detection and control to partial reliance on government agents and presumption that such agents will meet their long-term commitments. "Partial reliance" need not connect individuals directly to governments; the connections may run through parties, unions, communities, and other organizations that in turn rely on governmental ratification, toleration, support, or protection. People create associations that simultaneously organize risky enterprises and bargain with authorities, start investing family money in government securities, yield their sons to military service, seek government assistance in enforcement of religious obligations, organize mutual aid through publicly recognized labor unions, and so on.

Reversals de-democratize: when trust networks proliferate insulated from public politics, their proliferation saps governmental capacity, reduces citizens' incentives to collaborate in democratic processes they find costly in the short run, weakens protections for the bulk of the citizenry, and increases the opportunities of the rich and powerful to intervene selectively in public politics on their own behalf.

Let me underscore what this argument does *not* entail. It does *not* mean that the more governments absorb and dominate social life within their jurisdictions, the more democratic their regimes become. Trust networks reach their maximum effectiveness in promoting democracy when their participants can rightly assume that governmental agents will usually meet their commitments, but those same participants remain free to withdraw consent and to sanction officials who perform badly. When people segregate their trust networks entirely from public politics, they have strong incentives to evade responsibility for governmental performance and to seek short-term private advantage at the expense of long-term public good. In those circumstances, only the few who can turn governmental resources directly to their own advantage participate regularly in governmental activity. Up to a relatively high point, then, integration of trust networks into public politics provides both incentives and means for ordinary people to monitor, sanction, and collaborate with governmental production of public goods. Beyond that high point, I speculate, further integration of trust networks would (as libertarians and anarchists have often feared) reduce democracy; since no democratic regime has yet approached that point, we have no evidence on this speculation.

Nor does the argument mean that categorical inequality within a regime's subject population fatally hinders democratization or that collective action by members of subordinate categories threatens democracy. As we see below, in Europe protected consultation sometimes increased despite rising material inequality. The crucial question is whether categorical inequality translates directly into durable divisions within public politics – political organizations, rights, obligations, and relations with governmental agents sharply segregated by class, gender, ethnicity, or some other categorical division. Such inscription of categorical inequalities into public politics inhibits or reverses democratization.

Only where positive changes in trust network integration, inequality insulation, and the relevant internal transformations of public politics all intersect does effective, durable democracy emerge. Most changes in public politics, on the contrary, produce undemocratic outcomes. What is more, reversals in any of the three – for example, organization of public political blocs around major categorical inequalities – promote de-democratization. The explanatory problem, then, is to specify how, why, and when rare democracy-promoting alterations of categorical inequality, trust networks, and public politics coincide.

The questions "how?" "why?" and "when?" all point to a search for robust causal mechanisms: recurrent small-scale events that alter relations among stipulated elements of social life in essentially the same ways whenever and wherever they occur. In varying sequences and combinations, causal mechanisms compound into *processes:* concatenations of mechanisms that produce broadly similar short-term outcomes. The processes that interest us here are those that produce segregation or desegregation of categorical inequality from public politics, integration or separation of trust networks from public politics, and shifts in citizen-agent relations toward or away from broad, equal, binding, and protected interchanges. (Below I name the eight relevant processes.)

Causal mechanisms sort roughly into cognitive, environmental, and relational events. Cognitive mechanisms involve consequential shifts in perception, individual or shared, as when appearance of a new belief concerning the source of an injustice increases people's sensitivity to that injustice. Environmental mechanisms change relations between social units and their nonhuman surroundings, as when soil depletion reduces an agricultural village's crop yields. Relational mechanisms transform interactions among persons, groups, and social sites, as when members of previously segregated religious communities begin to intermarry. This book's search for

17

Table 1.1 *Mechanisms Segregating Categorical Inequality from Public Politics*

1. Dissolution of governmental controls (e.g., legal restrictions on property holding) that support current unequal relations among social categories; for example, wholesale confiscation and sale of church property weakens established ecclesiastical power
2. Equalization of assets and/or well-being across categories within the population at large; for example, booming demand for the products of peasant agriculture expands middle peasants
3. Reduction or governmental containment of privately controlled armed forces; for example, disbanding of magnates' personal armies weakens noble control over commoners
4. Adoption of devices that insulate public politics from categorical inequalities; for example, secret ballots, payment of officeholders, and free, equal access of candidates to media forward formation of cross-category coalitions
5. Formation of politically active coalitions and associations cross-cutting categorical inequality; for example, creation of region-wide mobilizations against governmental property seizures crosses categorical lines
6. Wholesale increases of political participation, rights, or obligations that cut across social categories; for example, governmental annexation of socially heterogeneous territories promotes categorically mixed politics

Negative versions of these mechanisms (e.g., proliferation of privately controlled armed forces and formation of class-segregated political coalitions or associations) facilitate translations of categorical inequality into public politics, and thus reverse democratization.

Major processes combining these mechanisms include (a) equalization of categories (chiefly mechanisms 1–3) and (b) buffering of politics from categorical inequality (chiefly mechanisms 3–6).

explanations of democratization and de-democratization concentrates on relational mechanisms, but gives due attention to cognitive and environmental mechanisms as well.

Tables 1.1–1.3 list mechanisms that recurrently produce democracy-favoring changes in regard to inequality, trust networks, and public politics. Under the heading of categorical inequality, mechanisms fall into two clusters: those that actively undermine previously existing categorical inequalities in general and those that erect barriers to translation of existing categorical inequalities into public politics. In European experience, the second cluster played a far larger part in democratization than the first. In fact, because of capitalism's simultaneous advance, material inequalities were often sharpening across Europe's national populations as democratization proceeded. Thus insulating mechanisms became crucial

Table 1.2 *Mechanisms Integrating Trust Networks into Public Politics*

1. Disintegration of existing segregated trust networks; for example, decay of patrons' ability to provide their clients with goods and protection promotes withdrawal of clients from patron-client ties
2. Expansion of population categories lacking access to effective trust networks for their major long-term risky enterprises; for example, growth of landless wage-workers in agrarian regions increases population without effective patronage and/or relations of mutual aid
3. Appearance of new long-term risky opportunities and threats that existing trust networks cannot handle; for example, substantial increases in war, famine, disease, and/or banditry visibly overwhelm protective capacity of patrons, diasporas, and local solidarities
4. Creation of external guarantees for governmental commitments; for example, conquest of shattered government by an occupying force committed to rebuilding provides backing for governmental protection from predators
5. Visible governmental meeting of commitments to the advantage of substantial new segments of the population; for example, creation of firm guarantees of rewards for military conscripts increases willingness of families to yield sons to military service
6. Governmental absorption or destruction of previously autonomous patron-client networks; for example, incorporation of regional ethnic leaders into governmental offices draws in their clients as well
7. Increase of governmental resources for risk reduction and/or compensation of loss; for example, creation of government-backed disaster insurance draws citizens into collaboration with government agents and/or established political actors
8. Extraction-resistance-bargaining cycles during which governmental agents demand resources under control of nongovernmental networks and committed to nongovernmental ends, holders of those resources resist, struggle ensues, and settlements emerge in which people yield resources but receive credible guarantees with respect to constraints on future extraction; for example, settlements of tax rebellions cement agreements on who will pay how much under what conditions

Negative versions of these mechanisms (e.g., governmental failure to meet commitments to previously protected segments of the population and decline of governmental resources for risk reduction and/or compensation of loss) promote detachment of trust networks from public politics, and thus de-democratize.

Major processes combining these mechanisms include (a) dissolution of insulated trust networks (chiefly mechanisms 1–3) and (b) creation of politically connected trust networks (chiefly mechanisms 4–8).

to European democracy. In 19th-century France and Britain, for example, cross-class coalitions eventually promoted democratization despite rising material inequality. The competition of British Liberals and Conservatives for workers' votes with which we began provides a case in point.

Table 1.3 *Mechanisms Increasing Breadth, Equality, Enforcement, and Security of Mutual Obligations Between Citizens and Governmental Agents*

1. Coalition formation between segments of ruling classes and constituted political actors that are currently excluded from power; for example, dissident bourgeois recruit backing from disfranchised workers, thus promoting political participation of those workers
2. Central co-optation or elimination of previously autonomous political intermediaries; for example, regional strongmen join governing coalitions, thus becoming committed to governmental programs
3. Brokerage of coalitions across unequal categories and/or distinct trust networks; for example, regional alliances form against governmental seizure of local assets, thus promoting employment of those alliances in other political struggles
4. Dissolution or segregation from government of nongovernmental patron-client networks; for example, regional religious leaders lose governmental patronage, thus making other political actors more crucial as allies and patrons
5. Mobilization-repression-bargaining cycles during which currently excluded actors act collectively in ways that threaten survival of the government and/or its ruling classes, governmental repression fails, struggle ensues, and settlements concede political standing and/or rights to mobilized actors; for example, negotiated settlement of resistance to governmental seizure of land establishes agreements concerning property rights
6. Imposition of uniform governmental structures and practices through the government's jurisdiction; for example, creation of uniform nationwide taxes increases likelihood of equity, visibility, and conformity
7. Bureaucratic containment of previously autonomous military forces; for example, incorporation of mercenaries into national armies reduces their independent leverage as political actors

Negative versions of these mechanisms (e.g., multiplication of autonomous political intermediaries and creation of special regimes for favored segments of the population) promote declines in breadth, equality, enforcement, and/or security of mutual obligations, hence de-democratize.

Major processes combining these mechanisms include (a) broadening (chiefly mechanisms 1–5), (b) equalization (chiefly mechanisms 2, 3, and 6), (c) enhancement of collective control (chiefly mechanisms 1, 4, 6, and 7), and (d) inhibition of arbitrary power (chiefly mechanisms 1 and 5–7).

A nice paradox, however, complicates relations among categorical inequality, public politics, and democratization: under some circumstances, unified categorical action temporarily inscribes inequality more deeply into public politics, but in the longer run promotes democracy (Tilly 2002b, 2003b). That happens when three conditions converge: (1) current political exclusion falls precisely at a categorical boundary, for instance, of class, religion, race, or gender; (2) members of the excluded category mobilize as such rather than forming united fronts of the excluded or joining coalitions with dissident members of included categories; and (3) the formerly excluded category then dissolves, splinters, or assimilates piecemeal into established political categories instead of acquiring distinctive political standing. In Europe, political exclusion did often fall along categorical lines (especially of class, gender, and religion). Mobilization within excluded categories did often occur. But when that happened, separate inscription of the new category rarely followed. It followed rarely because in the usual circumstances either existing holders of power co-opted some segment of the outsiders and repressed the rest or dissident insiders allied themselves with the outsiders. The longer-term result remained the same: decreased translation of categorical inequality into public politics.

A contrasting story applies to trust networks. Trust-bearing networks that remained segregated from public politics and governmental intervention hindered democratization by facilitating resistance to governmental initiatives and reducing the stakes of citizens in governmental performance. Over the long run of history, that has been the usual state of affairs: except for the privileged few whose networks actually controlled governments, people have jealously protected their networks of kinship, language, religion, trade, and mutual aid from governmental intervention and public politics.

Nevertheless, two clusters of mechanisms reversed those age-old circumstances: mechanisms that undermined the capacity of existing segregated networks to protect people's high-risk long-term enterprises and other mechanisms that made public political actors (e.g., trade unions) and governments themselves more attractive and/or reliable guarantors of those enterprises. In 19th-century France and Britain, proletarianization and urbanization were weakening old trust networks, promoting the politicization of others, and drawing governments into provision of new guarantees for credit, household survival, and religious choice. Although both countries (as we see below) underwent massive struggles over religiously based trust networks during the 19th century, eventually they dissolved some segregated networks, and at least partially integrated the rest.

The third group of crucial democratizing mechanisms operates at two different levels: the mechanisms in Table 1.3 transform public politics at large, but those transformations of public politics affect citizen-agent relations. The mechanisms alter interactions among constituted political actors, a process that in turn affects relations between citizens and governmental

21

agents. The changes promote breadth and equality of those relations, enforce collective decisions, and strengthen each side's protections from arbitrary action by the other side. The relevant mechanisms insert broad categories of people – at the limit, the whole citizenry – into roughly equivalent power-wielding positions within public politics. Privileges linking particular brokers or categories of people to particular agents of government become less prominent, as rights and obligations applying to broad segments of the population and to whole classes of governmental agents become more prominent. In 19th-century France and Britain, not only extension of the franchise but also equalization of rights to assemble, associate, and make demands resulted from mechanisms in this set.

The three sets of mechanisms compound into eight crucial processes:

Segregation of public politics from categorical inequality
1. equalization of categories
2. buffering of politics from categorical inequality

Integration of trust networks into public politics
3. dissolution of insulated trust networks
4. creation of politically connected trust networks

Alterations of public politics that change interactions between citizens and governmental agents
5. broadening of political participation
6. equalization of political participation
7. enhancement of collective control
8. inhibition of arbitrary power

This book's two most general claims follow: First, in varying combinations and sequences, the mechanisms listed in Tables 1.1–1.3 drive these crucial processes. Second, at least one of the processes under each of the first two headings (categorical inequality and trust networks) and *all* of the processes under the third heading (alterations of public politics) must occur for democratization to ensue. We therefore face the question: does this inventory of causes provide a valid explanation of variation in democratization and de-democratization across different parts of Europe between 1650 and 2000?

Changes in categorical inequality, trust networks, public politics, and citizen-agent relations obviously occupy different places in our explanatory problem. Democratization *consists of* shifts of citizen-agent relations toward greater breadth, equality, consultation, and protection. That much stands as true by definition. But the mechanisms in Table 1.3 do not simply restate the definition of democratization in other terms. Most of them produce changes in relations among actors *outside* government before they exert their impact on relations between citizens and governmental agents. Positive versions of those mechanisms then do act on citizen-agent relations – broadening those relations, equalizing them, enhancing citizens' collective control over the means of rule, and extending citizens' protections from arbitrary action by governmental agents. Alterations of categorical inequality and trust networks promote democratization more indirectly and slowly; they change the context within which transformations of public politics occur.

Changes in public politics, inequality, and trust networks clearly interact. Most of the time they interact to block democratization. Under most circumstances, for example, increases in governmental capacity encourage those who already exercise considerable political power to divert governmental activity on behalf of their own advantage and incite participants in trust networks to reinforce those networks while shielding them more energetically from governmental intervention. Either of those activities, if effective, diminishes or blocks democracy. If European experience provides sound guidance, even working democracies remain forever vulnerable to such reversals; rich minorities subvert democratic processes, or vindictive majorities exclude vulnerable minorities.

Across European experience since 1650, nevertheless, causal processes under the headings of inequality, trust networks, and public politics sometimes worked incrementally in the same direction, toward an increase in protected consultation. The reaching out of beleaguered political participants for tactical alliances with challengers, for instance, repeatedly promoted alteration of governmental operation, reduction of politically relevant forms of inequality, and incorporation of trust networks into public politics. Incorporation of trust networks into public politics occurred at a regional scale during the 17th century when France's regional magnates reacted to royal centralization by building up their own clienteles and even supporting popular rebellion. It occurred at a national scale during the 19th century when Britain's already enfranchised radical reformers recruited followings among the disenfranchised. Such incremental (and often temporary) increases in protected consultation frequently occurred in the aftermath of major struggles.

What sorts of struggles? In European experience since 1650, four recurrent circumstances have sometimes activated multiple democracy-promoting mechanisms: revolution, conquest, confrontation, and colonization. All involve abrupt shocks to existing social arrangements.

Revolution? As England's Glorious Revolution of 1688–89 and the Russian revolution of 1905 illustrate, revolutions do not universally promote moves toward broad, equal citizenship, binding consultation, and protection. Let us take revolutions to be large splits in control over means of government followed by substantial transfers of power over government. As compared with previous regimes, the net effect of most revolutions over the last few centuries has been at least a modicum of democratization, as here defined. Why so? Because they typically activate even a wider range of democracy-promoting mechanisms than do conquest, colonization, and confrontation.

Revolutions rarely or never occur, for example, without coalition formation between segments of ruling classes and constituted political actors that are currently excluded from power. But they also commonly dissolve or incorporate nongovernmental patron-client networks, contain previously autonomous military forces, equalize assets and/or well-being across the population at large, and attack existing trust networks. Revolutions sometimes sweep away old networks that block democratization and promote the formation of governing coalitions far more general than those that preceded them.

Conquest is the forcible reorganization of existing systems of public politics, inequality, and trust by an external power. In the history of European democratization, the most famous example is no doubt conquest by French revolutionary and Napoleonic armies outside France, which left governments on a semi-democratic French model in place through much of Western Europe after Napoleon's defeat. Reestablishment of France, Germany, Italy, and Japan on more or less democratic bases after World War II rivals French revolutionary exploits in this regard. Conquest promotes democratization when it does because it activates a whole series of democracy-promoting mechanisms, notably including the destruction of old trust networks and the provision of external guarantees that the new government will meet its commitments.

Confrontation has provided the textbook cases of democratization, as existing oligarchies have responded to challenges from excluded political actors with broadening of citizenship, equalization of citizenship, increase of binding consultation, and/or expansion of protection for citizens. Nineteenth-century British rulers' responses to large mobilizations by Protestant Dissenters, Catholics, merchants, and skilled workers fit the pattern approximately in Great Britain, but by no means always – and certainly not in Ireland. (Irish struggles figure prominently in Chapter 5.) Confrontation promotes democratization, when it does, because it generates new trust-bearing coalitions and weakens coercive controls supporting current systems of inequality.

Colonization with wholesale transplantation of population from mother country to colony has often promoted democratization, although commonly at the cost of destroying, expelling, or subordinating indigenous populations within the colonial territory. Except for Russia and adjacent territories, Europe's great experiences with internal colonization occurred well before our period of 1650–2000 (Bartlett 1993). But Europeans colonized the rest of the world and sometimes implanted democratic institutions elsewhere. Thus Canada, the United States, Australia, and New Zealand began European settlement with coercive, oligarchic regimes and energetically exterminated the native populations that blocked their ways, yet rapidly moved some distance toward broad citizenship, equal citizenship, binding consultation, and protection within their settler populations.

Let us never forget how far short of the maximum in these four regards all really existing democracies have always fallen; on a national scale, by these criteria, no near-democracy has ever existed anywhere. In the territory that became the United States, after all, much of the northern half colonized through massacre and expulsion of Amerindians, while much of the southern half colonized by means of plantation slavery. Colonization of this sort nevertheless makes a difference not merely because it exports political institutions containing some rudiments of democracy, but also because it weakens exclusive patron-client networks and promotes relative equality of material condition among the colonizers.

Paths to democracy varied significantly within Europe. After 1800, Britain moved toward democracy chiefly through confrontation, but so did Scandinavia. France provides the type case of democratization through revolution, yet much of Europe went through a similar, if temporary, cycle in 1848. Conquest also played a significant part in Europe, both as French revolutionary armies installed new regimes during the 1790s and as victorious Allies reorganized conquered politics after World War II. In France itself, Allied military victory helped recreate democratic institutions after four years of authoritarian rule – and through massive, often violent, struggles from 1944 to 1947. Britain became the great democratic colonizer in settler

25

regions of North America, the Caribbean, Australia, and New Zealand, despite imposing nondemocratic rule in most of its other colonies.

Although revolution and conquest generally involved more outright bloodshed in the short run than did colonization or confrontation, all four processes entailed sustained political contention. Sometimes rulers responded preemptively to as yet unrealized threats of mass action, but more often overt popular struggle figured importantly and directly in formation of democratic institutions. Not that masses regularly originated or responded to well-articulated projects of democratic reform; many steps toward democracy began as resistance to central power in the name of nondemocratic privileges and social arrangements: witness the British electoral expansion of 1867, initially engineered by Disraeli and his Conservatives in the interest of political victory over the Liberals. Or consider how often – as we see below happening across Europe – demands to bypass or replace hereditary political brokers cascaded into programs of direct representation and popular sovereignty.

Not all confrontation, conquest, colonization, or revolution, by any means, promotes democracy; it depends on which specific mechanisms the process activates. In watching democratization, we witness an erratic, improvisational, struggle-ridden process in which continuities and cumulative effects arise more from constraints set by widely shared but implicit understandings and existing social relations than from any clairvoyant vision of the future.

Figure 1.1 schematizes the explanatory problem before us, ignoring feedback and identifying only the main causal connections that later chapters of this book explore. We look at revolution, conquest, confrontation, and colonization primarily through the ways they activate and transform contentious making of claims rather than, for example, tracing their ideological heritages or their transformations of social organization. We follow the impact of contentious claim making on trust networks, categorical inequality, and public politics, while noting from time to time that influences other than contentious politics (the external arrows) also shape trust networks and categorical inequality. We look closely at the joint effects of changes in trust networks, categorical inequality, and public politics on citizen-agent relations. Within the zone of citizen-agent relations we observe the political changes that constitute democratization or dedemocratization. In each of these connections, we seek to specify and verify mechanisms and processes that regularly combine to produce the

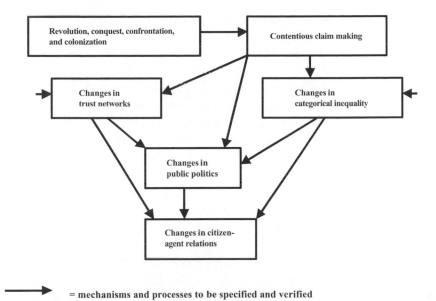

→ = mechanisms and processes to be specified and verified

Figure 1.1: Elements in the explanation of democratization and de-democratization.

crucial changes. We scrutinize European national histories since 1650 to accomplish these tasks.

Histories of Democratization

Seen from a European perspective, French and British histories of contention and democracy had plenty in common. The common conditions of 17th-century European regimes ranged from authoritarian government (relatively high governmental capacity combined with little protected consultation) to fragmented tyranny (neither high governmental capacity nor protected consultation, with many local individuals and organizations wielding coercive force). France and Britain fluctuated between those two extremes during the 17th century, but spent most of the century closer to authoritarian government than to fragmented tyranny. Both their central states displayed remarkable capacities to spring back from devastating civil wars into new rounds of authoritarianism.

Of course, differences between French and British experiences immediately strike the eye. (Chapters 4 and 5 examine French and British political histories from the 17th to the 20th century in detail.) Both countries underwent deep revolutionary crises between 1640 and 1690. French government emerged from the midcentury crisis a strengthened version of its early 17th-century self; by the 1680s, for example, Louis XIV was completing the dismantlement of Protestant political autonomy that Louis XIII had undertaken during the 1620s. In Britain, things went very differently: revolution and Dutch models of administration produced dramatic reorganization of public politics, including such enhancement of parliamentary power that 18th-century monarchs put much of their energy into packing, cajoling, or subverting Parliament.

During the 1790s, in a reversal of roles, France managed one of the most rapid and thorough national administrative reorganizations that had ever occurred anywhere, while the British regime contained challenges from its own radicals and revolutionaries. Britain then saw a dramatic renewal of popular demands after its wars with France ended. During the 19th century, French regimes faced repeated revolutionary challenges – and some outright revolutionary transitions – as British regimes survived and changed in the face of continuing struggle short of revolution. (Nevertheless, British rulers confronted multiple revolutionary situations in Ireland.) Meanwhile, both countries were capitalizing and industrializing, but with greater financial, spatial, and organizational concentration in Britain than in France.

Despite its reputation for aristocratic muddling through, Britain offers no exception to the rule that democracy emerges from contention. In the very act of taking credit for political pacification, Disraeli himself called attention to the intense conflict that produced the Reform Bill of 1832 and that accompanied working-class Chartism from 1838 to 1848; both affected the form of subsequent British institutions. If Disraeli had turned his gaze westward from Manchester, he could also have pointed out the fundamental influence of struggles in, with, and about Ireland on the character of British politics over a very long period. (Chapter 5 follows that interaction closely.) Contention shaped politics in both France and Britain. It left enduring marks on the forms of their democratic institutions – for example, the relatively armed, militarized, and centralized police of France as opposed to the mainly unarmed, demilitarized, and decentralized police of Britain.

Since favored participants in relatively democratic regimes regularly condemn unruly claim making as a threat to democracy, and since analysts of democracy often treat popular contention as irrelevant or inimical to democratization, let me insist: in Europe after 1650, all the main historical paths to democratic polities entailed sustained contention. Democracy results from, mobilizes, and reshapes popular contention. Yet one feature of that interdependence between democratization and contention helps account, paradoxically, for the impression that the two are incompatible. On the whole, democratization greatly limits life- and property-threatening forms of public, collective claim making, substituting for them highly visible but less directly destructive varieties of interaction. On the average, in democratic regimes threats and declared intentions to act in a certain way instead of nonnegotiable direct actions occupy much more central positions in popular politics than they do in nondemocratic regimes. Still, many such threats lead to open conflict from time to time, and would lack credibility if they did not. Thus contention is indispensable to democratic interchange, but democrats systematically downplay its importance.

More generally, democratization transforms repertoires of contention. Anyone who learns the political histories of France and Britain since 1650 soon recognizes that their prevailing means of making discontinuous, public, collective claims – that is, contentious repertoires – altered profoundly between the 17th and 20th centuries. Repertoires mutated from such old-regime interactions as mobbing of tax collectors, ceremonial shaming of moral reprobates, or creation of local militias with elected captains to such contemporary interactions as holding of mass meetings, staging of demonstrations, or organization of strikes.

Claim-making performances such as shaming ceremonies and demonstrations do not exhaust public political participation. Political participation includes a wide range of interactions between citizens and governmental agents: paying taxes, serving in the military, answering censuses, voting, supporting political parties, holding public office, and much more. Regimes vary significantly in the places they assign to different forms of political participation. Some they *prescribe*, for example, by insisting on tax paying and collective pledges of allegiance. Some they *tolerate*, for example, by allowing (but not forcing) people to form special-purpose associations or to publish newspapers. Some they *forbid*, for example, by outlawing creation of private militias. A regime's mix of prescribed, tolerated, and forbidden types of political participation already tells us much about its character; a regime that tolerates only a narrow range of citizen-initiated political participation and effectively either prescribes or forbids all the rest is usually authoritarian in other regards as well.

In all sorts of regimes, most of the time political participation goes on without contention – without public, collective, discontinuous making of claims. People pay their taxes, wait in line for public services, or watch legislative sessions without making discontinuous, public, collective claims on officials or other people. But relations between known forms of political participation and contentious politics vary significantly from one kind of regime to another. We can therefore profit from a distinction between democratic and nondemocratic repertoires of contention.

Democratic contention, for the most part, takes place in or adjacent to the regimes' prescribed and tolerated forms of political participation; public meetings, for example, provide vehicles for both established power holders and dissident groups, while election campaigns offer opportunities for electoral, para-electoral, and counterelectoral claim making by organized critics. Under undemocratic regimes, popular contentious politics rarely adopts prescribed and tolerated forms of political interaction, among other reasons because power holders generally bar ordinary people from those forms; courts reject poor people's lawsuits, guards block the door to royal audiences. A wide range of undemocratic contention enters forbidden territory, however selectively the regimes in question enforce their prohibitions; sometimes officials turn blind eyes to blood feuds and unruly shaming ceremonies, but they always try to crush armed resistance against governmental demands. As a consequence, under authoritarian regimes we commonly witness sharp division of the public dissent that occurs; either it adopts forbidden forms such as clandestine attacks on officials or it crowds into the relatively protected spaces of authorized public gatherings such as funerals, holidays, and civic ceremonies.

Table 1.4 refines the comparison somewhat. Based on studies of Western Europe over the last few centuries, it dares to summarize for Europe as a whole in undemocratic and democratic phases. Broadly speaking, it claims that under undemocratic regimes ordinary Europeans (as distinguished from ruling classes) have usually employed parochial, particular, and bifurcated means of making collective claims. Their usual means have been *parochial* in operating chiefly within a limited local context, and in varying significantly in form from one locality to another. They have been *particular* in applying to a narrow class of targets, complaints, and settings – appropriate for disciplining fellow workers, for example, but not for dealing with local dignitaries, who call up other forms of collective claim making. They have been *bifurcated* in dividing between relatively direct means of dealing with local actors and employment of honorable intermediaries to address distant and higher authorities.

In this schematic summary, democratic repertoires qualify as cosmopolitan, modular, and autonomous. *Cosmopolitan* means that popular claim

Table 1.4 *Contrasting Principles of Undemocratic and Democratic Repertoires in Europe*

Undemocratic	Democratic
1. Frequent employment of authorities' normal means of action, either as caricature or as a deliberate, if temporary, assumption of authorities' prerogatives in the name of the local community	1. Use of relatively autonomous means of action, of a kind rarely or never employed by authorities
2. Convergence on residences of wrongdoers and sites of wrongdoing, as opposed to seats and symbols of public power	2. Preference for previously planned action in visible public places
3. Extensive use of authorized public celebrations and assemblies for presentation of grievances and demands	3. Deliberate organization of assemblies for the articulation of claims
4. Common appearance of participants as members or representatives of constituted corporate groups and communities rather than of special interests	4. Participation as members or representatives of special interests, constituted public bodies, and named associations
5. Tendency to act directly against local enemies but to appeal to powerful patrons for redress of wrongs beyond the reach of the local community as especially for representation vis-a-vis outside authorities	5. Direct challenges to rivals or authorities, especially national authorities and their representatives
6. Repeated adoption of rich, irreverent symbolism in the form of effigies, dumb show, and ritual objects to state grievances and demands	6. Display of programs, slogans, and symbols of common membership such as flags, colors, and lettered banners
7. Shaping of interaction to particular circumstances and localities	7. Preference for forms of interaction easily transferred from one circumstance or locality to another
8. Summary: *parochial, particular, and bifurcated*	8. Summary: *cosmopolitan, modular, and autonomous*

making extends across a wide range of objects, claims, programs, and settings. *Modular* means that essentially similar forms of action (e.g., public meetings and special-purpose associations) operate in a great variety of circumstances. *Autonomous* means that ordinary people frequently take the initiative on their own rather than waiting for convocation by authorities or employing honored intermediaries.

Of course, any such two-paneled summary immediately calls for qualifications. Some undemocratic claim-making routines depended so heavily on specific forms of social organization that they remained absent from most of Europe; the routines of blood feuds, for example, only appeared where fairly large, autonomous, armed lineages prevailed. Sometimes people borrowed across the democratic-undemocratic divide, as when opponents of authoritarian regimes employed the demonstration as a form of protest. Specific forms of action such as shaming ceremonies, seizures of food, and attacks on the dwellings of dishonored people had their own histories and time schedules (see Blickle 1988, 1997; te Brake 1998; Muir 1997; Puls 1979; Ruff 2001; Tarrow 1998; Traugott 1995). Rapid transitions between undemocratic and democratic forms of government did not transform prevailing repertoires instantly, simultaneously, and automatically.

The approximate comparison between nondemocratic and democratic repertoires of contention nevertheless permits better specification of this book's central questions:

- How and with what effects do transitions from one sort of repertoire to the other connect with alterations of political power?
- What sorts of national differences exist in these regards, why, and with what consequences for subsequent political life?
- What patterns and outcomes of contention promote establishment of democratic polities, how, and why?
- What patterns and outcomes of contention promote moves away from democracy, how, and why?

Analyses to come establish significant country-to-country variation in both contentious repertoires and paths of democratization, close interdependence between contention and democratization or de-democratization, increasing international influence on both democratic institutions and forms of contention, convergence of democracies toward the sorts of cosmopolitan, modular, and autonomous claim making performances described earlier, but significant residual variation as a result of previous contentious histories.

It turns out, for example, that the long-term history of trust-bearing networks in a region made a large difference to the prospects for democracy and the processes by which democratic regimes formed, if they did. Both the structure (e.g., centralized or segmented) and the content (e.g., trade or kinship) of those networks mattered. Take the contrast between the Low Countries and the Balkans. Large urban-based networks of trade, kinship, and religious affiliation closely intertwined with local and regional government in the Low Countries. That intertwining deeply affected prevailing forms of contention from the 17th century onward, the character of democratic experiments during the 18th century, the response of inhabitants to French-imposed regimes from the 1790s to 1814, and the painful construction of more or less democratic institutions in the Netherlands, Luxembourg, and Belgium thereafter.

In the Balkans, religiously connected trade diasporas intersected with patron-client chains and lineage systems as principal bases for risky enterprises and popular struggle; large-scale government long operated through indirect rule mediated by arms-bearing regional magnates; some political entrepreneurs collaborated with outside powers in fashioning claims to national sovereignty as the Habsburg and Ottoman empires fell apart under military assault from their European neighbors; and only small areas have even today come close to protected consultation. So far, Balkan peoples have generally withheld their trust from government-connected networks, solving their collective problems instead by resort to nongovernmental and antigovernmental networks. Recent struggles in Albania, Bosnia, Croatia, Kosovo, and Macedonia illustrate the effects of disarticulation between trust networks and governmental institutions.

Throughout Europe, indeed, governmental attempts to extend control over people, activities, and resources within their nominal jurisdiction generally incited reinforcement and defense of nongovernmental networks of trust rather than moves toward democracy. Spirals of antidemocracy occurred. Only where conquest, revolution, or struggles between oligarchies and subordinate actors ended with external guarantees for governmental protection of risky enterprises did the elements of democracy begin to operate together. Although both France and the British Isles experienced revolution, conquest, and popular challenges to oligarchies after 1650, revolution played a more direct part in French democratization, struggles between challengers and established oligarchies a greater role in the democratization of Britain and Ireland.

Closer to democracy, however, contentious spirals of democratization also occurred; the entrustment of risky enterprises to such institutions as elections, political parties, voluntary associations, unions, and Parliaments, when effective for major political actors in the short run, encouraged both longer-run commitment to those institutions and demands by excluded parties for access to those institutions. Thus in Great Britain the expanding power of Parliament after 1750, driven at first by great increases in British military expenditure, drew an increasing range of claims away from local authorities and great patrons toward Parliament itself, while the growing significance of parliamentary elections generated demands for enlargement of the electorate and more extensive popular controls over the whole electoral process (Tilly 1997; Tilly and Wood 2003). Our problem is to map and explain variation in related processes across the whole of Europe between 1650 and 2000.

Explanatory Strategies

Any such explanatory program immediately raises historical, comparative, and analytical objections. Historically, one might follow many democratic theorists in arguing that democracy makes contentious politics superfluous and that democratization requires massive taming of contention. Comparatively, one might point out the contemporary concentration of truly lethal contention in such undemocratic regimes as Rwanda or Afghanistan rather than in the world's settled democracies. Analytically, one might argue that democracy's essential conditions include tight containment of contention and that large-scale contention threatens democracy's survival.

Each of these imagined objections contains elements of truth:

- Democratization has, in fact, generally entailed suppression of some forms of political contention and considerable containment of others.
- On the average, democratic regimes do engage their domestic political struggles in less deadly ways than do their nondemocratic neighbors.
- The process by which democracy emerges does include negotiation of significant limits on the destructiveness of contention.

Still, the histories of France, Britain, and other European countries since 1650 negate any conception of open struggle as irrelevant, antithetical, or fatal to democratization. On the contrary, those histories show that all of

Europe's historical paths to democracy passed through vigorous political contention.

Democracy, in any case, does not have a single history, one repeated in more or less the same conditions and sequences by each democratizing country. Democracy is unlike an oil field, which can form only under very specific conditions over centuries or even millennia. Nor is it like a garden, which skilled horticulturalists can bring to life in one form or another within a season or two in almost any environment. Democracy more closely resembles a lake. A lake is a large inland body of water. Lakes form in a limited number of contrasting ways – filling of a glacial basin or volcanic crater, damming of a river, human excavation, and so forth – but once in existence share many properties with other lakes: tidal expansion and contraction, regular vertical and horizontal currents, layering of temperatures and of organisms, formation of sand through wave action, and so on.

The proper analogy makes a difference, for if democracy is an oil field, lovers of democracy can search only for those rare favorable sites where democratic oil has not yet been tapped, and consign all other sites to undemocratic fates. If democracy is a garden, advocates can plan to cultivate it almost everywhere and on short order. If democracy forms like an oil field or a garden, this book may satisfy historical curiosity about the European past, but it will hold little interest for people who want to promote democracy in the future.

If, however, democracy actually resembles a lake, a set of historically contingent conditions that nevertheless operate with regularity once in place, then promoters of democracy should pay attention to accumulated historical experience. They must fit their interventions to the cultural and institutional context with great care if they are to foster democratization instead of some very different outcome. Flooding rivers do not usually form stable lakes. Here history should provide important guidance for future interventions – if only to say what sorts of intervention are unlikely to make much difference. I am betting that democracies resemble lakes, therefore that history matters.

How do we recognize a democratic lake when we come to it? We seek four markers: (1) relatively broad citizen-agent relations, (2) relatively equal citizen-agent relations, (3) binding, efficacious consultation of citizens with respect to governmental personnel, resources, and policy, and (4) protection of citizens, especially members of minorities, from arbitrary action by governmental agents. To the degree that a polity displays these attributes we call it democratic.

We concentrate on national governments, or states: coercion-wielding organizations, distinct from kinship groups, whose agents exercise priority over other organizations within a substantial, diversified, delimited territory. Nevertheless, we recognize that smaller-scale governments such as those of villages and cities sometimes sustain partial democracies (Cerutti, Descimon, and Prak 1995; Head 1995; Wells 1995). In detail, many practical democratic procedures – assemblies, voting, elections, caucuses, and much more – took shape in local politics before serving as models for national practices. Yet two surprises await us in these regards. First, institutions of local politics such as city councils rarely evolved into elements of democratic politics at the national scale, and often put up determined resistance to democratic changes that threatened their autonomies and privileges. Second, no regular connection prevailed between local and national democracy; relatively democratic peasant communities, for instance, repeatedly operated within authoritarian regimes.

We find our four democratic markers together chiefly in the presence of high-capacity states. Even when they assemble or inherit rudiments of democracy, low-capacity states remain vulnerable to narrowing of political participation, increasing inequality, barriers to effective consultation of political participants, and interruptions of protection – not to mention obliteration through conquest from outside or revolution from within.

Experts in comparative politics have already noticed a peculiarity in my method of analysis. Given an interest in the conditions that promote or inhibit democracy, a concern for relations between those conditions and changes in contentious politics, and arguments of the political-process genre I have laid out so far, an experienced reader of political analyses might reasonably expect the book to organize around (1) pursuit of similarities in French and British experience, (2) comparisons identifying similarities and differences among states that democratized through conquest, revolution, colonization, and confrontation, or, most ambitiously, (3) mapping of European experience as a whole since 1650 into contrasting structural conditions and trajectories, some of them leading to early democracy, some to late democracy, some to alternation between democratic and undemocratic regimes, some of them to no democracy at all. Instead I am concentrating on two relatively similar states, both of which produced more or less viable democracies, then seeking to apply elsewhere lessons drawn from that two-state comparison. Why not begin with similarities and differences on a larger scale? Why not undertake a whole series of paired comparisons?

John Stuart Mill, whom experts often invoke as the patron saint of yes-no paired comparisons, actually warned his own readers against applying his experimental methods to whole political systems. After laying out his (widely recognized) Methods of Agreement and of Differences, as well as his (often ignored) Methods of Residues and of Concomitant Variation, Mill reminded readers that his methods applied exclusively to experimental procedures. Mill confined them, furthermore, to relatively simple phenomena entailing little or no interaction among causes, which meant they would not much advance understanding of living organisms. He therefore issued a stern warning:

> If so little can be done by the experimental method to determine the conditions of an effect of many combined causes, in the case of medical science; still less is this method applicable to a class of phenomena more complicated than even those of physiology, the phenomena of politics and history. There, Plurality of Causes exists in almost boundless excess, and effects are, for the most part, inextricably interwoven with one another. To add to the embarrassment, most of the inquiries in political science relate to the production of effects of a most comprehensive description, such as the public wealth, public security, public morality, and the like: results likely to be affected directly or indirectly either in *plus* or in *minus* by nearly every fact which exists, or event which occurs, in human society.
>
> The vulgar notion, that the safe methods on political subjects are those of Baconian induction – that the true guide is not general reasoning, but specific experience – will one day be quoted as among the most unequivocal marks of a low state of the speculative faculties in any age in which it is accredited. Nothing can be more ludicrous than the sort of parodies on experimental reasoning which one is accustomed to meet with, not in popular discussion only, but in grave treatises, when the affairs of nations are the theme. "How," it is asked, "can an institution be bad, when the country has prospered under it?" "How can such or such causes have contributed to the prosperity of one country, when another has prospered without them?" Whoever makes use of an argument of this kind, not intending to deceive, should be sent back to learn the elements of some one of the more easy physical sciences. (Mill 1887: 324)

Later, Mill identified the chief difficulties in applying his experimental methods to human affairs: not only the complex interaction of causes, but also the fact that his methods required a priori a finite, specified set of hypothetical causes. Aimed at social processes, Mill's methods always remained, as he insisted, fatally vulnerable to the allegation that a hitherto unsuspected cause was operating.

Mill himself recommended explanation of complex social processes by means of the sorts of grand evolutionary schemes proposed by Auguste Comte and other 19th-century social theorists. Indeed, his own theory of democratization depended on an idea of cultural evolution in which nations moved from the subordinate conditions of Bedouins or Malays to the self-government of British or French citizens. We have, however, an alternative. Instead of supposing that whole structures and processes repeat themselves in conformity to giant laws, we can disaggregate complex causal processes, identifying recurrent causal mechanisms that concatenate differently in different circumstances (McAdam, Tarrow, and Tilly 2001; Tilly 2001a). Thus we can search for regularities in the ways that governmental agents' demands for resources generate resistance, concealment, and bargaining without assuming that such demands always fall into the same sequence or have the same outcomes.

Instead of assuming that every valid statement about political processes is either a particular description or a general law, furthermore, we can specify the scope conditions for sturdy causal analogies – whether, for example, they operate reasonably well among high-capacity undemocratic regimes, but require significant modification elsewhere. We seek to explain neither uniformity nor yes-no differences, but variety and change.

Any effective explanation of democratization must avoid four temptations to which its analysts have often succumbed: teleology, system functionalism, ideal-case reasoning, and the quest for sufficient conditions. *Teleology* works back from an outcome to its presumed causes, scanning antecedent circumstances for elements or causes of that outcome. We must shut our ears to teleology's siren song in order to avoid picking through the past selectively while ignoring crucial factors in political change that seem antithetical or irrelevant to democratization. We must also escape teleology in order to arrive at explanations identifying common properties in processes that sometimes yield democracy, but often lead to undemocratic polities.

System functionalism explains activities or institutions by their consequences for a society, a political system, or some similar encompassing entity. System functionalism tempts analysts because it is all too easy after the fact to argue that authoritarian institutions exist because the system needs stability, that democratic institutions exist because the system needs equity, and so on. Social arrangements do sometimes reproduce the conditions for their own survival, as when ruling classes extract surpluses from subordinate classes and employ part of those surpluses to reinforce their control over subordinate classes (Tilly 1998: chapter 4). In the realm of political change, nevertheless, two serious troubles dog all such functional arguments. First, the system in question always remains elusive: exactly what set of relations, activities, beliefs, or institutions is receiving the supposed benefits, and how do those elements interlock? Second, how does the system create or maintain the supposedly functional activities and institutions? Arguments in either regard turn out to be hard to specify and even harder to verify.

Ideal-case reasoning implicitly or explicitly takes a single country's experience, or an idealized summary of all positive experiences, as the model for movement from nondemocratic to democratic political arrangements, then arrays all other experiences by their approximation to that model. Thus we schematize the democratization of Western European countries before treating all other democratization as a partial replication of that idealized process. By now the analysis of economic growth as recapitulation of American, British, or idealized western experience has failed enough times to warn political analysts against taking up a similar logic. We have too many reasons to doubt that the next instance of democratization will somehow repeat the initial conditions or sequence of events that expanded democracy in the United States, Japan, or somewhere else.

A quest for *sufficient conditions* – or, worse yet, for both necessary and sufficient conditions – of democracy has several damning defects. It assumes existence of a single set of circumstances that, wherever and whenever repeated, produces similar outcomes. It therefore denies path-dependency and the influence of accumulated culture. It tilts analysis away from dynamic political processes toward static comparison. It denies the logic that permeates this book – not that the social world conforms to immutable general laws producing the same whole structures and sequences everywhere, but that the social world results from recurrent causal mechanisms concatenating differently, with different outcomes, depending on local circumstances. The secret of explanatory history and effective social science, in this book's view, is the discovery of comparable causal mechanisms, not similarities in whole structures and sequences, over a wide variety of times, places, and circumstances.

To be sure, my argument does claim to identify *necessary* conditions for democratization: at least partial integration of trust networks into public politics, some segregation of public politics from categorical inequality, plus broadening of participation, equalization of participation, enhancement of collective control, and inhibition of arbitrary power. It makes its most distinctive – and riskiest – contribution to analyses of democratization by proposing bundles of mechanisms that produce these necessary conditions and, if reversed, promote de-democratization. Here is the claim: in combination, the stipulated processes affecting relations among trust networks, categorical inequalities, and public politics are necessary for democratization, but alternative combinations of mechanisms and initial conditions generate those processes.

That statement of necessary conditions makes it easy in principle to refute or modify the book's main arguments. Any case of substantial democratization that occurs without the conditions just enumerated – without partial integration of trust networks into public politics, insulation of public politics from categorical inequality, plus broadening of participation, equalization of participation, enhancement of collective control, and inhibition of arbitrary power – suffices to refute the argument. So does any substantial democratization that occurs without significant popular contention, whether through calm consensus or inconspicuous incremental change.

Modifications? Any demonstration that some condition outside my list is necessary to substantial democratization modifies the argument. So does any demonstration either that (1) one or more of the mechanisms enumerated in Tables 1.1–1.3 does *not* promote alterations in categorical inequality, trust networks, or public politics in the manner claimed or that (2) additional mechanisms not listed in Tables 1.1–1.3 *do* promote similar alterations in categorical inequality, trust networks, or public politics. Surely, criticism and further research will modify the book's arguments in some regards. Indeed, later chapters introduce nuances and complications that this chapter's raw statement of the arguments has ignored. At best I hope that the main arguments, properly modified, will stimulate and serve a new, fruitful round of inquiry into democratization.

The agenda laid out so far breaks into two parts, one difficult, the other almost impossible. The difficult part, undertaken in the next two chapters, is to see whether the broad temporal and geographic correlations implied by my arguments are plausible. Do regimes vary in time and space as an orderly function of (1) concatenations of coercion, capital, and commitment or (2) previous histories of regimes within the same territories? Do change and variation in the character of regimes coincide sufficiently with alterations in the character of popular contention to suggest that the two interact closely? Do revolution, conquest, confrontation, and colonization play something like the roles that my story attributes to them?

The nearly impossible part, assigned to Chapters 4–7, is to trace out causal connections among the story's major elements: not only regime change, revolution, conquest, confrontation, and colonization, but also alterations in categorical inequality, trust networks, and public politics, the creation of citizenship, and the formation of durably democratic polities.

Eventually, we search for recurrent causal mechanisms that appear in different combinations and sequences to produce strong state, weak state, intermediate, and other paths from petty tyranny, authoritarianism, or locally protected consultation toward national democratic regimes. Before undertaking that search with any confidence, we must be sure that the long-term historical record reveals enough regularity to make the identification of recurrent causal mechanisms thinkable.

How, then, does this book conduct its search? In general, it supposes one complex or another of undemocratic contention to be humanity's usual condition, then asks under what rare conditions and by what robust causal mechanisms contention becomes democratic. Chapter 2 sketches general relations between types of regime and types of contention for Europe as a whole. Chapter 3 surveys the varieties of undemocratic regimes and their contention in Europe as a whole since 1650 before arriving at preliminary conclusions concerning interactions of regimes and contention. Chapter 4 proceeds to a close examination of French experience with regime change and contention since 1650. Chapter 5 undertakes a parallel analysis of the British Isles, including ever-contentious Ireland. Chapter 6 then zeroes in on Switzerland from 1830 to 1848, showing how the major mechanisms operate in detail. Chapter 7 returns to Europe in general since 1815, applying and modifying the causal account derived from French, British, and Swiss experiences. Along the way, the book offers narratives of democratization and de-democratization not only in those three areas but also for significant chunks of historical experience in the Low Countries, Iberia, the Balkans, Russia, and elsewhere.

Chapter 8 sums up with implications for analysis of contention and democratization on a world scale. The result is not a general theory of democracy, but a new program of inquiry into the delicate, crucial relations between democratization and contentious politics. It should be worth pursuing, because so many of the world's polities seem to be moving erratically toward democratization, because the survival of democracy remains uncertain in many countries that currently enjoy some of its benefits, and because democracy is one of humanity's most precious political creations.

2

Regimes and Their Contention

Armed with our 21st-century democracy-finder, suppose we speed back to 17th-century Europe. In one part of Europe or another, we will find roughly 200 regimes we can reasonably call independent states: relatively autonomous, centralized, and well-bounded governments exercising priority in some regards over all other organizations operating within their territories. On four counters marked "Breadth," "Equality," "Consultation," and "Protection," we take readings for the regimes we locate in a journey throughout the continent. Where and when do we encounter vigorous vibrations of democracy?

Let's say we land in the year 1650. We might think it an auspicious year for democratic initiatives: except for continuing struggle between France and Spain the major disruptions of the Thirty Years' War have just ended with the Treaties of Westphalia, great fissures have opened in the Habsburg empire, and the success of their 16th-century rebellion against Spain has finally brought the northern Netherlands international recognition as a highly decentralized independent republic. What do we find?

We find plenty of revolution and war, but few signs of settled democracy. Touring the British Isles, we discover a Scotland rebelling openly against English hegemony, and a Scottish military force in northern England backing Charles Stuart's claim to succeed his father Charles I; just last year, England's contentious revolutionaries united temporarily to decapitate King Charles. In Ireland, Catholic leaders are battling not only each other, but also the English invading force of Oliver Cromwell. (We are not surprised to learn that Thomas Hobbes's *Leviathan*, with its eloquent nostalgia for stable authority, is on its way to publication next year.) Not much breadth, equality, consultation, or protection in the British Isles of 1650!

42

Nor do our four dials reach democratic readings across the channel this year, what with the newly recognized Dutch Republic in disaggregation as William II fails in a bid for national power. We find France in the midst of its Fronde as the Prince of Condé and Cardinal Mazarin seek to eliminate each other from the national scene while all sorts of local people rebel against the growing demands of a war-making state. At the same time Catalonia and Portugal enter their eleventh year of open revolt against Castilian power, Savoy trembles in the grip of Waldensian uprisings, Poland and Russia fall prey to multiple rebellions by Cossacks and other inhabitants of their frontier regions, the Ottoman empire writhes in anarchy, and – despite the recently signed Westphalian treaties – small-scale interstate wars ravage many parts of the continent. Outside Europe itself, furthermore, Dutch and Portuguese forces are battling fiercely for control over sea lanes and trade in the Indian Ocean. In the short run, such mixtures of revolution, rebellion, war, and anarchy do not favor breadth, equality, consultation, or protection.

Where sharp splits in polities do not prevail, on the whole, some form of tyranny does. To coax any scintillation at all from our democracy-detector, we must reduce the scale, approaching the oligarchies formed by some North European mercantile cities, what little remains of republican forms in Italian city-states, and the unequal but consultative governments of some Central European peasant villages. Although a few national regimes score relatively high on consultation and protection for members of their oligarchies, none qualify as democratic with regard to breadth and equality of political participation. Except as radical doctrine and as distant kin of civic republicanism, nothing like democracy exists at a national scale in the Europe of 1650.

Nor would moving backward in time do us much good. If we returned to the local scale and moved back a century or so to the Protestant Reformation, to be sure, we could find a number of villages and towns that temporarily created relatively autonomous, broad, and equal communities of believers with their own binding forms of consultation and even some degree of protection for their members (Blickle 1988, 1997; te Brake 1998; Wells 1995). In a long series of English revolts and in some elements of the recent English revolution we could identify demands for radical equality, broad participation, and strong consultation. Yet nowhere on a large scale for a sustained period would we detect a state featuring the combination of broad, equal citizenship with binding consultation and protection of citizens. Only piercing hindsight allows 20th-century analysts to look back to the 17th century or before and find nascent democracy.

Hindsight can easily distort, if it consists of looking back into history for specific institutional forms such as elections, representatives, terms of office, deliberative assemblies, and associations. All these forms actually existed widely in Europe before any national democratic regime took shape. Most of them appeared in villages, cities, or regional jurisdictions, but some even operated at a national scale; the most spectacular national examples consisted of Estates that met with rulers to bargain out taxes, military support, or responses to crisis. When democratic regimes did take shape, such institutions often served as procedural models. As they worked before the 19th century, however, they did not in themselves constitute democratic regimes beyond any but the smallest scale. Above that scale, they always coexisted with narrow, unequal political participation, manipulation by oligarchies, and uncertain protection from arbitrary action by governmental agents. Nor did those institutions often evolve into democratic practice at a national scale. Britain's Parliament notwithstanding, on the whole creation of national democratic institutions almost always resulted from crises in which people solved problems by emulating models available from elsewhere.

Europe before the 19th century, then, offers a bounteous array of nondemocratic contention. Although we spend a certain amount of time touring across the continent and through earlier centuries as we inventory different varieties of contentious politics, our chief mission in this chapter falls into two parts. First we stop time in 1650, examining connections among locations of regimes with respect to protected consultation and governmental capacity, general conditions of social life, and forms of contentious politics. Second, we restart time between 1650 and 1850, scrutinizing mutual transformations of regimes and of contentious politics.

Here we concentrate on nondemocratic regimes – the vast majority of European regimes year by year and place by place – but peer now and then into regions and times of democratic expansion. The idea is to clarify trajectories followed by European regimes since 1650 and to place alterations of contention firmly within that field of variation.

This chapter pursues two distinct but complementary questions:

1. Over the period between 1650 and 1850, what accounts for variation and change in the location of European regimes within the two-dimensional analytical space defined by degree of protected consultation and governmental capacity?

2. How, to what extent, and why did (a) alterations of contentious politics and (b) changes of position within that two-dimensional space affect each other?

Now and then we adopt finer distinctions, for example, by looking separately at changes in breadth, equality, consultation, and protection. For the most part, however, we keep a complex history manageable by lumping protected consultation into a single dimension of change, then mapping regimes into the two-dimensional space defined by degree of protected consultation and governmental capacity.

The most general answer to question 1 runs as follows: regional variation in the accumulation and concentration of coercion, capital, and commitment strongly affected the sorts of governmental institutions that formed in different parts of Europe through the centuries, but the presence of certain sorts of regimes in a region shaped what kinds of regimes formed later. The most general answer to question 2 runs: negotiation and struggle – emphatically including contention by ordinary people – over means of government generated the institutions of regimes, which then channeled the character of collective claim making. Those effects operated, however, within strong constraints set by regional social contexts.

On grounds already explored in Chapter 1, we might therefore expect similarities in forms and trajectories of contentious politics to cluster geographically as well. They did. Not only did significantly different combinations of governmental capacity and protected consultation characterize regimes in separate regions of Europe at any given point in time, but strong state trajectories, weak state trajectories, and middling trajectories into the zone of citizenship clustered geographically as well. Balkan regimes took very different paths toward substantial citizenship than did their Low Country confreres. Those paths involved different qualities and sequences of contention.

Coercion, Capital, and Commitment

Before examining variations in contentious politics, let us look at variation in regimes. Regimes are polities seen from the perspective of relations between governmental agents and other political actors. Three variable elements of regimes' social environments strongly affect their organization: coercion, capital, and commitment.

Coercion includes all concerted means of action that commonly cause loss or damage to the persons or possessions of social actors. We stress means such as weapons, armed forces, prisons, damaging information, and organized routines for imposing sanctions. *Accumulation* of such means within a given polity varies in principle from nonexistent to huge, with low accumulation signifying that over a specified population the total volume of such means is small, and high accumulation signifying that the population contains extensive coercive means. *Concentration* of coercion means likewise varies from trivial to total, with low concentration signifying that whatever means exist disperse across the population, and high concentration signifying that all coercive means – however extensive – come close to forming a single clump under one agent's control. The multiple of accumulation and concentration defines the extent of coercion in a regime's territory. Low accumulation combined with low concentration describes a situation close to anarchy. High accumulation combined with high concentration describes a well-armed tyranny ruling a disarmed populace.

Coercion's organization helps to define the nature of regimes. With low accumulations of coercion, all regimes are insubstantial, while with high levels of coercive accumulation and concentration all regimes are formidable. But since no government ever gains control of all the coercive means within its territory, the organization of coercion constitutes not only a feature of regimes but also part of each regime's immediate environment. All other things equal, for example, regimes in circumstances of high coercive accumulation and low coercive concentration spend a good deal of their effort fighting off, repressing, evading, or making deals with violent entrepreneurs who are operating within the regime's territory but outside the government. Southern Italian regimes long operated in just such circumstances.

Capital refers to tangible, transferable resources that in combination with effort can produce increases in use value plus enforceable claims on such resources. As with coercion, accumulation of capital varies in principle from nonexistent to huge. Capital's concentration likewise varies from trivial to total. In Europe since 1650, the organization of capital in a region shaped the region's regimes in several different ways: by determining the prominence of capitalists and cities as presences with which agents of government had to contend; by affecting the extent and form of resources that were available for governmental activities such as war, infrastructural investment, or enrichment of rulers; and by affecting relations of nongovernmental activity (e.g., industrial production, trade, agriculture, migration) within the government's jurisdiction to activities outside that jurisdiction.

46

By *commitment* I mean relations among social sites (persons, groups, structures, or positions) that promote their taking account of each other. Commitment's local organization varies as dramatically as do structures of coercion and capital. Commitments can take the form of shared religion or ethnicity, trading ties, work-generated solidarities, communities of taste, and much more. They include networks of trust, those webs of connection on which people rely when engaging in long-term, high-risk, socially contingent activities. Accumulation in this regard varies in principle from nonexistent – every person an isolate, and no collective structures at all – to an overwhelming maximum – vast collective organization, including ties of every person to every other one. But concentration likewise occurs: from an even dispersion of relations across all social sites to binding of everyone and everything that is connected at all into a single centralized system.

How does commitment impinge on regimes? First, by confronting agents of government with varying cleavages and solidarities inside the government's subject population – for example, the presence or absence of large religious, linguistic, racial, ethnic, or cultural minorities. Second, by affecting the degree to which members of the subject population maintain strong relations with persons, groups, or organizations outside the government's own territory. Third, by influencing the means through which (and therefore the ease with which) governmental agents incorporate members of the subject population into the governmental structure. A fragmented population faces high costs of communication and resistance on a large scale but also presents formidable coordination costs to its government. In contrast, a population that resembles an evenly and intensely connected grid combines lower communication and resistance costs with vulnerability to observation and infiltration by governmental agents. Regionally concentrated clumps of commitment in the form of religious, linguistic, racial, ethnic, or cultural minorities almost always pose obstacles to uniform centralized rule.

Coercion, capital, and commitment co-vary to some degree over time and space. As great chunks of accumulated coercion form, so in general do clusters of accumulated capital and webs of accumulated commitment. Yet in European experience as a whole, plenty of independent variation occurred in these regards: regions, periods, and structures combining high capital concentration with relatively little coercion, others combining extensive commitment with little capital accumulation, and so on. Our later comparison of the Low Countries with Iberia between 1650 and 1850 will feature a region combining extensive capital and commitment with relatively weak coercion (the Low Countries) and another region (Iberia) offering extensive coercive means but very uneven – and, on the average, less – capital and commitment. That variability gives us reason enough not to lump changes in coercion, capital, and commitment together in portmanteau process terms such as state formation, centralization, and modernization.

As of 1650, how did the geography of coercion, capital, and commitment affect the character of regimes? No large European regime of that time greatly resembled a 20th-century state; none exercised anything like routine 20th-century state controls over resources, activities, and populations within its nominal territories, and none afforded anything like the extent of popular participation in national affairs that became commonplace after 1900. But prevailing combinations of coercion, capital, and commitment in a region significantly affected the character of that region's regimes. In general, governmental capacity ran higher at intermediate levels of coercion, capital, and commitment. At very low levels of any (and especially all) of them, would-be rulers lacked the means to assemble organizations that could control resources, persons, and activities within their claimed territories; petty, fluctuating tyrannies characterized such marginal regions in the Europe of 1650. Much of the interior Balkans, buffer areas between the Russian and Ottoman empires, high mountain valleys, and pastoral islands such as Corsica and Sardinia conformed to this pattern.

Very high values on just one of the elements – coercion, capital, or commitment – likewise blocked the creation of high-capacity governments; high accumulations and concentrations of coercion, as in 17th-century Poland, yielded war-making magnates who bowed reluctantly to central control and interfered incessantly in each other's regional rule. Disproportionate strength of capital yielded merchant-dominated political structures with great propensities to factionalism – although the case of the Venetian Republic shows that merchant oligarchies could also muster fierce, if intermittent, coordination for warfare. In the absence of equivalent coercion and capital, extensive commitment typically meant that local people had the means of escape from or resistance to the exactions of would-be state-builders, as when persecuted Waldensians, Jews, or Protestants received aid from their co-religionists elsewhere.

Intermediate and relatively equal levels of coercion, capital, and commitment facilitated creation of governmental capacity through synergy. Creators of effective states used their coercive means to draw resources from their capitalists in exchange for protection of commerce. But they also employed moderately centralized webs of commitment to integrate subject populations into their governmental enterprises through stable in-direct rule. Although Scandinavian, Burgundian, Habsburg, Ottoman, and Northern Italian rulers had at various times over the two previous centuries made partially successful attempts to create stable national governmental capacity, in 1650 the two leading European exemplars were no doubt France and Britain.

Until the 19th century, Europe's large states worked their will on sub-ject populations chiefly through indirect rule; they empowered existing, relatively autonomous local and regional authorities to collect taxes, gather troops, administer justice, and maintain order on their behalf without dis-patching central agents for local or regional administration more than in-termittently. Rulers ruled directly in their capitals, indirectly elsewhere. Such an arrangement reduced the cost and personnel of government from the center's perspective, but it also set stringent limits on the resources central authorities could extract from their nominal jurisdictions, reduced the amount of standardized control those authorities could exert over ac-tivities within remote regions, promoted or tolerated the formation of variable rights and obligations connecting different clusters of subjects to agents of the central power, and augmented the influence of privileged intermediaries.

European colonizers exported a very similar system to conquered terri-tories outside Europe. Mahmood Mamdani sums up for Africa:

Colonialism was not just about the identity of governors, that they were white or European; it was even more so about the institutions they created to enable a minority to rule over a majority. During indirect rule, these institutions unified the minority as rights-bearing citizens and fragmented the majority as so many custom-driven ethnicities. I have suggested that this is what the legal discourse on race and ethnicity was all about. Instead of racializing the colonized into a majority identity called "natives," as did 19th-century direct rule, 20th-century indirect rule dismantled this racialized majority into so many ethnicized minorities. Thus it was said that there were no majorities, only minorities, in the African colonies. (Mamdani 2001: 663; see also Mamdani 1996: 18)

Although European "natives" sometimes belonged to the same broad lin-guistic and cultural groups as their rulers, the partition between direct and indirect rule operated quite similarly within the colonizer's own continent.

More so than in European-conquered regions of Africa, however, European indirect rule resulted from the interaction of top-down and bottom-up politics. From the top, expanding states selectively incorpo-rated constituted leaders and their followers into governmental structures while granting retention of previously existing rights and customs. From the bottom, constituted political actors bargained for particular rights as the price of peace when they could not fight off their would-be conquerors. Even centralizing Britain and France fashioned special systems of rule for such conquered territories as Ireland, Brittany, and Franche-Comté.

The geography of commitment significantly affected the character and effectiveness of indirect rule. Where geographically segregated cultural networks prevailed, rulers could usually find members of a cultural elite – priests, chiefs, merchants, and others – to collaborate with them in exchange for a degree of autonomy and recognition as authoritative interlocutors for the population at large. Where such commitments overlapped each other spatially, each such arrangement promoted resistance on the part of excluded minorities; still, the Ottoman empire's millet system managed separate representation of territorially mingled populations.

The greatest obstacles arose where cultural fragmentation and spatial dispersion went farthest: such populations usually did not mount effective opposition to conquest, but ruling after conquest entailed consolidating disparate populations and their connecting networks into territorially contiguous administrative units. After the Boer War, South African regimes fashioned just that sort of consolidation among multiple African peoples, including their assignment to nominal homelands. At its extreme, that system gained the name "apartheid" (Ashforth 1990; Jung 2000; Marks and Trapido 1987; Marx 1998). Although they never reached the extremes of apartheid, tsarist and Bolshevik regimes likewise segregated previously mingled populations, assigned many of them home territories, and in the process created or fortified nationalities. Just as South Africa's created African nationalities became significant actors in the destruction of apartheid, republic-based nationalities constituted a major force in the Soviet Union's disintegration (Beissinger 1993, 2001; Kaiser 1994; Khazanov 1995; Suny 1993, 1995; Tishkov 1997, 1999).

Since 1650, accumulations and concentrations of coercion, capital, and commitment have all increased enormously in Europe as a whole. Formation of standing armies, police forces, and weapons of mass destruction certainly registers great expansions of coercive means. But the sensational growth has occurred on the side of capital; as measured by total wealth, current income, productive plant, or domination of production and distribution, capital's influence over European life has multiplied (Bairoch 1976; Bairoch and Lévy-Leboyer 1981; Dodgshon 1987; Hohenberg and Lees 1985; Kellenbenz 1976; Landes 1998; Pomeranz 2000; de Vries 1984).

Commitment has altered in a more mixed fashion. On one side, an undoubted multiplication of connections among Europeans by means of political organization, commercial ties, and improved means of communication has occurred. On the other, we observe undermining of transnational trade diasporas, linguistic networks, and crafts in favor of segmentation of social life within a limited number of well-bordered, increasingly monolingual states. Culture homogenized within states. Boundaries of commitment thereby moved into increasing correspondence and interdependence with national political structures (Armstrong 1982; Watkins 1990). States themselves promoted that homogenization by favoring national languages, celebrating national histories, establishing national educational systems, conscripting men into national armies, and restricting movement across national frontiers. Until the recent past, changes in coercion, capital, and commitment have on balance interacted to make the particular state to which European citizens were attached more and more salient in all varieties of contentious politics. Whether the European Union and international capital are now reversing that centuries-old trend remains to be seen (Imig and Tarrow 2001).

Imagine a two-dimensional space defined by variations in governmental capacity and protected consultation. Figure 2.1 schematizes that space. Relative concentrations of coercion, capital, and commitment in the social environments of European regimes limited their possible locations within the capacity-protection space, hence their proximities to petty tyranny, authoritarianism, citizenship, and democracy. On the whole, disproportionate concentration of coercive means in its region brought a regime closer to the zone of authoritarianism – that is, of high capacity combined with limited protection and consultation. Remember that capacity refers to the extent of governmental agents' control over persons, activities, and resources within the government's claimed territorial jurisdiction. No regime reached very high governmental capacity (and therefore full authoritarianism) without substantial control over capital as well. Although Prussia and Russia accumulated great coercive means during the two centuries after 1650, combinations of coercion and capital brought France and Britain higher-capacity states over the same period.

Where capital and commitment outstripped coercion, however, governmental capacity generally suffered, while protected consultation had more room for expansion. Europe's commercial band from northern Italy across the Alps to the Low Countries, with its often vigorous urban oligarchies, exemplified that pattern. Within those limits, the histories of

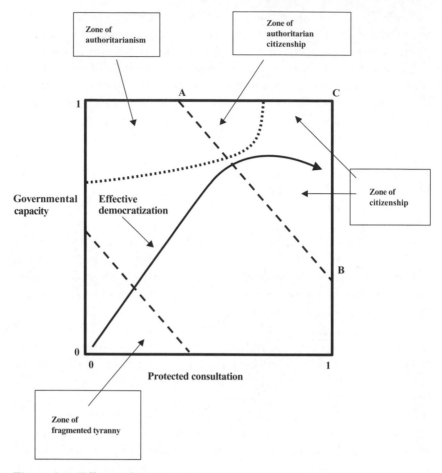

Zone of
authoritarianism

Zone of
authoritarian
citizenship

1

A

C

Governmental
capacity

Effective
democratization

Zone of
citizenship

0

B

0

1

Protected consultation

Zone of
fragmented tyranny

Figure 2.1: Effective democratization.

particular regimes and their dynasties made a difference; even within
the well-connected Low Countries, for example, the Habsburgs imposed
more centralized controls over their domains than did the House of
Orange.

Taking only central states into account, Figure 2.2 sketches two idealized paths out of fragmented tyranny into democracy. The "strong state"
path involves early increases of governmental capacity, often at the expense
of whatever protected consultation existed in previous regimes; it passes
through an extended phase of authoritarianism. Below we see expansion of
protected consultation as struggle produces broadening and equalization

52

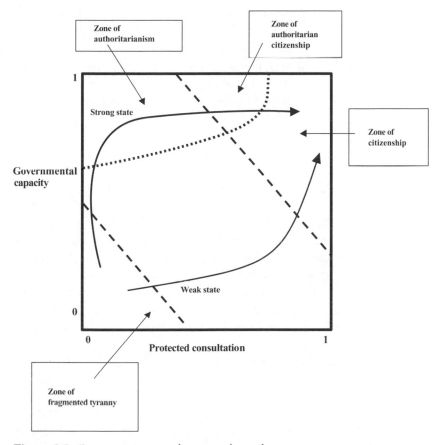

Figure 2.2: Strong state vs. weak state paths to democracy.

of access to governmental agents, services, and resources while binding consultation and protection generalize. In such historical experiences, goes the hypothesis, even the resulting democratic state bears distinct marks of its authoritarian history in the form of centralized institutions and serious constraints on the range of tolerated political performances. Russia and Prussia stand as exemplars of the strong state path toward citizenship and democracy.

The weak state trajectory entails elaboration of protected consultation – relatively broad and equal access to governmental agents, binding consultation, and creation of protections from arbitrary governmental action – before any great expansion of governmental capacity. Given low levels of governmental capacity, the weak state trajectory toward democracy probably entails more reversals and hesitations than the strong state trajectory, simply because the government does not lock in democratic institutions as firmly. Here again, nevertheless, we expect to see residues of previous history in the workings of democracy and citizenship, with greater restraints on the state's power of intervention in local affairs and greater accommodation of difference. In this case, Switzerland will serve as a model.

Even where they eventuated in democracy, most European experiences followed more irregular paths somewhere between the two idealized trajectories. In Great Britain, 18th-century wars and colonial expansion built up a strong central state apparatus amid local autonomies that had previously been vested in landlords, magistrates, municipalities, and (especially after 1689) elements of the Anglican church. In the Low Countries, municipal oligarchies predominated until French conquests under the Revolution and Napoleon established centralized regimes that endured into the 19th century. In Scandinavia, the Protestant Reformation promoted alliances between war-making rulers and state-serving pastors in the construction of relatively high-capacity states, but (especially in Norway and Sweden) peasants acquired corporate representation in return for provision of military service. Russia went from tribute-taking regimes that left great autonomy to landlords and warlords to extensive incorporation of landlords and bureaucrats into a repressive administrative hierarchy (Kivelson 2002; Raeff 1983; Wirtschafter 1997). Both the Balkans and much of Iberia featured sharp alternations between imperial expansion and petty tyrannies, with effects on democratic politics that endure today. In short, strong state and weak state paths to democracy present cartoons of limiting cases.

How Regimes and Contention Interacted

Distributions of coercion, capital, and commitment limited trajectories of regimes with respect to governmental capacity and protected consultation, which in turn significantly affected the forms of contentious politics. Let us think about the varieties of popular contentious politics (i.e., excluding maneuvers among elites) in an idealized medium- to high-capacity undemocratic state at a single point of time between 1650 and 1850. Figure 2.3 offers a simplified view for Europe as a whole. It makes the following observations:

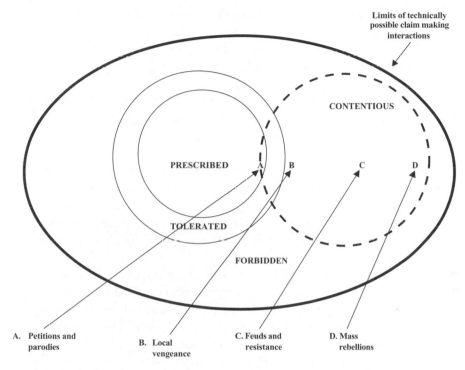

Figure 2.3: Typical forms of popular contentious politics in Europe's medium- to high-capacity undemocratic regimes, 1650–1800.

1. Such regimes typically prescribed a substantial range of political performances (e.g., popular attendance at royal processions and ritual executions) but tolerated few performances they did not prescribe; they generally declined, for example, to intervene in local political squabbles or covert expressions of political preference during public celebrations so long as the actions and claims involved remained within bounds. That left a wide range of technically possible claim-making interactions (e.g., bribes and attacks on corrupt officials) legally forbidden.

2. In such regimes, contentious politics rarely overlapped with state-prescribed forms of political participation, such as court assemblies and military maneuvers. Although a substantial minority of contention took place in the small tolerated zone, contentious claim making went on largely in legally forbidden territory.

3. Within the narrow range of tolerated performances, ordinary people had the option of humble petitions or legal suits, but rarely reached higher authorities without the endorsement or direct mediation of notables – of cultural or political brokers.
4. At the same edge of tolerated performances, contention commonly took the form of parodies and subversions, as when masked revelers at Mardi Gras cast verbal or visual barbs at dignitaries or theater audiences cheered actors' lines carrying politically resonant double meanings.
5. Boundaries between tolerated and forbidden performances blurred, both because the regime's capacity to monitor and control claim making throughout its territory and over all groups remained very uneven, and because the regime's toleration or repression of different performances (e.g., deliberative assemblies and armed gatherings) varied significantly by group.
6. Much contentious interaction enacted routines of collective local vengeance (e.g., rough music, seizures of high-priced grain, or burning in effigy), which authorities typically forbade formally and suppressed when it threatened public order, national officials, or local agents of the central power, but otherwise monitored without active intervention. Such contentious forms often mimicked established legal procedures – not only burning in effigy, but also official commandeering of grain supplies, demeaning punishments, and solemn judgments of offenders.
7. Feuds and similar violent struggles among constituted actors, as well as forcible resistance to governmental agents such as tax collectors and recruiting sergeants, generally fell under authorities' interdiction and discredited governmental agents who failed to contain them. At times, however, dissident authorities tacitly encouraged or tolerated such forms of contention.
8. Mass rebellions sometimes began as purely popular resistance to state authority, but never became massive without brokerage – without significant involvement of disaffected elites or external allies. Established authorities always tried to repress mass rebellions, but commonly checked them by negotiating (or pretending to negotiate) with rebel leaders. Although very few mass rebellions produced revolutionary outcomes (significant transfers of power over states, hence important realignments of polities), revolutionary situations (splits in polities such that each segment or coalition controlled

substantial means of government) ordinarily emerged from mass rebellions.

Needless to say, mass rebellions occurred much less frequently than parodies, local vengeance, or feuds and resistance. Whether they also occurred less frequently than petitions and their equivalents varied dramatically from regime to regime and period to period; where and when elaborate judicial systems or extensive patron-client chains prevailed as means of government, so too did varieties of petitioning (Heerma van Voss 2001; Zaret 2000).

To sense some of that historical particularism, let us make a brief excursion to the county of Hauenstein, Outer Austria (a region of Habsburg crown lands across the Rhine from Switzerland, to the east of Basel) during the 1730s. Politics in Hauenstein shared many features with the contention of its Swiss neighbors. As part of a conflict that began earlier and lasted longer, between 1728 and 1745 two shifting factions within Hauenstein fought an intermittent civil war. To simplify radically an exquisitely complex and mobile set of alignments, the conflict involved four principal actors: (1) the nearby abbey of St. Blasien, which claimed feudal control over persons and property of many Hauensteiners; (2) a peasant faction (known as *müllerisch* for the early prominence of miller Joseph Tröndle) led by elected cantonal officeholders who in general served as brokers between the abbey and the regional peasantry; (3) a second peasant faction (known as *salpeterisch* for the initial influence of Hans Albiez, a substantial peasant who dealt in saltpeter); and (4) the Austrian imperial administration. Official intermediaries between Hauenstein's villagers and the imperial administration (and, in fact, between villagers and the monastery as well) consisted of a Forest Steward, peasant bailiffs chosen by the steward from cantonal nominees, and the Octovirs, or Eight, made up of one spokesman elected by manhood suffrage from each of the eight cantons.

After much local bickering and repeated delegations to Vienna, *müllerisch* leaders had negotiated a commutation of servile status for St. Blasien's subjects within Hauenstein at the price of a large fee and what *salpeterisch* leaders interpreted as acknowledgment of the whole county's collective subjection to St. Blasien. *Salpeterisch* activists thereupon rejected the deal and called for complete emancipation without compensation to the overlord. On the morning of 22 July 1738, the feast of Mary Magdelene,

A great crowd gathered to hear a report from several *salpeterisch* peasants who had recently returned from a diplomatic mission to Vienna, where they had petitioned Emperor Charles VI to rescind the manumission treaty concluded between the *müllerisch* Eight, St. Blasien, and the provincial government on 15 January. To open the proceedings, one Hans Friedle Gerspach, a native of Bergalingen who had also traveled to Vienna, enjoined all who were loyal to "God, the emperor, and the rights of Hauenstein," to recite an *Ave Maria* and the Lord's Prayer. Then Gerspach gave a speech that was meant to prove Emperor Charles VI's opposition to the servile condition of most Hauensteiners. . . . Finally, the assembly elected some two hundred delegates to present to Forest Steward von Schönau their demand that he confirm in office four rebels who had been elected Octovir the previous April. Before it disbanded, the group swore "no longer to follow the old [*müllerisch*] Octovirs." (Luebke 1997: 182–83)

The occasion's religious references confirmed the cause's upright solemnity, as did the factions' frequent incorporation into their claim making of pilgrimages (complete with white-gowned village virgins) to shrines of the Virgin Mary. In this case, regional brokers organized contention around a series of performances ranging from solemn gatherings to mass marches to attacks on the enemy. All these performances drew strength from their rooting in established local practices, discourses, and symbols. As the death of Hans Albiez in prison and the later banishment or imprisonment of many other *salpeterisch* activists indicates, however, such dissident collective actions fell clearly into the zone of claim making forbidden by the Austrian regime.

With its strong orientation to decision makers in far-off Vienna, Hauenstein's civil war radically challenges any equation between particularism and social isolation. It alerts us, however, to the crucial place of brokerage in connecting local conflicts with national and international centers of power (see te Brake 1998 for many examples). Brokerage involves creating connections among social sites that were not previously as well connected. Brokerage played different parts in undemocratic contention depending on the form and locus of interaction. On the rare occasions when ordinary people collectively entered a regime's prescribed and tolerated forms of claim making at a national scale by drafting petitions, appealing to law courts, or similar procedures, they generally recruited cultural brokers – priests, schoolteachers, landlords, notaries, or other notables – to present their demands. Parodies and subversions usually aimed at local targets, and thus did not require brokers. Ordinary people usually produced local vengeance or feuds and resistance on their own; in these cases, brokers most often entered after the fact as mediators or as defenders of local culprits against retaliation from higher authorities.

58

Mass rebellions, however, regularly involved two contrasting styles of brokerage: deliberate alliance with a dissident polity member (e.g., a rebuffed pretender to the crown or a regional magnate who was resisting royal infringement on his powers) and designation of leaders or interlocutors from among the mass of rebels. In the latter case, the elected, conscripted, or self-designated captain or delegate ordinarily enjoyed some sort of prior distinction (e.g., retired soldiers chosen to lead military maneuvers) and ran the risk of exemplary punishment if, as usual, the rebellion failed.

Identities in Politics

By creating or activating connections among previously scattered clusters of people, brokers formed new *political identities* (for much greater detail, see Tilly 2002b). Identities are collective answers to the questions "Who are you?," "Who are we?," and "Who are they?" They become *political* identities to the extent that they involve ties – hostile or friendly – to governments. As such, they define boundaries between categories of people, relations among people on each side of the boundary, relations across the boundary, and shared stories about all those elements. *Müllerisch* Hauensteiners established a boundary separating themselves from their *salpeterisch* rivals, relations within the *müllerisch* world, collective relations between members of the two categories, plus a set of stories about boundaries and relations. At the start, brokers Joseph Tröndle and Hans Albiez helped establish boundaries, relations, and stories. The identities became political identities because they connected people with Hauenstein's regional and imperial governments.

Here we need a distinction between two contrasting types of political identities: embedded and detached. *Embedded* identities such as membership in a particular shop or household figured in a wide range of social interactions and significantly affected the behavior of parties to those interactions. *Detached* identities rarely or never figured in routine social interaction but became salient in coordinated claim making; participants organized and portrayed themselves as vassals of Lord Q, Crusaders, or assembled inhabitants of an officially constituted community. *Embedded* and *detached* mark ends of a fluid continuum, with identities such as member of a parish occupying intermediate positions, with embedded identities sometimes becoming more detached (as when all of a region's parish priests began coordinating their demands on the bishop), and with detached identities sometimes increasing their embeddedness (as when a spreading heresy became a way of life). In Hauenstein, we see initially quite detached identities – *müllerisch* and *salpeterisch* – becoming deeply, if temporarily, embedded in routine social life.

The relative salience of embedded and detached identities varied greatly across undemocratic Europe's contrasting varieties of contention. At the two extremes of petitioning and mass rebellion, detached identities often came into play, as participants made demands in the guise of assembled communities, subjects of long-conquered principalities, or clients of great lords. In the course of vengeance or feuds, participants more often organized and portrayed themselves in embedded identities, those governing a wide range of everyday social relations: member of household P, craft A, and so on.

As bases of mobilization for contention, detached identities had the advantage of spanning a variety of local situations (as, e.g., when members of many villages subject to the same lord joined to march on his seat of power) but had the disadvantage of depending on specialized brokers, communication lines, and symbol systems not readily available in routine social life. Conversely, embedded identities had the advantages of ready availability (as, e.g., when a tax collector unexpectedly showed up at the Wednesday market only to be assaulted by regular participants in the market) and had the disadvantages of great particularity. The particularity of embedded identities greatly limited the scale of coordinated action in the names of those identities.

Embedded political identities also hindered democratization. Equal, broad, protected, binding consultation depends on the creation of detached identities, most notably the cross-cutting identity of citizen. The more that embedded identities organized around boundaries of religion, ethnicity, kinship, gender, trade, or class figure directly in public politics, the greater the propensity of political actors to deploy and reproduce existing social inequalities in claim making, to rely on segmented interpersonal networks of trust for political advantage, and to bend governmental means to the ends of their own category members. Embedded identities hinder democratization especially when they combine local controls over social interaction within hierarchies and internal communication systems that incorporate localities into nationally constituted political actors.

Leaders of such embedded conglomerates have strong incentives to strike collective bargains with governments and restrain their followers from independent political participation. Democratic politics by no means blocks the pursuit of collective advantage by members of well-organized categories, but it sets limits on interest-seeking in two ways: by encouraging countervailing action on behalf of the disadvantaged and by facilitating the formation of actors consisting of temporary coalitions connected by shared but relatively narrow interests. In relatively democratic regimes, those temporary coalitions – characterized by such labels as X Front, Campaign for Y, People United Against Z, and the like – activate detached identities. Social movements and political parties regularly surge up around just such detached identities.

Detached identities figure doubly in democratization. First, the very formation of political coalitions, parties, special-interest associations, regional groupings, and movement identities frequently activates the crucial democracy-promoting processes – insulating categorical inequalities from public politics, integrating trust networks into public politics, and directly fostering broad, equal consultation and protection. (The major exceptions, obviously, are those detached identities that fortify existing categorical inequalities, translating them durably into public politics as corporate entities by class, race, religion, gender, or other fundamental divisions.) Second, citizenship itself established at least two detached identities (citizen and noncitizen) entailing shared relations to agents of a given government. The replacement of particularized relations to governmental agents by citizenship does not in itself guarantee democracy, since it sometimes occurs through top-down incorporation without protection or binding consultation; authoritarian citizenship results. On the whole, however, the creation of citizenship facilitates democratization as well.

Prevalence of embedded identities in undemocratic politics did not, however, condemn their regimes to monotonous political rituals. In Europe's undemocratic regimes, contentious performances such as Hauenstein's acrimonious assemblies always involved improvisation. Although participants in Outer Austria's 18th-century dissident assemblies obviously shared a series of scripts, they improvised incessantly on those scripts. Performances sometimes merged and occasionally shifted position with respect to prescribed, tolerated, and forbidden political routines. Because all of them engaged at least two parties in strategic interaction and most of them took place before audiences whose reactions could affect outcomes, surprise and attention-getting drama gave advantages to their creators.

Shaming ceremonies such as Swiss-German *Katzenmusik* – cousins of rough music, charivari, and shivaree elsewhere – ordinarily targeted offenders of local morality but on occasion turned to concerted resistance against hated authorities. They could also shift direction, as when hostile *Katzenmusik* turned into a laudatory or grateful serenade. Mass rebellions sometimes began with legal assemblies of inhabitants or musters of militias that moved into the zone of forbidden and contentious performances only when they voiced audacious complaints, joined forces with adjacent militias, and elected leaders to coordinate their actions.

As compared with a relative standardization of contentious forms in democratic polities, all of these political performances varied widely by locality, actor, and issue in Europe's undemocratic regimes. Consider one striking example: the 16th-century *Fähnlilupf* (or *Strafgericht*) of Switzerland's Graubünden:

In general, the process began when a number of districts raised their military banners and gathered in some central spot such as Chur or Thusis: this first stage was known in Rhaetian German dialect as a *Fähnlilupf* (literally, a "banner-raising"). The gathered militia usually encouraged more communes to join them, and if they were successful, a sort of chain reaction would bring nearly all of the communes to the assembly. The second stage involved public assemblies of the citizen-soldiers, who often draft a bill of articles intended to cleanse the Freestate of corruption and treachery. Finally, the third stage consisted in the appointment of a court, the actual *Strafgericht*, consisting of jurors from each commune and a larger number of "overseers" (*Gäumer*), who allegedly ensured honesty and incorruptibility. These courts, which often included hundreds of jurors and overseers, indicted, tried, and condemned anyone they felt had acted against the fatherland's interests. (Head 1995: 147–48)

Such popular courts often continued for months, until their members felt justice had been done by condemning, fining, or even executing suspects. They established temporary, decorous countergovernments. The canton's legislature (*Bundestag*) often followed up a *Strafgericht* by appointing a court to monitor and modify the outcome. Although Randolph Head's description emphasizes the action of dissidents, the *Strafgericht* clearly established a complex round of interaction not only among dissidents but also between them and other members of the community, including local authorities. This remarkable form of interaction shared some properties with militia assemblies elsewhere, with industrial turnouts, and with the recurrent invention of popular tribunals to mock, counter, or supplement the work of official courts and judges.

But the *Strafgericht* also exuded the distinctive odor of Switzerland's local history. Repeatedly, indignant Swiss citizens called assemblies to demand justice in the name of old laws, charters, and rights. In 1653, for example, peasants from the region dominated by Lucerne used their own local assemblies to raise a rebellion against the city's inflationary imposition of debased currency – the Swiss Peasant War. In that large conflict, rebellious peasants invoked and enacted the myth of Swiss liberator William Tell, but they built their action on local courts they had long used for the adjudication of everyday affairs. Citing previous documents and old established rights, the courts of Escholzmatt, Schüpfheim, and Entlebuch sent forty sworn delegates, quickly rebuffed, to ask justice of Lucerne's authorities (Suter 1997: 59–102). They then mounted armed rebellion. The Swiss Confederation's army finally defeated a peasant force of thousands in June 1653.

Consistent with their frequent activation of embedded identities, particularism marked the contentious repertoires of nondemocratic Europe. Each locality accumulated its own variations, for example, of collective local vengeance against violators of sexual and marital codes, depending on the organization of youth groups, class structure, religious composition, and previous histories of conflict. Feuds among clans or corporate youth groups varied enormously in prevalence, form, and intensity from one region to the next. Mass rebellions always built on locally accumulated grievances, social ties, and previous histories of struggle. They generally built on locally embedded – hence usually rather particular – identities. To assign these forms of contention general names, then, is not to say that they shared nearly as many structures and routines as do lobbying or demonstrating under democratic regimes.

Variations in trajectories of contentious politics corresponded closely to the contrasting histories of regimes we have already examined. Detailed study of those correspondences occupies central space in later chapters. Within the range of undemocratic regimes, let us settle here for three illustrations: (1) the impact of increasing governmental capacity on contentious identities and repertoires, (2) paradoxical differences between strong state and weak state trajectories with respect to established means of contention, and (3) interplay between consultation and contention on the basis of categorically established rights.

First, substantial increases in governmental capacity promote formation of political actors having detached collective identities and of repertoires that span multiple localities, populations, and issues. So doing, they generalize and standardize forms of contentious politics throughout polities. In Europe, the sorts of increases in governmental capacity that resulted from

63

successful preparation for war promoted detached identities because their threats to valued local routines gave common cause to disparate populations, because they involved simultaneous and similar demands by governmental agents within a polity's diverse niches, because they activated brokers between rulers and whole categories of the population, and because increased governmental capacity itself created new forms of commitment across the government's subject population.

Repertoires became more uniform for much the same reasons, as an innovation in petitioning or subversion became increasingly visible and relevant to linked populations for which distant innovations in local vengeance or intercommunity competition would have had little meaning. As national authorities installed new, weighty systems of conscription, taxation, or population registration, they inadvertently created and advertised circumstances shared by disparate and previously unconnected populations. That process facilitated diffusion of innovations in contentious performances from one population to the next.

Second, relatively strong state and weak state trajectories toward joint increases in governmental capacity and protected consultation exhibit paradoxical differences in emerging means of contentious claim making. By definition a strong state trajectory features an early increase in governmental capacity followed (if at all) by a later proliferation of protected consultation, whereas a weak state trajectory features creation of protected consultation before significant expansion of governmental capacity. Under these circumstances, we might reasonably expect the weak state process to produce democratic institutions ready-made for installation at a national scale, the strong state process to necessitate intricate engineering or titanic struggle over the character of those institutions.

Not so. In fact, the opposite commonly happened: an early expansion of governmental capacity enhanced the role of successful brokers, promoted the formation of detached political identities, and rendered the political frameworks of local contention irrelevant to mobilization on a national scale. It created undemocratic but connecting national institutions that then became the frameworks of further struggle. High-capacity tyranny helped form conditions for its own overturn. In contrast, early development of protected consultation always occurred on a local or regional scale, provided ineffectual models for claim making on a national level, rendered its participants vulnerable to outside conquest, and therefore increased the likelihood of internecine struggle at the threshold of democracy. That locally democratic Switzerland passed through multiple coups, military raids, and a civil war between 1798 and 1847 signals the difficulties of translation from local to national. (Chapter 6 analyzes that turbulent period of Swiss history.)

Third, extraction of means for war or other weighty governmental enterprises bore a dialectical relation to the establishment of collective rights. Under undemocratic regimes, any expansion of governmental demands in the form of taxation, conscription, or other extraction violated some existing rights and obligations. For example, governmental agents often incited popular resistance by withdrawing from local availability resources that were already committed to marriages, communal ceremonies, and routines of mutual aid. Often rapid increases in governmental demands violated compacts, customs, and consultative institutions that had previously governed the population's contributions to governmental activities.

Short of the sheer extortion sometimes imposed by warlords, Mongol invaders, bandits, and mercenaries, however, any ruler who anticipated returning to the same sources of wealth for future needs negotiated some sort of agreement with the suppliers or their brokers. Those agreements then became the ground for future demands as well as for resistance to those demands. Such negotiation established not only the terms of agreement – rights and obligations of the parties – but also the parties' identities. Thus they specified *in what collective capacities* they would exercise relevant rights and obligations. The more governmental command over people, activities, and resources advanced, the more often those collective capacities would activate detached identities linking whole categories of a regional or national population but quite distinct from identities embedded in everyday social relations. Negotiation over massive means of governmental enterprise thereby altered the constituted actors in a regime, redefined relations among them, and created some elements of citizenship.

This process generally did little to advance breadth of political participation, equality of political participation, or protection of political participants from arbitrary action by governmental agents – on the contrary! But it did create a modicum of binding consultation oriented not to particular ties between ruler and subject but to categorical definitions of mutual obligation. The strong state path, despite all its cruelty in other regards, thereby created opportunities for full-fledged citizenship. National citizenship constituted an extreme and crucial case of detached political identity – rarely significant in day-to-day relations on a local scale, but fundamental in differentiating who had what rights and obligations vis-à-vis the state. Citizenship, in turn, established necessary but far from sufficient – conditions for democracy.

Democratic Winds

No recognizably democratic national regimes existed in the Europe of 1650. Only on the scale of individual communities and within protected oligarchies did any institutions combining breadth, equality, consultation, and protection prevail. But, alerted by the *Strafgericht* and the *müllerisch-salpeterisch* controversy, we must now refine and qualify that observation. In 17th-century Europe, distant cousins (but by no means identical twins) of democracy did appear in three settings: in the oligarchies of mercantile municipalities, in peasant communities that enjoyed protection against lordly power, and in intermittent rebellions against expanding states. Mercantile communities never installed genuine equality or even breadth of political participation; on the whole their power holders constituted small, wealthy, mutually selected minorities drawn overwhelmingly from among male heads of prosperous enterprises. Nevertheless, burghers did commonly govern collectively and rotate offices, while protecting persons and property of their members. Study 17th-century paintings of urban militia companies (a standard genre, e.g., in the Netherlands) for a test; you will not see cross-sections of urban populations, but the proud, well-fed faces of local oligarchs. Their protected consultation crystallized into constitutional oligarchy (Prak 1999).

Agrarian, pastoral, and fishing communities sometimes escaped subordination to great lords because they formed in or adjacent to geographically inaccessible areas, because production remained too precarious to sustain an exploiting class, or because they could play one lord off against another. Something like peasant democracy therefore developed from time to time in Europe's mountain regions, in some German and Italian areas of intensely fragmented sovereignty, and at the more distant edges of great forests or vast seas.

Still, we must qualify any portrait of peasant democracy in two crucial ways. First, we are dealing with small-scale oligarchies in which women, children, poor people, and mobile workers (the latter increasingly abundant in Europe from the 16th-century onward) had little or no say. Second (as Benjamin Barber points out forcefully for a cluster of small communities around the town of Chur that eventually entered Switzerland as part of the canton of Graubünden), protections and liberties installed by such communities established collective rather than individual rights (Barber 1974; see also Head 1995). They defended prerogatives of the community as a whole against inside or outside encroachment, but did not protect local deviants from persecution or keep communities from exploiting out-siders that fell under their control. The same villagers of Graubünden that fiercely defended their peasant liberties against outsiders' encroachments ruled tyranically in the adjacent dependent territory of Valtellina.

In times of rebellion against expanding states, European peasants, work-ers, and dissident elites repeatedly articulated semi-democratic doctrines – at least to the extent of claiming that rapacious rulers were violating rights attached inherently and/or by custom to existing communities. For the duration of open resistance, rebels commonly formed leagues featuring mechanisms of representation and consent, extensive deliberation, and election of military or diplomatic leaders. During the 16th century, the Castilian Comuneros of 1520, the German Peasants' Revolt of 1525, Dutch rebels against Spanish authority, and many previously Catholic communi-ties that converted to Protestantism followed such a pattern. During the 17th century these forms of rebellion persisted, but the most widely fol-lowed quasidemocratic programs emerged during the English civil wars of 1640 to 1660.

Consider, for example, the coalition of English radicals known (signif-icantly, if derisively) as Levellers. In 1647, Levellers presented to a fa-mous series of debates at Putney their Agreement of the People, which "asserted popular sovereignty and parliamentary supremacy...set aside the monarchy, invested Parliament with executive and administrative authority – though no coercive power over religion – and advocated elec-toral reforms based on the principle of manhood suffrage" (Kishlansky 1996: 176). Breadth, equality, consultation, and protection all figure promi-nently in the Leveller program.

As practices and social networks, none of these quasidemocratic pro-grams outlasted their rebellions. Yet they mattered for later democratization because they made available both models of resistance to arbitrary author-ity and doctrines, however muted, of popular sovereignty. In repressing them, furthermore, rulers ordinarily established new forms of agreement with local and regional authorities. Although those forms usually bound the general population more tightly to central control, they also created channels, relations, understandings, and institutions that affected the next rounds of remonstrance. As they specified why past rebellions were illegiti-mate, indeed, they almost inevitably stated the rare conditions under which rebellions *would* be legitimate.

Both the presence of democratic practices within some institutions and the pursuit of democratic programs by rebels made those practices and programs available for appropriation by government authorities. But many barriers intervened between the sheer availability of democratic ideas, practices, and programs, on one side, and their implementation in national politics, on the other. Let me repeat one more time: democratization is a change in the character of relations between people subject to the authority of a given government and agents of that government. This book's task is precisely to track down the processes that inhibited or forwarded the formation of broad, equal, binding, and protective relations between citizens and agents of governments.

For the moment, however, our task is not yet to examine the processes that moved regimes durably into the zone of citizenship and democracy. It is to trace relations between regimes and contention outside that zone, within the undemocratic territory that has included most of Europe for most of the period since 1650. Inside that territory, we should find changes in governmental capacity and protected consultation strongly associated – as both causes and effects – with alterations in contentious politics. On the whole, we should find that where governmental capacity increased, governmental agents became increasingly salient as objects and participants in contention, while the division sharpened between forms of contention conforming to government-prescribed or government-tolerated routines of public politics, on one side, and government-forbidden routines, on the other. We should also expect detached identities (e.g., workers at large or subjects of the king rather than members of particular local craft groups) to become increasingly prominent as bases of contentious claims.

With increases in protected consultation, we should expect a rather different set of effects:

- more frequent alliances between existing power holders and mobilized but politically excluded claimants
- greater clustering of open contention at the edges of prescribed and tolerated political forms
- shifts of claim-making performances from parochial, particular, and bifurcated to cosmopolitan, modular, and autonomous
- more rapid responses to shifts in the composition of ruling coalitions

These expectations rest on the idea that rising protected consultation, on the average, lowers the risk to aggrieved but relatively powerless groups of entering public politics as currently constituted. The process is dialectical: every extension of the political actors covered by protected consultation sharpens the discrepancy between them and those currently excluded.

On similar grounds we should expect that rapid moves from one position in the capacity-consultation space to another will coincide with surges of contention. That should be true for two reasons: because such alterations of regimes offer opportunities and threats to a wide range of political actors and because widespread contention in the form of confrontation, conquest, or revolution itself causes transformations of regimes. Most likely, furthermore, such effects intensify as a regime approaches the zone of democracy, since in that vicinity a higher proportion of the population belongs to established political actors, a higher proportion of political actors maintain relatively high mobilization, and political actors generally stay more closely attuned to shifts in the behavior of governments, their agents, and other political actors.

So, at least, run our theoretical expectations. In this first mapping of the relationship between regime change and contention, we look for no more than broad evidence that some such correspondence exists. In upcoming chapters we seek to identify some of its causal dynamics. Let us scan experiences of the Low Countries and Iberia between 1650 and 1850 for evidence of connections between variation in the character of regimes and variation in the texture of contentious politics. That is Chapter 3's business.

3

Undemocratic Contention in Europe, 1650–1850

From the perspective of contentious politics, Europe had more than one Old Regime. According to the arguments just unfolded, Europe's undemocratic regimes should have displayed systematically different sorts of contention. Different combinations of coercion, capital, and commitment should have affected the trajectories of various governments within the limits set by an idealized strong state (expanding capacity with little or no increase in protected consultation) and an idealized weak state (expanding consultation with little or no increase in capacity). Changes in capacity and/or consultation, in their turn, should have altered the character of contention. Finally, contention itself should have affected the character of regimes, even short of conquest, colonization, or revolution. Let us try out these expectations on the contrasting histories of the Low Countries and Iberia between 1650 and 1850. The Low Countries and Iberia created very different regimes after 1650, and experienced contrasting forms of contentious politics. Do the histories of the Low Countries and Iberia confirm our expectations? At least roughly, they do.

As of 1650, the 1648 treaties of Westphalia had finally confirmed outcomes of the momentous 17th-century Dutch revolt against Spain. The treaties provided de jure certification for the Low Countries' longstanding de facto division into the autonomous United Provinces in the north, a Habsburg-controlled Spanish Netherlands in the south, plus imperially connected but semi-autonomous Luxembourg and several city-states, likewise to the south. At midcentury, Holland was arguably Europe's predominant economic power (Davids 1995; Kindleberger 1996: 100–103; de Vries and van der Woude 1997: 665–80). The urban, commercial, seafaring region generally lived under the sway of urban merchant oligarchies, although landed nobles and churchmen carried more weight in southern and inland areas. Coastal traders maintained intensive connections with the Atlantic, the Pacific, the Indian Ocean, the Mediterranean, the Baltic, but most notably with Scandinavia, north Germany, and the British Isles. Those connections animated one of Europe's most prosperous populations.

Relative to most other European areas, as of 1650 the Low Countries' regimes operated in environments of substantial capital and widespread connections of commitment, but fragmented coercive means; even making war at an international scale resembled business enterprises of the time. War making involved piecing together intricate coalitions among multiple holders of coercive force, pooling capital to rent mercenary forces from elsewhere, and overcoming the resistance of local merchants and municipalities to disruption of their peaceful commerce. Because of multiple jurisdictions, prescribed and tolerated forms of public politics varied significantly from place to place – depending, for example, on whether the regional government had installed its own official church. On average, however, public politics followed the familiar routines of local bourgeois oligarchies wherever they existed throughout the continent (te Brake 1998).

Between 1650 and 1850 the Low Countries underwent momentous political changes. After the failure of Stadhouder William II's attempt to consolidate his power over the entire north in 1650, that region remained an uneasy but influential confederation of city-states and provinces until the 1790s. In 1688, the Dutch Republic gave England a new king, William III of Orange, and forged a close alliance with its former enemy across the North Sea. During the 1780s, bourgeois-democratic revolutionary regimes took over many of the north's provinces, only to be crushed by a Prussian invasion of 1787. The next invasion arrived in 1795, when French revolutionary forces established a Batavian Republic. The Republic gave way to a French satellite Kingdom of Holland (1806), to direct incorporation into France (1810–13), then to a bifurcated kingdom that until 1839 nominally included both the north and the south. From the French takeover onward, the Dutch state assumed a much more centralized administrative structure than had prevailed in the heyday of autonomous provinces.

History ran differently in the southern Netherlands. During the later 17th century French forces repeatedly attacked the south, incorporating the region around Lille into France. With the Treaty of Utrecht (1713), remaining sections of the south (except Luxembourg and the bishopric of Liège) passed from Spain to the Habsburgs' Austrian branch. For another half-century Dutch forces occupied eight strategic fortresses across the Austrian Netherlands. During the 1780s, Emperor Joseph II expelled the Dutch occupiers, but his attempt to install a more centralized administration generated resistance and even insurrection through much of the south. As revolutionaries came to power in adjacent France, their southern Netherlands counterparts tried to make a revolution as well, only to be crushed by Austrian troops. The region became a battleground for France and Austria between 1792 and 1795, from which point the French controlled it until 1814.

As in the north, French occupation and incorporation of the south brought a vast centralization and standardization of governmental structure. Integrated into the Kingdom of the Netherlands at the next year's peace settlement, the Belgians (as they increasingly called themselves) began open rebellion in 1830, then endured Dutch and French invasions over the next few years. But in 1839 they achieved independence as a kingdom, with English Queen Victoria's uncle Leopold of Saxe-Coburg (who had declined the Greek crown in 1830) conveniently stepping in as king. Although splintered politically by creed, region, language, and economic interest, the Low Countries' regimes lived out the remainder of the 19th century in recognizable versions of European bourgeois politics.

What happened to contentious repertoires over the two centuries? Frequencies of public claim making increased enormously, but in great surges separated by periods of considerable decline. As governmental capacities rose, a visible shift of contention toward regional and national scales occurred. Particularism of contention's forms and issues declined as common routines and programs became more prominent throughout the region. Local power holders continued to mediate a significant share of contention, yet direct claim making on national authorities by organized local people greatly increased as centralized, high-capacity governments displaced the fragmented polities that predominated before the late 18th century. Cosmopolitan, modular, and autonomous claim making performances began to replace the parochial, particular, and bifurcated forms of contention that had long prevailed.

Let us begin with major displacements of control over ostensible national governments such as the Dutch Republic and the Spanish Netherlands. The arguments laid out earlier imply that such displacements coincide as both causes and effects, with surges of contention going well beyond attempted seizures of power over the governments themselves. The central struggles within revolutionary transfers of power emerge from or cause opportunities and threats to the positions of multiple political actors. Seen from the top, the Low Countries moved from dynastic struggles to intermittently revolutionary politics mobilizing substantial blocs of the general population in bids for control over central governments.

Suppose we recognize as revolutionary situations those instances when for a month or more at least two blocs of people backed by armed force and receiving support from a substantial part of the general population exercised control over important segments of state organization. By that rough test, likely candidates for revolutionary situations in the Low Countries between 1650 and 1850 include:

1650	failed coup of William II
1672	Orangist seizures of power in many towns
1702	displacement of Orangist clients in Gelderland and Overijssel
1747–50	Orange revolt in United Provinces, after French invasion precipitates naming of William IV of Orange as Stadhouder
1785–87	Dutch Patriot Revolution, terminated by Prussian invasion
1789–90	Brabant Revolution in south
1790–91	revolution in Principality of Liège, terminated by Austrian troops
1792–95	French-Austrian wars, culminating in French takeover of Low Countries, which produced variants of French and French-style rule
1795–98	Batavian Revolution in north
1830–33	Belgian Revolution against Holland, with French and British intervention

Observed from close by, to be sure, these clustered events consisted of much meeting, marching, petitioning, confronting, fighting, sacking, arguing, and organizing. The largest changes in texture consisted of shifts from mobilization of aristocratic military clienteles and burgher militias to sustained integration of ordinary householders into national struggles for power. In conformity with our general argument, increases in governmental capacity promoted shifts toward mobilization on the basis of detached identities and by means of nationally standardized repertoires.

Seen from a local perspective, collective contention occurred far more frequently, and changed character even more dramatically. Rudolf Dekker (1982) has cataloged dozens of "revolts" – events during which at least twenty people gathered publicly, voiced complaints against others, and harmed persons or property – in the province of Holland during the 17th and 18th centuries. By comparison with all of Europe's contentious repertoires from 1650 to the present, the events in question generally qualify as small, local, variable in form from one place or group to another, and bifurcated between (many) direct attacks on local targets and (few) mediated appeals to higher authorities. Concretely, Dekker's catalog emphasizes five sorts of events: (1) forcible seizures of marketed food or attacks on its sellers, (2) resistance to newly imposed taxes, (3) attacks by members of one religious category on persons, property, or symbols of another, (4) attempts to displace political authorities, and (5) collective vengeance – for example, sacking of houses – on figures who had outraged public morality.

Sacking of houses also often accompanied protests against tax farmers and other public figures targeted in the first four categories of violent events; in that regard, Dutch 18th-century popular actions greatly resembled their French, British, and North American counterparts. Like students of old regime contention in these other areas, Dekker calls attention to the festival atmosphere of many such rituals: "A participant in an Orangist disturbance of 1787 declared," he reports, "'I've never had so much fun at a fair as in tearing down that sacked house'" (Dekker 1982: 92).

More generally, Dekker's events conformed recognizably to prevailing old-regime repertoires of popular contention in Western Europe as a whole. Along the standard range from (1) petitions and parodies to (2) local vengeance to (3) feuds and resistance to (4) mass rebellion, they clustered at the edges of prescribed and tolerated forms of public politics. Nevertheless, in such times of general political struggle as the Orange revolt of 1747–50, they merged into open rebellion.

So far as Dekker's catalog indicates, Holland's struggles over food concentrated from 1693 to 1768 in market towns and in periods of rising prices when local authorities failed to guarantee affordable supplies to the local poor. His catalog's tax rebellions (which Dekker worries may only have been "the tip of the iceberg"; Dekker 1982: 28) focused on farmed-out excise taxes rather than direct taxation, and clustered in times of general struggle over political authority such as 1747–50. In Holland, about half the population belonged to the established Dutch Reformed Church, perhaps 10 percent to other Protestant denominations, 40 percent to the Roman Catholic Church, and a small number to Jewish congregations.

Full local citizenship, furthermore, commonly depended on membership in the locally official church. Ostensibly religious conflicts therefore often included struggles for voice in local affairs as well as responses to religiously identified external events, for example, Savoy's massacre of Waldensian heretics in 1655. Like tax rebellion, however, religious contention surged in times of general political struggle such as 1747–50. At such times, every political actor's stake in the regime faces risk. As a result, a wide range of place-holding and place-taking action occurs regardless of how the cycle of contention began.

Events that Dekker classifies as openly political pivoted on the House of Orange. Under Habsburg rule, the absent king had typically delegated power within each province of the Netherlands to a Stadhouder (city-holder = lieu-tenant = ruler's lieutenant or deputy). From their 16th-century revolt against Habsburg Spain onward, Dutch provinces had commonly (although by no means always or automatically) named the current prince of the Orange line their Stadhouder, their provisional holder of state power; that happened especially in time of war. Whether or not a prince of Orange was currently Stadhouder, his clientele always constituted a major faction in regional politics, and opposition to it often formed around an alliance of people outside the Reformed church, organized artisans, and exploited rural people. During the struggles of 1747–50, contention over the Stadhouder's claims to rule merged with opposition to tax farmers and demands for popular representation in provincial politics. Such events underwent greater transformation between 1650 and 1800 than did food-, tax-, and religion-centered events.

During the later 18th century, we see emerging concerted demands for broad participation in local and provincial government, so much so that R. R. Palmer's *Age of the Democratic Revolution* (1959, 1964) bracketed the Dutch Patriot Revolt of the 1780s with the American Revolution (1775–83) as significant representatives of the revolutionary current. Wayne te Brake's systematic analysis of the Dutch revolution in the province of Overijssel identifies the 1780s as a historical pivot in popular claim making. Public meetings, petitioning, and militia marches did much of the day-to-day political work, but in company with older forms of vengeance and intim-idation. In the small city of Zwolle, te Brake reports that in November 1786:

A gathering of more than 1,000 persons in the Grote Kerk produced a declara-tion that a scheduled election to fill a vacancy on the Sworn Council by the old method of co-optation would not be recognized as legitimate. When the govern-ment nevertheless proceeded with the election in mid-December, the chosen candi-date was intimidated by Patriot crowds and forced to resign immediately. (te Brake 1989: 108)

When Prussian troops ended the revolution with an invasion of September 1787, however, the Patriots' Orangist opponents took their own vengeance by sacking the houses of Patriot activists. Leaders on both sides altered the stakes and routines of public politics by reaching out for popular support. Speaking of nearby Deventer, te Brake concludes that:

The "People" of Deventer had entered politics to stay. Not simply the rhetorical invention of self-serving Patriot pamphleteers or constitution-writers, "*het Volk*" had in the course of the 1780s become an armed and organized reality which proved to be easily capable, when united, of breaking into the urban political space. As unity gave way to division and conflict at all levels of society, however, the force and significance of the new popular politics was by no means extinguished. Thus, as we have seen, the counter-revolution in Deventer represented the victory of one segment of a newly politicized and activated "People" over another – not simply a restoration of aristocratic politics as usual. Indeed, the Orangist counter-revolution in Deventer unwittingly consolidated two momentous changes in the politics of this provincial city, the combination of which suggests that the character of urban politics was forever transformed: the private, aristocratic politics of the past had been shattered and the foundation had been laid for the public, participatory politics of the future. (te Brake 1989: 168)

In public politics at a regional and national scale, both repertoire and participation in contention were changing noticeably.

During the later 18th century, organized workers and their strikes also became more prominent in Dutch political struggles (Dekker 1982: 50). A significant transformation of contentious repertoires was under way even before French influence so profoundly altered the Low Countries' contentious politics. On balance, newer performances in the Low Countries' repertoires mobilized more people from more different settings, built on detached rather than embedded identities, targeted more regional and national figures and issues, adopted forms that were more standardized across the whole region, and involved direct rather than mediated presentation of claims. Specialized political entrepreneurs (as opposed to established local and regional authorities) were emerging as critical actors in popular contention. A cosmopolitan, modular, autonomous array of claim-making performances was gaining currency.

In a study parallel to Dekker's, Karin van Honacker has cataloged about 115 "collective actions" directed against central authorities farther south, in Brabant – more precisely, in Brussels, Antwerp, and Louvain – from 1601 to 1784. Some actions took place in a single outing, but many consisted of clusters spread over several days or weeks. Van Honacker classifies her events under four headings: resistance to violation of local political rights, fiscal conflicts, civil-military struggles, and fights over food supply. The first two categories overlap considerably, since in Brussels the dominant guilds (the Nine Nations) frequently resisted taxes on the basis of what they claimed to be their chartered rights. "Fiscal grievances stated by full citizens of the cities," remarks van Honacker,

sometimes lay far from the central concerns of ordinary city-dwellers. In 1680, for example, the complaint made by the heads of Brussels guilds about a five percent tax on transactions in the hinterland accented less the tax as such than the fact that the city's third estate – that is, representatives of the guilds – had not yet approved it. That is why the action, which involved sacking the house of the patricians's mayor, which occurred again at renewal of a tax on beer, and which used a fiscal question as its screen, ought to be considered collective action on behalf of political rights. (van Honacker 2000: 50).

Religious struggles of the sort that figured prominently in Holland escape van Honacker's net because they typically set members of the urban population against each other rather than against public authorities. With Brabant under Spanish, then Austrian, control, struggles of civilians with royal soldiers, disputes over their quartering or payment, freeing of captured military deserters, and competition of urban militias with royal troops for jurisdiction all loomed much larger than in Holland. Fights over food supply, however, greatly resembled each other in north and south; repeatedly city dwellers attacked merchants who raised their prices and outsiders who sought to buy in local markets.

On the whole, van Honacker's catalog of events from 17th- and 18th-century Brabant reveals less change in the character of popular demands than Dekker's findings from Holland. In the three southern cities we see repeated resistance to royal centralization in the name of established privilege, but no obvious swelling of demands for popular sovereignty. Claim making followed Western Europe's characteristic undemocratic old regime repertoire, in van Honacker's account:

- frequent employment or parody of authorities' own political means and symbols
- participation of people as members of established communities and corporate groups (i.e., mainly embedded identities
- concentration of claim making in holidays and authorized gatherings
- rich symbolism, often including shaming ceremonies
- orientation of avenging actions to dwellings of perpetrators and to places where alleged offenses occurred (van Honacker 1994: 541–43).

The old regime repertoire did not last much longer in the Southern Netherlands. Gita Deneckere has assembled a catalog of "collective actions" in Belgium as a whole from 1831 through 1918 from a wide range of archives, official publications, periodicals, and historical works. Her catalog includes about 440 occasions on which people gathered and made collective demands "in the socio-economic field of conflict," which means largely workers' actions and actions concerning work (Deneckere 1997: 10). Such a selection principle excludes, for example, widespread violence surrounding the Netherlands' separation of church and state in 1834, just as the uneasy union of north and south was breaking up. Within Deneckere's chosen field, nevertheless, her evidence demonstrates a significant alteration in Belgian repertoires of contention.

Or, rather, two alterations. Up to the revolution of 1848, Deneckere's contentious events feature workers' assemblies and marches to present petitions, attacks on the goods or persons of high-priced food merchants, and work stoppages by people in multiple shops of the same craft. Workers' actions frequently took the form of turnouts: occasions on which a small number of initiators from a local craft went from shop to shop demanding that fellow craft workers leave their employment to join the swelling crowd. The round completed, turnout participants assembled in some safe place (often a field at the edge of town), aired their grievances, formulated demands, and presented those demands to masters in the trade (often through a meeting of delegations from both sides), staying away from work until the masters had replied satisfactorily or forced them to return.

Between the revolution of 1848 and the 1890s, turnouts practically disappeared as demonstrations and large-firm strikes became much more frequent and prominent. Although strikes and demonstrations continued apace into the 20th century, from the 1890s onward regionally and nationally coordinated general strikes emerged as major forms of contentious action. As Deneckere says, workers and socialist leaders designed general strikes to be large, standard in form, coordinated across multiple localities, and oriented toward national holders of power. These new actions built on detached identities as socialists or as workers at large. They represented a significant shift of repertoire.

Of course these changes reflected major 19th-century social changes such as rapid urbanization and expansion of capital-intensive industry. But the changing repertoire of contention also had a political history. Deneckere sees increasingly tight interdependence between popular contention and national politics. In the 1890s:

> The correspondence between successive socialist mass actions and the parliamentary breakthrough to universal suffrage is too striking for anyone to miss the causal connection. On the basis of published and unpublished correspondence from ruling circles one can conclude that the general strike had a genuine impact, in fact more significant than contemporary socialists themselves realized. Time after time socialist workers' protests confronted power-holders with a revolutionary threat that laid the foundation for abrupt expansion of democracy. (Deneckere 1997: 384)

Thus, in Belgium, street politics and parliamentary politics came to depend on each other. Power holders' efforts to forestall revolutionary threats, in short, produced democratization as a second-best compromise. Deneckere's analysis takes us past our assigned cutoff of 1850, but does so fruitfully; it indicates that both before and during democratization, major alterations of repertoires interact with deep transformations of political power. It identifies confrontation as a spur to democratization.

Methodologically, the analyses of Dekker, van Honacker, and Deneckere offer us both hope and caution. All three use catalogs of contentious events to gauge political trends and variations in the character of conflict (Franzosi 1998; McCarthy, McPhail, and Smith 1996; Olzak 1989; Rucht and Koopmans 1999; Rucht, Koopmans, and Neidhardt 1998). Clearly, such catalogs discipline the search for variation and change in contentious politics. But comparison of the three catalogs also establishes how sensitive such enumerations are to the definitions and sources adopted. Dekker's search of Dutch archives for events involving at least twenty people in violent encounters, regardless of issues, brings him a wide range of actions and some evidence of change, but it excludes smaller scale and nonviolent making of claims. Van Honacker's combing of similar Belgian archives for collective challenges to public authorities nets her plenty of smaller scale and nonviolent episodes, but omits industrial and intergroup conflicts. Deneckere's sources and methods, in contrast, concentrate her catalog on industrial events.

None of the three choices is intrinsically superior to the others, but each makes a difference to the evidence at hand. When trying to make comparisons over time, space, and type of setting, we must make allowance for the selectivity of all such catalogs (Tilly 2002a). We are, nevertheless, far better off with the catalogs than without them. The Low Countries are among the few regions where scholars have inventoried contentious events on a substantial scale before the 20th century. France and Great Britain, as it happens, are two of the others. For most of Europe's remainder, we must settle for pickings from general histories and for occasional specialized studies of particular localities, issues, and populations.

What do Dutch and Belgian experiences teach us about regimes, contention, and democracy? In the Low Countries, great accumulations of capital and commitment early coincided with relatively fragmented coercive means, especially in the northern regions that acquired recognition in 1648 as an independent Dutch Republic. Throughout the Low Countries, prosperous, mercantile, urban oligarchies wielded great influence over their immediate hinterlands and held off the demands of their nominal overlords. Even in the southern regions that formed into an independent Belgium during the 1830s, 17th- and 18th-century Habsburg overlords (first Spanish, then Austrian) had to bargain hard with their feisty subjects.

Before the 19th century, the Low Countries' popular contention centered on four foci: struggles within and among privileged municipalities, efforts of would-be national rulers to extract resources and impose central coordination of local activities, attempts to impose or subvert religious establishments, and local rights with respect to food, work, taxation, and land. With acceleration of the Low Countries' already precocious commercialization and industrialization during the 19th century, confrontations of labor and capital occupied an increasingly central place in popular contention. The forms of claim making we associate with social movements became more and more prevalent (for more recent repertoire changes, see Kriesi 1993; Kriesi et al. 1995).

Relations to Britain and France significantly affected interactions of contention and democracy in the Low Countries. Britain's Glorious Revolution of 1688–89 brought in a Dutch ruler and Dutch-style administrative reforms while ending the Anglo-Dutch wars that had wracked the previous decades and establishing the British as powerful Dutch allies in most subsequent wars. French intervention arguably shaped contention and democracy in the Low Countries even more profoundly: Dutch patriots of the 1780s took encouragement from the American Revolution to effect bourgeois-democratic revolutions of their own in a number of provinces and their capitals, only to be snuffed out by a Prussian invasion; French revolutionary armies overran both the Austrian (southern) Netherlands and the Dutch Republic. They imposed a series of satellite regimes with French-style centralized administrations. In 1815, Napoleon's victorious enemies constituted a Kingdom of the Netherlands retaining far more

80

centralized structures than had existed before 1795 and installing the representative institutions of a constitutional monarchy. Over the long run, the Low Countries' democratization combined conquest, revolution, confrontation, and unceasing popular contention (van der Laarse 2000).

The Low Countries' experience thus contradicts one widely held idea: that solidly democratic local institutions provide the foundation of national democracy. As Maarten Prak has argued forcefully, little of the constitutional apparatus that characterized Dutch urban oligarchical rule carried over into the 19th century's democratic forms (Prak 1999; see also Cerutti et al. 1995). Instead, the boost to governmental capacity and the models for political organization imposed by French conquest in the 1790s set a new political dynamic going. With the victorious allies' establishment of a Kingdom of the Netherlands, a limited constitutional democracy of a recognizably Western European type took over where the fissiparous United Provinces, Austrian Netherlands, and other splinters had flourished before the French Revolution. In this case, conquest opened the way to further democratization through both confrontation and (in the case of Belgium) revolution.

Iberian Contention

Iberia wrote a very different script. Overall, Iberia's political history displays affinities with Europe's coercion-intensive trajectories of regime change. Nevertheless, Iberia differed from coercion-intensive Russia or Poland in two crucial regards: first, great contrast and tension between coastal regions with extensive international connections and interior regions pursuing landlord-dominated agriculture; second, repeated and effective military intervention from Iberia's belligerent neighbor, France. The two circumstances intertwined to produce little protected consultation for any but nobles, priests, and chartered municipalities. They also conspired to generate wide swings in governmental capacity. If on the whole Iberia's regime change between 1650 and 1850 hewed more closely to the strong state trajectory than the weak state trajectory cartooned earlier, a diagram of Iberian trajectories would exhibit even more zigzags than a comparable diagram for France, Britain, or the Low Countries.

From 1640 to 1659, Spanish (i.e., Castilian and Aragonese) forces were beating down an ultimately unsuccessful Catalan secession, which had been abetted by Catalonia's French allies and resulted in Aragon's loss of Roussillon to France. From 1640 to 1668 Spanish forces were likewise battling rebellious Portugal, which held out successfully for independence. By 1650, Iberia had lived centuries of conquest – first in expulsion of Muslim rulers from the peninsula, then in colonization of the Americas, Africa, and Asia. That violent political history had created a striking combination of:

- fragmented but substantial coercive power, featuring close integration between military organization and control over public order
- sharp division between mercantile-imperial coastal regions and an interior dominated by litigious nobles who drew their wealth from rents and the wool of wide-ranging sheep herds
- within that interior, a Castilian (and eventually Spanish) capital, Madrid, that first operated a command economy but later became a major center of market-mediated consumption
- two regimes limited greatly in their power within the peninsula by chartered privileges of municipalities, noble lineages, and guilds while relying heavily for operating funds on international bankers who loaned against the security of vast but fluctuating colonial revenues
- incessant military pressure from neighboring France into the 18th century, followed by several 18th-century wars allied with France and/or against England

Into the 18th century, what became Spain served as the seat of a dual Habsburg empire, both within Europe and throughout the non-European world. Portugal, in contrast, drew its international strength chiefly from Brazil and from far-flung trading networks in Africa, Asia, and elsewhere in Latin America. Much less populous Portugal colonized far less aggressively than Spain. Except at the scale of some peasant villages, nothing remotely resembling democracy existed in Iberia before the 19th century.

From the perspective of regimes, the years from 1650 to 1850 brought two moments of major transition: the War of the Spanish Succession (1701–14) and the multiple struggles (1793–1814) that began with a French war and ended with a battered Spanish state plus a splintered Latin American empire. The definitive installation of a Bourbon regime in 1714 marked a shift to more centralized, direct forms of rule, in which both provincial autonomies and the powers of privileged intermediaries dwindled. Among other things, Bourbon king Philip V created a standing army recruited from his own country and centralized the administration of state finances.

The troubles of the French Revolution and Napoleon eventually led to further centralization and increases in governmental capacity, but with a crucial peculiarity: great political autonomy for the armed forces and the men who ran them. Gloria Martínez Dorado argues that:

there was a fracture of the state in 1808: a state crisis followed by open conflict between rulers and elites, on one side, and popular groups, on the other, ending with a new phase of state reconstruction through negotiation between rulers and the principal social sectors. (Martínez Dorado 1993: 108)

As compared with the rest of Western Europe of the time, however, the "social sector" of the military played an exceptionally prominent and independent part in the new settlement.

In tracing the Iberian history of contention between 1650 and 1850, we must place our largest marker at the French revolutionary and Napoleonic wars. Before 1793, the peninsula experienced numerous rebellions and international wars, especially with its two countries' commercial-imperial rivals France, Britain, and the Dutch Republic. At local and regional levels, Iberia also featured struggles over food and land, violent encounters between bandits and their intended prey, and concerted resistance against grasping officials, rapacious soldiers, and greedy landlords.

After 1793, a period of war, occupation, and deep political reorganization under French influence sent Portugal's rulers into Brazilian exile, freed Spain's South American colonies to throw off the imperial yoke, and gave Iberia's multiple military forces room to bid for political power. Under pressure of war debts, Spain began in 1798 to sell off entailed lands belonging to religious orders, municipal corporations, and nobles; over the next decade, perhaps 15 percent of all Castile's Church property and 3 percent of all real property changed hands (Herr 1989: 129–36; 19th-century regimes almost entirely dispossessed the church). In the Spanish interior, that expansion of private property interacted with a decisive shift from sheep grazing to wheat farming as dominant agricultural activities (Ringrose 1996: 282–85).

From 1807 into the 20th century, both Spain and Portugal produced a dazzling array of popular rebellions, civil wars, military coups, and ill-fated attempts to establish constitutional regimes, compounded by the increasing involvement of organized agricultural and industrial workers in political strife. Revolutionary regimes of the 1830s stripped the Spanish Catholic Church of most of its civil powers, lands, and rents, leaving it greatly weakened as a political actor. In distinctive ways, both Spain and Portugal participated in the 19th-century's characteristic political movements: liberalism, socialism, anarchism, and clerical or royalist conservatism. In May 1848, for example, skilled workers supporting progressive colonel Gándara erected barricades in Madrid's Plaza de Santa Ana and raised a call for revolution. They failed. But then in 19th-century Iberia no popular regime ever remained in power very long.

Summed as revolutionary situations between 1650 and 1850, Iberia's major struggles followed the tumultuous timetable of Table 3.1. In Iberia, absence of the detailed catalogs that Dekker, van Honacker, and Deneckere have prepared for the Low Countries hides the fine grain of smaller scale contention and its changes from the historical eye. Note, for example, the eye-catching elements of Juan Díaz del Moral's account of 6 May 1652 in Córdoba:

A poor Gallegan woman crossed the barrio of San Lorenzo mourning inconsolably, displaying the corpse of her son, who had just died of hunger, and demanding justice with wild cries. A powerful, sweeping revolt broke out. Indignant, frenetic local women scored their men's cowardice and incited them to act against injustice and iniquity. The men armed themselves with knives, pikes, halberds, and axes, went as a body to the house of the Corregidor (who on hearing of the uprising had fled to Trinity Convent), broke open the doors, sacked the house, and destroyed everything in it. The growing troop, including women who encouraged the action, ran through streets shouting insults and complaints against nobles, placemen, benefice holders, even against bishop Don Pedro de Tapia; they attacked houses and granaries, took stored wheat from the church of San Lorenzo and also from the houses they assailed. (Díaz del Moral 1984: 68–69)

Richard Herr's account of events in Madrid a century and a half later identifies significant continuities in the performances of Spain's urban crowds:

On Friday evening, 18 March 1808, reports reached Madrid of rioting in Aranjuez and, on Saturday afternoon, of the discovery and arrest of Manuel Godoy, believed by large numbers of Spaniards to be the cause of their country's ills. The populace was already alarmed by news that French troops were approaching the capital after occupying various cities in the north of the country, reputedly on a mission to protect Spain from a possible British invasion. The news from Aranjuez drew a crowd to the palace of Godoy – today the ministry of war on the Plaza de Cibeles – which it entered and sacked, tossing into a huge bonfire his papers, paintings, and precious furniture. That evening, while Carlos IV was signing his abdication in Aranjuez, the crowd spread through Madrid, laying waste the houses of Godoy's relatives and supporters and those of royal officials to whom the public allocated a share of the blame for its suffering. (Herr 1989: 712)

Both reports contain familiar elements: gathering in the streets, sacking of houses as vengeance against moral offenders, popular display of support of or opposition to political programs by means of concerted

Undemocratic Contention in Europe, 1650–1850

Table 3.1 *Revolutionary Situations in Iberia, 1650–1850*

1640–59	Catalan revolt
1647–52	*Alteraciones urbanas* of Andalucía: popular rebellions against taxation, high food prices, and oligarchic control in Córdoba, Seville, and elsewhere
1649–68	Revolt of Portugal
1667	Seizure of power as Portuguese regent by Pedro, brother of king Afonso
1688–89	*Barretines* of Catalonia, in which rural people occupy Mataro, take over a number of other towns, and march on Barcelona in response to troop billeting and war-driven taxes
1693	Second Germania of Valencia (the first having occurred in 1519–22): in the course of widespread local and legal resistance to dispossession of peasants by landlords, 2,000 country people form an *Eixércit dels Agermanats* that takes over lands of the duke of Gandía
1701–14	War of the Spanish Succession, including invasions of Spain and Portugal; civil war, ending with the loss of Spanish Netherlands to Austrian Habsburgs, integration of Catalonia and Valencia into Castilian regime
1758	So-called conspiracy of the Tavoras in Portugal and aristocratic resistance to central power, crushed by Pombal
1793–1814	Intermittent war with France, including invasion, British counterinvasions, popular resistance, eventual dismemberment, and rebellions in Latin America
1801	War of the Oranges, Portugal vs. Spain
1807	French invasion of Portugal, flight of royal family to Brazil
1808	Uprising against Godoy (Aranjuez), popular insurrection in Spain, abdication of king Carlos IV in favor of Fernando VII, forced abdication of Fernando in favor of Joseph Bonaparte, British invasion of Portugal, beginning of war – at once civil and international – which lasted until 1813
1820	Mutiny of Spanish troops under Colonel Rafael Riego, generalizing revolution to 1823, termination by French invasion
1820	Revolution begun at Oporto, Portugal, seizes national power
1822–23	Royalist rising in Spain
1823–24	Portuguese civil war
1827	British landing in Portugal, supporting constitutionalists
1827	Revolt of Malcontents in Spain
1828	Portuguese coup d'état by Dom Miguel, followed by civil wars until 1834, dissolution of monasteries, and extensive sale of crown lands
1833–39	Carlist war in Spain
1834–53	Frequent insurrections in Portugal
1836	Progressist insurrections in Andalucía, Aragon, Catalonia, and Castile, ending in Spanish constitution of 1837

(continued)

Table 3.1 (continued)

1840	Revolt of General Baldomero Espartero, who seized power in Spain
1841	Spanish coup on behalf of Queen Cristina, defeated
1842	Rising in Barcelona, temporary declaration of republic, crushed by Espartero
1843	Coalition deposes Espartero; Narvaez president until 1851
1846–50	Portuguese civil wars

direct action. Clearly, Córdobanos and Madrileños drew on their own variants of the undemocratic claim-making repertoire that prevailed elsewhere in Western Europe through much of the 18th century and well into the 19th.

Of the four clusters of undemocratic politics distinguished in Chapter 2 – petitions and parodies, local vengeance, feuds and resistance, mass rebellions – the available record surely understates prevalence of local vengeance as well as feuds and resistance. Even the highly selective list of revolutionary situations, however, signals some differences between the commercialized, consummately connected, and coercion-resisting Low Countries, on one side, and coercion-intensive Spain or Portugal, on the other. In general, Iberian regimes came closer to the strong state trajectory from petty tyranny toward the zone of citizenship – but with the important qualifications that (1) the government's reach varied and fluctuated enormously from one region to another, exercising control more securely, for example, in the hinterlands of Madrid and Lisbon than in the Pyrenees or in distant commercial centers such as Barcelona and Oporto; (2) shifts in returns from colonies and overseas commerce significantly affected governmental capacity; and (3) wars with France repeatedly changed the direction of regime transformation in Iberia.

Revolutionary catalogs also miss widespread handworkers' attacks on mechanized shops between 1798 and 1844, not to mention the organization of strikes and demonstrations by Catalonia's urban workers (Pérez Ledesma 1990: 180–81). During the 19th century, finally, the propensity of Iberia's agricultural wage workers to organize, act, and support various programs of political decentralization distinguished them from their counterparts in France, Britain, or the Low Countries while giving them something in common with Italian *braccianti*.

Broadly speaking, forms of Iberian contention changed and varied in accordance with expectations set by the earlier analysis of connections between regime change and contentious politics. More so than the Low Countries, Iberia exemplifies the main characteristics of popular contention in Europe's low- to medium-capacity undemocratic regimes. Such regimes typically prescribed a substantial range of political performances (e.g., royal processions and ritual executions) but tolerated few performances they did not prescribe. However, a good deal of popular contention took place outside the regime's effective span of control. Only during periods of substantial increase in governmental capacity did Iberian regimes police day-to-day popular contention effectively.

Over the period from 1650 to 1850, Iberian regimes generally failed, for example, to intervene in local political squabbles or covert expressions of political preference during public celebrations so long as the actions and claims involved remained within bounds. That left a wide range of technically possible claim-making interactions (e.g., dissident gatherings, formation of conspiratorial associations, and attacks on corrupt officials) legally forbidden but only intermittently controlled. Even Spain's self-consciously liberal regimes of the early 19th century generally tried to impose extensive restrictions on popular assemblies and public speech, often relying on declarations of emergency to suspend the few guarantees of contentious voice their constitutions offered (Ballbé 1983: 37–86).

In such regimes, popular contentious politics rarely overlapped with government-prescribed forms of political participation, such as court assemblies and military maneuvers. Although a substantial minority of contention took place in the small tolerated zone, contentious claim making went on largely in legally forbidden territory. Within the narrow range of tolerated performances, ordinary people had the option of humble petitions or legal suits, but rarely reached higher authorities without the endorsement or direct mediation of notables – of cultural or political brokers. Only from the 1840s onward did the erratic movement of Spain and Portugal toward protected consultation facilitate direct dialogue between national authorities and groups of ordinary people by means of associations, demonstrations, public meetings, strikes, and related performances from more recent Western European repertoires. Even then, top-down brokerage loomed larger in Iberia than elsewhere in Western Europe until well into the 20th century.

At the same edge of tolerated performances, contention commonly took the form of parodies and subversions, as when masked revelers at Mardi Gras cast verbal or visual barbs at dignitaries or theater audiences cheered lines carrying politically resonant double meanings. Much contentious interaction enacted routines of collective local vengeance (e.g., sacking of houses and seizures of high-priced grain), which authorities typically forbade formally and suppressed when it threatened public order, national officials, or local dignitaries, but otherwise monitored without active intervention. Such contentious forms often mimicked established legal procedures – not only burning in effigy, but also official commandeering of grain supplies, demeaning punishments, and solemn judgments of offenders.

Vendettas, intervillage youth fights, and similar violent struggles among constituted actors, as well as forcible resistance to governmental agents such as tax collectors and recruiting sergeants, generally fell under authorities' interdiction and discredited governmental agents who failed to contain them from escalating into threats to royal power. At times, however, dissident authorities tacitly encouraged or tolerated such forms of contention. In the multilayered governments of Iberia, local authorities repeatedly conspired with popular contention in just such ways.

As Iberia's many revolutionary situations make clear, mass rebellions themselves sometimes began in purely popular resistance to government authority, but never became massive without brokerage – without significant involvement of disaffected elites or external allies. Established authorities always tried to repress mass rebellions, but commonly checked them by negotiating (or pretending to negotiate) with rebel leaders. Although very few mass rebellions produced revolutionary outcomes (significant transfers of power over governments, hence important realignments of polities), when revolutionary situations (splits in polities such that each segment or coalition controlled substantial means of government) did occur, they ordinarily emerged from mass rebellions.

Iberia's repeated revolutionary situations between 1650 through 1850 depended heavily on brokerage by dissident elites and external allies. From the French revolutionary invasion onward, they depended increasingly on military leaders. During the first half of the 19th century, progressive military officers and royalist leaders sometimes attracted popular followings, as in the constitution-promoting revolution of 1820–23, the royalist rising of 1822–23, and the Carlist wars of 1833–39. But those movements proceeded chiefly from the top down. Although Iberia's earlier history had produced its share of bottom-up rebellions – for example, the *Germanias* of 1519 and 1693, the *Alteraciones urbanas andaluzas* of 1647–52, and the *barretines* of Catalonia, 1688–89 – popularly initiated mobilizations at a regional or national scale played little part in the peninsula's national politics between 1700 and 1850.

The sketchy evidence of repertoire changes in Iberian contention between 1650 and 1850 points toward correspondences between transformations of regimes and alterations in the texture of contentious politics. Doubly so. First, major regime changes such as French invasions, loss of American colonies, and 19th-century liberal revolutions introduced significant shifts in predominant patterns of contention, as when after 1820 military *pronunciamientos* doubled with public expressions of popular support for the makers of coups in a new sort of transition from regime to regime. Second, in an attenuated way, Iberia's 19th-century establishment of constitutional regimes facilitated the formation of associations, public meetings, and demonstrations as instruments of popular claim making (González 1998: 535–51; 1999: 635–45).

Iberia versus the Low Countries

What differences in contention between the Low Countries and Iberia mark the period from 1650 to 1850? First, configurations of coercion, capital, and commitment in regime environments did, as expected, condition the sorts of regime that prevailed in one region or another, and consequently the textures of their contentious politics; in Iberia, only capital- and commitment-rich Catalonia produced regimes and popular politics vaguely resembling those of the Low Countries. Second, revolutionary situations formed much more frequently in Iberia, especially in times of war and regime succession. Third, despite recurrent efforts of the House of Orange to gain hereditary power and despite the 1830–33 Belgian rebellion, dynastic struggles for the right to rule figured much more centrally in large-scale Iberian contention than in the United Provinces or the Southern Netherlands between 1650 and 1850. Fourth, beginning with French conquests of 1793–1814 and armed resistance to them, military forces came to play a much more autonomous part in Iberia than they did in the Low Countries; Iberian generals, moreover, recurrently allied themselves not with reactionary landlords but with bourgeois reformers. Finally, rural people (who predominated numerically in Spain and Portugal) more often took up arms against landlords and government authorities in Iberia than in the Low Countries.

Calendars of revolutionary situations miss the greater frequency of subsistence struggles in the free-trading Low Countries than in the tightly regulated markets of Iberia. Although price rises did stimulate occasional local struggles such as those of those of Córdoba and Seville in May 1652 or Barcelona in February–March 1789, only in 1766 did Spain experience anything like the long chains of local attacks on bakers, millers, grain merchants, and local authorities that often occurred in the Low Countries, France, and England at times when market deregulation coincided with rapidly rising prices (Pérez Ledesma 1990: 125–26; Ringrose 1996: 318). Such struggles did, however, become much more common in liberalizing 19th-century Spain; they reached peaks in Catalonia (1835) and Andalucía (1847). Again comparisons between regions and across time provide evidence of interdependence between the organization of regimes, on one hand, and forms of popular contention, on the other.

More narrowly, my earlier arguments suggested these relationships:

1. Where governmental capacity increased, (a) governmental agents became increasingly salient as objects and participants in contention, (b) division sharpened between forms of contention conforming to government-prescribed or government-tolerated routines, on one side, and government forbidden routines, on the other, (c) bargaining over resources between governmental agents and major segments of the subject population generated categorical rights and obligations, (d) repertoires standardized across localities, groups, and types of claims – they became more modular and assumed larger scales, and (e) detached identities became increasingly prominent as bases of contentious claims.

2. With increases in protected consultation, (a) alliances between existing power holders and mobilized but politically excluded claimants become more frequent, (b) open contention clusters more heavily at the edges of prescribed and tolerated political forms, (c) shifts in the composition of ruling coalitions receive more rapid responses, (d) the average intensity of claim making increases.

3. Major surges in contention coincide as cause and effect with transformations of regimes that significantly shift their location in the capacity-consultation space.

Although the evidence on contention far away from government in the Low Countries and (especially) Iberia remains too thin for certainty, these theoretically motivated conjectures seem consistent with the evidence we have reviewed. Between 1650 and 1850 governmental capacity increased decisively in the Low Countries and more erratically in Iberia. Governmental agents became more salient objects of claims in both regions; governments did act to narrow the range of politically acceptable claim making at the same time as the circle of acceptable actors widened. Whether bargaining over resources generated categorically defined rights and obligations remains to be seen, but such rights and obligations did approach citizenship in Iberia and, especially, the Low Countries. The democratic repertoire of meetings, marches, associations, petitions, and strikes did acquire dominance and generality, especially in the Low Countries. Such detached identities as worker and socialist did, indeed, become more prevalent as bases of claim making.

Similarly, at a national scale, protected consultation greatly expanded in the Low Countries between 1650 and 1850. As for Iberia, the peninsula's history is more volatile, with great spurts and recessions of protected consultation. In both regions, however, it does look as though during expansions of protected consultation, alliances between existing power holders and mobilized but politically excluded claimants (e.g., between bourgeois and organized workers) became more frequent, that open contention came to cluster more heavily at the edges of prescribed and tolerated political forms (e.g., the house-sacking that once figured centrally in popular vengeance disappeared, and popular rebellions decreased greatly in frequency), while shifts in the composition of ruling coalitions received more rapid responses from other political actors (e.g., popular mobilizations clustered increasingly around changes of national government).

Finally, great surges of contention going far beyond struggles for central control did coincide, as expected, with major regime transformations such as the French conquests of both the Low Countries and Iberia or the creation of an independent Belgium. Cause-effect relations seem, moreover, to have run in both directions, from such struggles as the Orangist bid for power in the Dutch Republic from 1747 to 1750 and from popular rebellions to civil war and regime change in Spain from 1808 onward. Thus the line of inquiry remains promising.

Our comparison of the Low Countries with Iberia also calls attention to a set of connections that my earlier arguments understated. How military organizations developed clearly affected the character of contentious politics and the prospects for democracy in the two regions. Burgher militias played crucial parts in Dutch politics up to the 1790s, then virtually disappeared as successive Dutch and Belgian governments created national armed forces under civilian bureaucratic control. In Iberia, military force long intertwined with civil control, but professional soldiers figured much more prominently in national politics and maintained their political autonomy much longer. Policing of what authorities called "public order" also remained a military activity much longer in Iberia. Surely, military political autonomy and engagement in policing of contentious politics deserve attention in our wider comparisons of paths toward democracy.

Let me not claim too much. Evidence from the Low Countries and Iberia falls far short of clinching a case for causal interdependence between regime change and alterations in the character of contentious politics. It runs the risk, furthermore, of tumbling into tautology: placing observations of regime characteristics on both sides of the equation. Only historians who see no political content in workaday popular contention are likely to find surprising, after all, that regimes built around urban commercial oligarchies experience significantly different kinds of popular claim making than regimes based on privileged landholders and royally controlled colonial revenues. Let us place the argument and evidence exactly where they belong: as a puzzle worth pursuing.

From there we must move on to identify causal mechanisms that connected operations of polities with forms of contention: how much of the effect of changing capacity, for example, resulted from invention of effective police forces that separated from the national military, engaged in anticipatory surveillance of possible claim makers, and negotiated regularly with organized political actors before they aired their claims? Then we must examine whether something like the interactions between regime change and contention that promoted democratization in the Low Countries operated when democratization occurred elsewhere in Europe. We must eventually look separately, moreover, at the components of democratization: changes in breadth of political participation, equality of political participation, binding consultation, and protection.

Such a description may call up a frightening image of chapters to come: complex models, dense statistical tables, mind-numbing chronologies. Never fear! The remainder of this book does its work mainly by means of analytically informed national narratives. The point is to identify broad correspondences and connections among:

1. changing locations of national governments with respect to capacity and consultation
2. alterations in contentious repertoires

3. impacts of contention at the scale of individual events and campaigns on regimes
4. impacts of major crises – revolution, confrontation, conquest, and colonization – on regimes
5. shifts in relations among trust networks, categorical inequality, and public politics

We seek connections among these five elements in the form of recurrent mechanisms such as brokerage and cross-class coalition formation. Which mechanisms promote democratization or de-democratization under what conditions?

The Low Countries and Iberia have offered a few hints, for example, by pointing up the barriers to democratization set by autonomous military forces, and the regularity with which effectively democratizing regimes subordinate military forces (including police) to civilian control. For other tales of contention and democratization or its absence, we might turn to the authoritarian and revolutionary history of Russia, the turbulent disintegration of the Ottoman empire, the Swiss movement from deeply fragmented sovereignty to civil war to oligarchic versions of democracy, or the Scandinavian creation of social democracy in late-industrializing agrarian countries. Each offers its own causal story, its own peregrination within the territory delimited by strong state and weak state models of change, its own combination of conquest, revolution, colonization, and confrontation. Clearly, Britain and France occupy a narrow band in the range of intersections among regimes, contentious politics, and approaches to democracy. Our quick sketches of Britain, France, the Low Countries, and Iberia neither exhaust the trajectories of political change nor tell us how and why contention and democratization intersected. They do, however, help specify what sorts of variation we must explain.

What, precisely? Even if the correlations of regime change with alterations of contention I have claimed to detect in the Low Countries and Iberia hold up, exactly what produced those correlations requires close scrutiny. While getting a first grip on shifts in public politics, we have hardly touched the changes in categorical inequality and trust networks I earlier identified as crucial to democratization. While some of our stories about Iberia and the Low Countries confirm the importance of conquest, confrontation, and revolution in transformations of popular contention, furthermore, they do not establish either (1) that acceleration of the same causal mechanisms favorable to more incremental mutations of protected consultation occurs in those crucial shocks or (2) that subsequent politics looks different as a function of the relative historical importance of colonization, confrontation, revolution, and conquest in the production of democratic arrangements. In short, the major analytical work remains to be done. The next chapter begins that work by scrutinizing France's contentious history since 1600.

4

France

For the princess of Longueville's pleasure, from 1650 to 1665 Jean Loret set down wry commentaries on current news in rhyming couplets. The princess belonged to a family figuring significantly in the princely Fronde of 1649–52. That phase of France's great civil war centered on fierce noble opposition to young Louis XIV, his mother the Queen-Regent Anne of Austria, and their chief minister, his Eminence Cardinal Mazarin. On 6 August 1650 Loret offered the princess these lines:

Bordeaux tient toujours en balance	Bordeaux now holds within its gate
La fortune de l'Eminence	The keys to his Eminence's fate.
Et le cas est encor douteux	It still remains quite far from clear
Sçavoir qui crevera des deux.	Which one of them will yield in fear.

"Despite civil war," Loret continued sarcastically,

the mayor and city council set off in pomp to visit the queen and king, who are now at Libourne, but the people said "Come back!" and swore at their first step, "By God, you won't go!" Thus an uncivil mob kept the municipal gentlemen from going to offer their compliments. Oh, what base scoundrels! (Loret 1857: I, 32)

The royalist *Gazette de France* predictably took a different line. It devoted its issue of 14 September 1650 to reports of efforts by beleaguered twelve-year-old Louis XIV to pacify Guyenne, the rich, rebellious province of which Bordeaux was the capital. In a letter dated from Libourne, Guyenne, on 9 August, the young king (prompted by his mother and Cardinal Mazarin) addressed his subjects in Bordeaux. He – or rather they – complained that despite all the queen's efforts a few malcontents had

usurped violent authority over the populace, using it whenever possible to promote tumults and uprisings, to destroy the freedom of honorable figures such as the Parlement and the city administration, and to bend all public proceedings and resolutions to their own will. (*Gazette* no. 138, p. 1230)

What is more, the people of Bordeaux ("stirred up and led by a few ringleaders") had opened the city's gates to rebel troops and their commanders. They had, worse yet, aligned themselves with leaders of the princely Fronde. Bordeaux's malcontents had thereby actually committed treason: in effect, they had endorsed treaties of the Fronde's leaders with Spain, a country currently at war with France.

More than a few malcontents had turned against royal authority in 1650. From 1648 onward the Parlement of Bordeaux had allied itself with judicial bodies elsewhere in taking extraordinary, if formally legal, moves to block royal taxes and enhance provincial autonomy. The Parlement had clashed repeatedly with the Duke d'Épernon, provincial military governor. The governor had forestalled possible junctions of the Bordelais with the king's enemies by blockading both sea and land routes to the city; the fortress at Libourne where the governor based himself with the royal party commanded access to the Atlantic. Bordeaux's inhabitants had responded to royal pressure with extraordinary municipal assemblies, resistance against war-driven taxation, popular attacks on royal troops, great expansion of urban militia units, expulsion of the garrison from the royal citadel (Château Trompette), and even an occasional armed foray against royal strongholds in the hinterland. In July 1649 armed Bordelais had driven the governor and his troops from the city when the governor came to reassert royal authority.

The situation grew more dangerous during 1650. In January, the regent had imprisoned onetime supporters the prince of Condé, his brother Conti, and the duke of Longueville. The Condé party began making gestures toward alignment with Spain, when France and Spain were still actively at war. In May, the princess of Condé and her young son arrived at the gates of Bordeaux, thus visibly violating their assignment to forced residence hundreds of miles away. After solemn deliberation, dignitaries and residents of the city escorted the aristocratic outlaw and her military escort into the city with pomp and celebration. (One of the burdens and delights of 17th-century historiography is the abundant availability of printed step-by-step accounts for just such *entrées*, which historians decode with the same zest that Kremlinologists once expended on the lineup at the Politburo's latest public appearance.) The arrival of a Spanish diplomat to speak with the princess and her entourage had divided the bulk of the city's population from the wary Parlement and precipitated an invasion of the Palais de Justice by local supporters of Spain. Royal forces encircled Bordeaux, but the city itself was becoming a rebel bastion.

In these circumstances, the principals negotiated withdrawal of the Condé party from Bordeaux. At the end of September 1650, city fathers staged another *entrée* – but this time for Anne of Austria, Louis XIV, and his younger brother the duke of Anjou:

Arches of triumph, speeches, banquets, and fountains of wine brought animation to the city. Had anything really changed? Had Mazarin finally given up his support for Épernon? Would the new taxes on wine once again be collected? Had the monarchy really given up the proposed new parlementary offices? The ceremonies suspended, but could not cancel, these issues. Who was master of Bordeaux? The king had arrived via the river, in a magnificently appointed and decorated galley, not at the head of an army. (Ranum 1993: 247)

It took another three years of struggle to determine that Bordeaux would return to reluctant conformity with royal will. During 1652 the militia-backed Ormée – a popular body named for the elms (*ormeaux*) under which its members sometimes met and deliberated – took over the city and held control for a year. In the name of ancient freedoms since trampled by authoritarian rule, the Ormée announced a doctrine of liberty, fraternity, and even to some degree equality. It asserted the right of all male citizens to gather and make law. Fatefully, it also allied itself with the Fronde and went so far as to appeal, vainly as it happened, for aid from Cromwell's England.

Did Bordeaux's revolutionary surge issue a precocious demand for democracy? "The Ormée," concludes its historian Sal Westrich,

was a movement of artisans, shopkeepers, petty officials, and small merchants seeking protection from patrician justice, the uncertainties of mercantile capitalism, and the increasingly heavy burden of the royal fisc. Its solution was to return to the particularism of an earlier era: to corporate control in the social and economic spheres, to municipal sovereignty on the level of national politics. Although differing from the *Parlement* in its desire to free society from oligarchical control, the Ormée was one with its rival in opposing the forces that were gradually coming to dominate the course of French history. Undoubtedly, this was the ultimate reason for its failure, as it was for the failure of the *Parlement*. The future would belong to the centralized state and not to the cities, to free trade and not to guild controls, to the liberty of the individual rather than to the liberties of the community. (Westrich 1972: 59)

Despite backward-looking elements in the Ormée's program, nevertheless, realization of its principal claims would have moved Guyenne, or at least Bordeaux, significantly toward democracy – toward relatively broad and equal relations between governmental agents and constituted political actors, binding consultation of the governed with respect to governmental personnel, resources, and resources, as well as protection from arbitrary action by governmental agents. It would have moved the region in that direction, however, along a weak state trajectory, without significant augmentation of governmental capacity. Note the prominence of popular militias, a standard accompaniment of decentralist politics in old regime Europe. In 17th-century Europe deliberate decentralization was, as Westrich suggests, a good way to become prey for conquest – or reconquest.

Instead, France's post-Fronde rulers built up the government's capacity for conquest at the expense of protected consultation. After the Fronde's formal termination in 1653, reconquering rebellious provinces, reestablishing fiscal control, and rebuilding the national military establishment occupied Louis XIV and Mazarin for the rest of the 1650s (Lynn 1997). The end of war with Spain in 1659 reduced stress on the government's fiscal apparatus, although France was soon joining or fomenting other wars in the Low Countries, the Balkans, Italy, the Mediterranean, the British Isles, and North America as well as with England, Spain, and Holland on the high seas.

With Mazarin's death, Louis XIV's personal rule, and the beginning of Jean-Baptiste Colbert's ascendancy in 1661, the regime fortified its military and administrative capacity. Louis XIV resumed his predecessors' attacks on Protestant autonomies, revoking the Edict of Nantes in 1685 and pursuing nonconforming Protestants by force of arms to the end of his regime. Great regional magnates likewise lost their autonomy, nobles and priests became increasingly beholden to the crown for their authority, and the alliances of aggrieved commoners with dissident lords that had threatened French rulers for centuries began to dissolve. Louis XIV greatly expanded the French state's capacity, at the expense of protected consultation.

My book *The Contentious French* (1986) traced French struggles more or less continuously from 1600 to the 1960s. We need not repeat that effort here. This chapter summarizes major crises and regime changes in France, giving special attention to how the Revolution of 1789–99 affected the prospects and characteristics of French democracy. It shows how France's strong state trajectory brought the regime repeatedly into authoritarian rule, and thus shaped popular politics as resistance to authoritarianism. Revolution loomed large in French history, especially before the 20th century.

Table 4.1 provides a calendar of France's major revolutionary situations from 1650 to 2000. As in the cases of the Low Countries and Iberia, it includes only those occasions on which at least two competing political clusters whose leaders made incompatible claims to govern held control of some substantial geographic areas and/or governmental means within metropolitan France for a month or more. It therefore excludes numerous urban insurrections lasting less than a month as well as many fierce divisions within – or with – France's overseas territories. Despite that very high threshold, per fifty-year interval, France turns up with the following numbers of years containing revolutionary situations:

Years with revolutionary situations

1650–99	22
1700–1749	5
1750–99	11
1800–1849	3
1850–99	3
1900–1949	2
1950–1999	0

During the 17th century, France passed through a significant revolutionary situation almost one year in two. From Louis XIV's consolidation of power, revolutionary situations and forcible transfers of state power became less frequent. Even the great upheavals of the 1790s did not reverse the long-term trend. Still, the fifty-year period from 1950 to 1999 was the first half-century since 1650 (and well before) during which France did *not* pass through at least one deep revolutionary situation. By the latter half of the 20th century, French involvement in revolutionary situations had shifted from the metropole to such colonies as Algeria and Vietnam.

As of 1600, France had occupied an intermediate position in Europe with respect to the interlacing of commitment, coercion, and capital. Commitments fragmented along religious, linguistic, and regional lines, yet compared with many other parts of the continent, centuries of shared history had given French people many unifying ties. Despite the battering of 16th-century religious wars, the crown still commanded the largest

Table 4.1 *Revolutionary Situations Within Metropolitan France, 1648–2000*

1648–53	The Fronde
1655–57	Tardanizat rebellion (Guyenne)
1658	Sabotiers rebellion (Sologne)
1661–62	Bénauge rebellion (Guyenne)
1662	Lustucru rebellion (Boulonnais)
1663	Audijos rebellion (Gascony)
1663–72	Angelets guerrilla warfare (Roussillon)
1675	Papier Timbré and Bonnets Rouges (or Torrében) rebellions (Brittany)
1702–6	Camisard rebellions of Cévennes and Languedoc
1768–69	Corsican rebellion
1789–99	Multiple French revolutions and counterrevolutions
1815	Hundred Days
1830	July Revolution
1848	French Revolution
1851	Louis Napoleon coup d'état and insurrection
1870	State collapse, occupation, and republican revolutions
1870–71	Multiple Communes
1944–45	Resistance and liberation

concentrations of coercive means in a country where many regional magnates and local lords also controlled their own armed force. Unlike Russia or inland Iberia, however, France hosted considerable concentrations of capital in a well-developed web of trading cities. The country's seacoasts, major rivers, and the northeast at large all sustained extensive commercial activity.

Over the following four centuries, France's commitment, coercion, and capital underwent a two-phase transformation. The first phase (into the 18th century) brought the government's partial capture of interpersonal commitments as the crown simultaneously reduced Protestant strength and increased its control over the Catholic Church's apparatus, the subordination of existing capital to government ends, and the buildup of the central government's coercive power at the expense of previously autonomous warriors. The second phase (from the later 18th century onward) continued expansion of the government's coercive means but also saw unprecedented growth in capital and, eventually, further integration between existing interpersonal commitments and governmental activity. The second phase included repeated alternations between democratization and de-democratization, but finally produced a substantial net movement toward protected consultation.

France

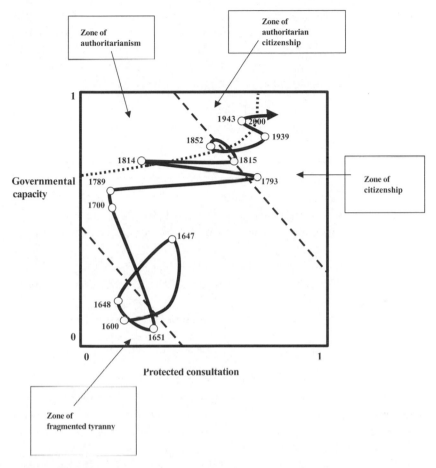

Figure 4.1: Fluctuations in French national regimes, 1600–2000.

A Multitude of Regimes

We might schematize the fluctuation of French regimes between 1600 and 2000 as in Figure 4.1. The scheme represents an elusive but interesting pair of numbers: capacity and protection as manifested in relations between the central governmental organization(s) and the average person subject to French governmental jurisdiction within the national territory. The graph arbitrarily sets bottom and top at, respectively, the lowest and highest levels of capacity France reached during the four centuries. It also sets left and right borders at, respectively, the lowest and highest levels of protected consultation ever prevailing in the country over the same period. Obviously,

101

other European regimes reached lower and higher levels in both regards during the 400 years after 1600, not to mention before then. Thus sketched, France's overall trajectory resembles the schematic strong state path to democracy sketched in Chapter 2, but with far more twists, turns, and reversals than that idealized map. In Figure 4.1 we see

- military-administrative expansion of governmental capacity (despite fierce resistance and multiple setbacks) from 1600 into the 1640s
- devastating collapse of governmental capacity followed by temporary concessions to protected consultation during the Fronde (1648–53, with the crown regaining power during 1652 and 1653)
- rebuilding of capacity and curtailment of consultation after 1653
- radical democratization between 1789 and 1793
- rapid (if struggle-filled) return to a high-capacity undemocratic regime between 1793 and 1814
- partial, but temporary, democratization at Napoleon's defeat
- rapid and multiple alternations between de-democratization and democratization, 1815–60s
- incremental and often contested democratization, 1870s–1939
- authoritarian regime under German control, 1940–43
- emergence of high-capacity democratic regimes, 1944-present

Despite its curlicues, such a graphic representation actually exaggerates the uniformity and continuity of trends. During the 16th century, France had swung repeatedly in and out of civil war, probably ending the century with no greater governmental capacity than it began. The next few centuries did bring substantial increases in governmental capacity, but only at the price of intermittent rebellion and repeated flirtation with fiscal collapse. During the 17th century, Louis XIII and Louis XIV used brute force to extract revenues for war making and to stamp out Protestant political autonomy. Their increasingly successful efforts incited resistance that ran from local foot-dragging to national insurrection. In regions of high Protestant concentration such as the Cévennes and Vivarais, for example, Louis XIV faced bloody conflicts and rebellions in 1653, 1656, 1670, 1671, 1685, 1686, and, especially, 1701–9 (for details, see Tilly 1986: 146–78).

Nevertheless, over the long run, the French state made impressive gains in capacity. Consider the central government's budget over the century beginning in 1610. Expressed as a laborer's days' wages per year per capita, royal expenditure swung widely over twenty year intervals: two days per capita in 1610, up to eight days in 1650, back down to five in 1670. (Since the "per capita" includes children and the elderly, the burden on the average household may have run three times as high.) Per capita taxes quadrupled between 1610 and 1650, only to drop by a third with the Fronde, then accelerate after Louis XIV and Colbert began exerting control during the 1670s. Colbert died in 1683, but by then he had laid down an effective national network of royal patronage and administration. The state continued to expand. At Louis XIV's death in 1715, a hypothetical average French person was working more than seven times as many days per year to support the national state as did a subject of Louis XIII one century earlier. By 1789, that same imaginary person was working twenty-four days per year for the government, up another half or more (Tilly 1986: 61–63).

Between 1600 and the revolution of 1789–99, then, French regimes moved erratically but definitively toward higher capacity – more extensive control over persons, activities, and resources within their territory. When it comes to protected consultation, however, whether any increase occurred over the same period remains debatable. Figure 4.1 incorporates my judgment that after 1653 protected consultation receded visibly at a national scale as governmental capacity underwent a spectacular increase. The French regime became more authoritarian. On one side, the crown continued its practice of raising quick money for military forces and central administration by selling or renting privileges – public offices, farmed taxes, guild monopolies, and the like. That practice placed political veto power in the hands of nobles, courts, officeholders, tax farmers, municipalities, and guilds. It set significant obstacles to further expansion of governmental capacity.

On the other side, the crown succeeded largely in disarming its potential opposition, increasing its own coercive power, and regularizing its extraction of resources from the subject population. It managed to co-opt or break the princes and lords who had still controlled autonomous armed force and independent patronage networks during the earlier 17th century. Only the overrunning of their extractive capacity by debt, corruption, foot-dragging, and elite opposition led late 18th-century regimes to a series of temporary, ineffectual experiments in consultation and representation. The early revolution certainly introduced governmental institutions that eventually became models for high-capacity democracy across the world. But the 1790s ended with Napoleon starting to consolidate a new round of authoritarian rule.

Alterations and continuities in popular claim-making repertoires corresponded to these changes in the national structure of power. At a local scale, forms of resistance, retaliation, and local control based on embedded identities continued to prevail:

- collective attacks on hoarders and gougers in times of food shortage
- sacking of houses and persons of officials or entrepreneurs who tried to collect disapproved taxes
- disruption of public ceremonies and celebrations such as Mardi Gras by mocking the powerful, voicing popular complaints, or subverting the proceedings
- shaming ceremonies (e.g., charivari) for individuals who violated local expectations concerning work, sexual behavior, or marital relations
- mass invasion of enclosed commons
- turnouts in which workers belonging to the same trade countered some joint action of the trade's masters by parading from shop to shop, recruiting the craftsmen therein, assembling in some protected place, then presenting collective demands to the masters on the threat of withdrawing from production until the demands were satisfied.

All these performances should now be familiar as standards in Europe's old regime undemocratic repertoire.

Amid these continuities, three significant and related shifts in contentious repertoires occurred between 1650 and the Revolution: (1) Until its temporary revival in 1789, the old routine of meeting emergencies by summoning or creating local militias with elected captains virtually disappeared. (2) So did the related practice of erecting chains or barricades to protect urban neighborhoods from invaders. (3) Although local resistance to new taxes continued apace, the propensity of nobles to join, lead, or even foment tax rebellions declined to insignificance. Forcibly and otherwise, French regimes had co-opted their nobility and sapped their subjects' capacity for autonomous military action.

Yet a revolution occurred. A fiscal crisis aligned a surprising (if shifting) coalition of old regime institutions, bourgeois, and peasants against the regime, rapidly destroying the monarchy. At first, privileged institutions such as the Parlements spearheaded the opposition, insisting on extensive administrative reforms (not to mention protections of their own rights) as the price of new revenues for the crown. They received widespread popular support. Then the king's attempt to bypass that confrontation spurred bottom-up mobilization.

Louis XVI's calling of an Estates General for the spring of 1789 did not merely accelerate a national debate over the terms of rule. More than

40,000 local and regional assemblies gathered to record grievances. In Third Estate (commoners') assemblies something like a sixth not only stated their complaints and demands but also formed committees of correspondence on the American revolutionary model; they thereby created durable connections between France's localities and the deputies who represented them in Versailles even before revolutionaries began forming their own institutions (Shapiro and Markoff 2001: 99). Thus the bottom-up revolutionary process began.

John Markoff's detailed analysis of French popular mobilization between 1789 and 1793 established that

- stated rural grievances of 1789 centered on taxes and the seigneurial regime
- the grievances of 1789 exhibited distinct class and regional differences in their (generally informed and critical) views of the existing national structure of power and privilege
- French rural people acted vigorously against seigneurial rights and privileges (much more so than against the persons of lords) from 1789 onward
- an active interplay continued between legislation of successive national administrations and rural demands (as expressed in both claims on authorities and direct actions against local targets)
- national authorities monitored, feared, and responded with anti-seigneurial legislation to rural uprisings
- on the whole, rural people in regions of extensive market activity and heavier state control participated more actively in revolutionary struggles
- a shifting but strong peasant-bourgeois alliance played a major part in steering the early revolution (Markoff 1996a)

In short, a judicious synthesis of Alexis de Tocqueville and Karl Marx provides a valuable guide to revolutionary situation, process, and outcome in France during the fateful years from 1788 to 1793.

What happened to France's system of rule during the revolutionary years? Before 1789, the French state, like almost all other governments, ruled indirectly at the local level, relying especially on priests and nobles for mediation, at most allowing representatives of trades, local communities, and other corporate bodies to negotiate with royal representatives over such matters as taxation. From the end of the American war, the government's efforts to collect money for its war debts crystallized an antigovernmental coalition that initially included the parlements and other power holders, but shifted toward a more popular composition as the confrontation between regime and opponents sharpened (Comninel 1987; Doyle 1986; Egret 1962; Frêche 1974; Stone 1981). The state's visible vulnerability in 1788–89 encouraged any group that had a stifled claim or grievance against the state, its agents, or its allies to articulate its demands and join others in calling for change. The rural revolts – the Great Fear, grain seizures, tax rebellions, attacks on landlords, and so on – of spring and summer 1789 occurred disproportionately in regions with large towns, commercialized agriculture, navigable waterways, and many roads (Markoff 1996a). Their geography reflected a composite but largely bourgeois-led settling of scores.

At the same time, those whose social survival depended most directly on the old regime government – nobles, officeholders, and higher clergy are the obvious examples – generally aligned themselves with the king (Dawson 1972: chapter 8). A revolutionary situation began to form: two distinct blocs both claimed power and both received support from some significant part of the population. With significant defections of military men from the Crown and formation of militias devoted to the popular cause, the opposition acquired armed force of its own. The popular bloc, connected and often led by members of the bourgeoisie, started to gain control over parts of the government apparatus.

Thus began a turbulent, divisive, incomplete, but still unprecedented experiment in direct rule and democratization at a national scale. At least temporarily, French revolutionaries insulated public politics from the old regime system of inequalities, shattered some old segregated trust networks, integrated others into public politics, and introduced measures promoting the breadth, equality, enforcement, and security of mutual obligations between citizens and governmental agents – at least those who stood by the bourgeois-led Revolution.

Bourgeois Revolution

The lawyers, officials, and other bourgeois who seized the government apparatus in 1789–90 rapidly displaced old intermediaries: landlords, seigneurial officials, venal officeholders, clergy, and sometimes municipal oligarchies as well. "It was not a rural class of English-style gentlemen," declares Lynn Hunt, "who gained political prominence on either the national or the regional level, but rather thousands of city professionals who seized the opportunity to develop political careers" (Hunt 1984: 155; see also Hunt

1978; Vovelle 1987). At the local level, the so-called Municipal Revolution widely transferred power to enemies of the old rulers; patriot coalitions based in militias, clubs, or revolutionary committees, and linked to Parisian activists, ousted the old municipalities.

Even where old power holders managed to survive the Revolution's early turmoil, relations between each locality and the national capital altered abruptly. Village "republics" of the Alps, for example, found their ancient liberties – including ostensibly free consent to taxes – crumbling as outsiders clamped them into the new administrative machine (Rosenberg 1988: 72–89). Then Parisian revolutionaries faced the problem of governing without intermediaries; they experimented with the clubs, committees, and militias that had formed in the mobilization of 1789, but found them hard to control from the center. More or less simultaneously, they recast the French map into a nested system of departments, districts, cantons, and communes, while sending out *représentants en mission* to forward revolutionary reorganization. They installed direct rule.

Given the unequal spatial distribution of cities, merchants, and capital, furthermore, the imposition of a uniform geographic grid altered relations between cities' economic and political power, placing commercially insignificant Mende and Niort at the same administrative level as mighty Lyon and Bordeaux (Margadant 1992; Ozouf-Marignier 1986; Schultz 1982). Bernard Lepetit once established a "functional" hierarchy for the prerevolutionary period that weighed both commercial importance and administrative position, but gave pride of place to administration; we can therefore take the discrepancy between a city's size and its position on Lepetit's scale as a rough indication of its relative emphasis on trade. A city that ranked higher in total population than on Lepetit's combined scale of importance, for example, had almost certainly grown large from commercial rather than administrative activity.

Within old regime France, cities whose size outran their administrative stature included Nîmes, Saint-Étienne, Roubaix, and Castres. In such cities, royal officials found themselves surrounded by well-connected merchants and other bourgeois who could easily evade finicky central control. Cities occupying higher administrative than commercial rank included Tulle, Saint-Amand-en-Berry, Saint-Flour, and Soissons (Lepetit 1988: 167–68). In such cities, royal administrators could more easily bring the central government's coercive means into play against local elites.

The Revolution, however, reordered that relationship. Revolutionary reformers established eighty-six nominally equal departments with capital cities occupying the same national administrative level regardless of their size and commercial importance. Larger cities that failed to win departmental capitals clustered disproportionately in more urban northern France, with Atlantic and Mediterranean seaports likewise providing more than their share (Lepetit 1988: 208). As a result of the realignment, the balance of forces in regional capitals shifted significantly. In the great commercial centers, where merchants, lawyers, and professionals already clustered, departmental officials (who, in any case, frequently came from the same milieux) had no choice but to bargain with the locals. Where the National Assembly carved departments out of relatively uncommercialized rural regions, the Revolution's administrators overshadowed other residents of the new capitals and could plausibly threaten to use force if the locals became recalcitrant. But officials of those regions lacked the bourgeois allies who helped their confreres do the Revolution's work elsewhere. They also confronted old intermediaries who still commanded significant followings.

In great mercantile centers such as Marseille and Lyon, political processes operated very differently. By and large, the Federalist movement, with its protests against Jacobin centralism and its demands for regional autonomy, took root in departmental capitals whose commercial positions greatly outraced their administrative rank. In dealing with these alternative obstacles to direct rule, Parisian revolutionaries improvised three parallel, and sometimes conflicting, systems of central control: (1) committees and militias, (2) a geographically defined hierarchy of elected officials and representatives, and (3) roving commissioners from the central government. To collect information and gain support, all three relied extensively on existing personal networks of lawyers, professionals, and merchants.

As the system lurched into operation, revolutionary leaders strove to routinize their control and contain independent action by local enthusiasts, who often resisted. Using both co-optation and repression, they gradually squeezed out committees and militias. Mobilization for war put great pressure on the system, incited new resistance, and increased national leaders' incentives for a tight system of control. Starting in 1792, the central administration (which until then had continued in a form greatly resembling that of the old regime) underwent its own revolution: its staff expanded enormously, and a genuine hierarchical bureaucracy took shape. In the process, revolutionaries installed one of the first systems of direct rule ever to take shape in a large state.

That shift entailed changes in systems of taxation, justice, public works, and much more. Consider policing. Outside the Paris region, France's old regime government had almost no specialized police of its own; it dispatched royal marshals (the *Maréchaussée*) to pursue tax evaders, vagabonds, and other violators of royal will and occasionally authorized the army to quell rebellious subjects, but otherwise relied on local and regional authorities to deploy armed force against civilians. The revolutionaries changed things. With respect to ordinary people, they moved from reactive to proactive policing and information gathering: instead of simply waiting until a rebellion or collective violation of the law occurred, then retaliating ferociously but selectively, they began to station agents whose job was to anticipate and prevent threatening popular collective action.

During the Revolution's early years, old regime police forces generally dissolved as popular committees, National Guards, and revolutionary tribunals took over their day-to-day activities. But with the Directory, the government concentrated surveillance and apprehension in a single centralized organization. Fouché of Nantes became minister of police in 1799. Through the Napoleonic regime, he ran a ministry whose powers extended throughout France and its conquered territories. By the time of Fouché, France had become one of the world's most closely policed countries.

Overcoming Resistance to Revolution

Going to war accelerated the move from indirect to direct rule. Almost any government that makes war finds that it cannot pay for the effort from its accumulated reserves and current revenues. Almost all war-making governments borrow extensively, raise taxes, and seize the means of combat – including men – from reluctant citizens who prefer other uses for their resources. Prerevolutionary France followed these rules faithfully, to the point of accumulating debts that eventually forced calling of the Estates General. Nor did the Revolution repeal the rules: once France declared war on Austria in 1792, the government's demands for revenues and manpower excited resistance just as fierce as that which had broken out under the old regime. Of the 500,000 young men eligible for military conscription in 1793–94, for example, some 200,000 evaded service, often by fleeing into the bush (Woloch 1994: 386).

In March 1793 the Republic's call for a great levy of troops to face the expanded demands of war had touched off widespread resistance. The greatest anti-Republican rising formed in the western region that became known collectively as the Vendée, a name drawn from one of the half-dozen western departments that divided lethally between self-declared revolutionaries and counterrevolutionaries. But the south also produced extensive strug-gles over military conscription during the spring of 1793. In Languedoc, sharp divisions between Protestants and Catholics as well as between city and country people emerged in response to military conscription.

The Languedoc village of Seysses illustrates popular resistance to mil-itary service. The village lay about seventeen kilometers southwest of Toulouse, capital of the Haute-Garonne department. On 8 April 1793 the people of Seysses were scheduled to choose military recruits for the con-tingent assigned them by a decree of 19 March. On the 8th, Jean Sautet of Seysses complained to the departmental attorney general (*procureur-général-syndic*) that on the previous day he was waiting for confession by the village's constitutional priest when in the village street appeared a large mob (*attroupement*)

of citizens armed with sabers, guns, and other weapons who were shouting pub-licly that they should kill all the patriots. When the curé went out to send them away, they continued, shouting even louder that since by means of conscription [the government] was exposing citizens to the risk of death people should exterminate the patriots. (Archives Muncipales, Toulouse (hereafter AMT) 2/1/33)

(Strictly speaking, the government was not yet "conscripting" soldiers but following the model of the old regime national militia by requiring each locality to supply its quota of troops through voluntary enlistment, public election, drawing of lots among single able-bodied men, or other means; it still allowed, furthermore, the purchase of replacements. "Patriots," in the (not always complimentary) jargon of 1793, meant active supporters and beneficiaries of the revolutionary regime; in a nice irony, patriots often called their enemies, however plebeian, "aristocrats.")

Similar events, with the additional fillip of objections to the new taxes levied in support of military levies, occurred in Toulouse, St. Sulpice, Cadours, and the district of Muret (Lyons 1978: 39). In Seysses, Sautet blamed the gathering on "refractory priests or émigrés who remain hidden around Seysses, the self-confidence they lend to enemies of public welfare, and the opportunity [the regime's enemies] have so far been given to abuse the arms they bear" (AMT 2/1/33). The department's governing council commissioned its member Citizen Goulard to proceed to Seysses with a detachment of at least 200 National Guards, to search for weapons, and to arrest refractory priests, émigrés, the "authors and instigators of the riot," and other suspicious persons the municipal officers or constitutional priest might identify, then bring them back to jail in Toulouse – all this at the expense of Seysses's residents. In overcoming resistance to conscription and taxes, revolutionaries built yet another set of centralized controls.

The French used their own new system as a template for reconstruction of other governments. As revolutionary and imperial armies conquered, they tried to build replicas of that system of direct rule elsewhere in Europe. Napoleon's government consolidated the system and turned into a reliable instrument of rule. Almost everywhere, it significantly increased the central government's capacity. The system survived the Revolution and Empire in France and, to some degree, elsewhere; Europe as a whole shifted massively toward centralized direct rule with at least a modicum of representation for the ruled.

Resistance and counterrevolutionary action followed directly from the process by which the new government established direct rule. Remember how much change revolutionaries introduced in a very short time. They eliminated all previous territorial jurisdictions, consolidated many old parishes into larger communes, abolished the tithe and feudal dues, dissolved corporations and their privileges, constructed a top-to-bottom administrative and electoral system, expanded and standardized taxes through that system, seized properties of emigrant nobles and of the Church, disbanded monastic orders, subjected clergy to the government and imposed on them an oath to defend the new state church, conscripted young men at an unprecedented rate, and displaced both nobles and priests from automatic exercise of local leadership. All this occurred between 1789 and 1794.

Subsequent regimes added more ephemeral changes such as the revolutionary calendar and the cult of the Supreme Being, but the early Revolution's overhaul of the government endured into the 19th century. French reorganization set the pattern for many other European governments. The greatest reversals of the early Revolution's changes concerned throttling of local militias and revolutionary committees, restoration or compensation of some confiscated properties, and Napoleon's Concordat with the Catholic Church. All in all, these changes constituted a dramatic, rapid substitution of uniform, centralized direct rule for a system of government mediated by local and regional notables. What is more, the new state hierarchy consisted largely of lawyers, physicians, notaries, merchants, and other bourgeois.

Like their prerevolutionary counterparts, these fundamental changes attacked many existing interests and opened opportunities to groups that had previously had little access to government-sanctioned power – especially the village and small-town bourgeoisie. As a result, they precipitated both resistance and struggles for power. Artois (the department of Pas-de-Calais) underwent a moderate version of the transition (Jessenne 1987). Before the Revolution, Artesian nobles and churchmen held a little over half of all land as against a third for peasants. Up to 60 to 80 percent of all farms had fewer than five hectares (which implies that a similar large majority of farm operators worked part-time for others), and a quarter of household heads worked primarily as agricultural wage laborers. Taxes, tithes, rents, and feudal dues took a relatively low 30 percent of the income from leased land in Artois, with a fifth of rural land on sale at the revolutionary seizure of church and noble properties. Artesian agricultural capitalism, in short, had advanced far by 1770.

In such a region, large leaseholders (*fermiers-lieutenants*) dominated local politics, but only within limits set by their noble and ecclesiastical landlords. By sweeping away the privileges of those patrons, the Revolution threatened leaseholders' power. They survived the challenge, however, as a class, if not as a particular set of individuals. Many officeholders lost their posts during the early Revolution's struggles, especially where the community was already at odds with its lord. Yet their replacements came disproportionately from the same class of comfortable leaseholders. In the 1790 communal elections, for example, voters chose leaseholders as 86 of the department's 138 newly elected mayors (Jessenne 1987: 62).

The struggle of wage laborers and smallholders against the "village roosters" that Georges Lefebvre discovered in the adjacent Nord occurred with less intensity, or less effectiveness, in the Pas-de-Calais. Local revolutionary zealots did label as "aristocrats" those farmers who maintained contact with their exiled former landlords and peasants who sneaked into Belgium for the ministrations of exiled priests, but no counterrevolutionary force organized in Artois. Although the larger farmers, viewed with suspicion by national authorities, lost some of their grip on public office during the Terror and again under the Directory, they regained it later and continued to rule their roosts through the middle of the 19th century. By that time, nobles and ecclesiastics had lost much of their capacity to contain local powerholders, but manufacturers, merchants, and other capitalists had taken their places. The displacement of old intermediaries opened the way to a new alliance between large farmers and bourgeoisie.

Under the lead of Paris, the transition to direct rule went relatively smoothly in Artois. Elsewhere, intense struggle accompanied the change. The career of Claude Javogues, agent of the Revolution in his native department of the Loire, reveals that struggle and the political process that incited it (Lucas 1973). Javogues was a huge, violent, hard-drinking roustabout whose close kin were lawyers, notaries, and merchants in Forez, a region not far to the west of Lyon. The family was climbing socially during the 18th century. In 1789, Claude himself was a well-connected thirty-year-old lawyer in Montbrison. The Convention dispatched this bourgeois bull to the Loire in July 1793 and recalled him in February 1794. During those six months, Javogues relied heavily on his existing connections, concentrated on repression of the Revolution's enemies, acted to a large degree on the theory that priests, nobles, and rich landlords were enemies, neglected and bungled administrative matters such as the organization of food supply, and left behind him a reputation for arbitrariness and cruelty.

Yet Javogues and his coworkers did, in fact, reorganize local life. As we follow his actions in the Loire, we encounter clubs, surveillance committees, revolutionary armed forces, commissars, courts, and *représentants en mission*. We see almost unbelievable attempts to extend the direct administrative purview of the central government to everyday individual life. We recognize the importance of popular mobilization against the Revolution's enemies – real or imagined – as a force that displaced the old intermediaries. We therefore gain insight into the conflict between two objectives of the Terror: extirpation of the Revolution's opponents and forging of instruments to do the Revolution's work. We discover the great importance of control over food as an administrative challenge, as a point of political contention, and as an incentive to popular action.

Contrary to the old image of a unitary people welcoming arrival of long-awaited reform, local histories of the Revolution make clear that France's revolutionaries established their power through struggle, and frequently over stubborn popular resistance. Most of the resistance, it is true, took the form of evasion, cheating, and sabotage rather than outright rebellion. But people through most of France resisted one feature or another of revolutionary direct rule. In the bustling port of Collioure, on the Mediterranean close to the Spanish border, popular collective action during the Revolution "consciously or not, pursued the goal of preserving a certain cultural, economic, and institutional independence. In other words, popular action sought to challenge the French government's claims to intervene in local life in order to raise troops for international wars, to change religious organization, or to control trade across the Pyrenees" (McPhee 1988: 247).

Issues differed from region to region as a function of previous history, including previous relations of capital, coercion, and commitment. Where fault lines ran deep, resistance consolidated into counterrevolution: the formation of effective alternative authorities to those put in place by the Revolution. Counterrevolution occurred not where everyone opposed the Revolution but where irreconcilable differences divided well-defined blocs of supporters and opponents on a large geographic scale.

Counterrevolution

France's south and west, through similar processes, produced the largest zones of sustained counterrevolution (Lebrun and Dupuy 1985; Lewis and Lucas 1983; Nicolas 1985). The geography of executions under the Terror provides a reasonable picture of counterrevolutionary activity. Departments having more than 200 executions included Loire Inférieure (3,548), Seine (2,639), Maine-et-Loire (1,886), Rhône (1,880), Vendée (1,616), Ille-et-Vilaine (509), Mayenne (495), Vaucluse (442), Bouches-du-Rhône (409), Pas-de-Calais (392), Var (309), Gironde (299), and Sarthe (225). These departments accounted for 89 percent of all executions under the Terror (Greer 1935: 147).

Except for the Seine (essentially Paris) and the Pas-de-Calais (largely Arras), high-execution departments concentrated in the South, the Southwest, and, especially, the West. In the South and Southwest, Languedoc, Provence, Gascony, and the Lyonnais hosted military insurrections against the Revolution, insurrections the geography of which corresponded closely to support for federalism (Forrest 1975; Hood 1971, 1979; Lewis 1978; Lyons 1980; Scott 1973). Federalist movements began during the spring of 1793, when Jacobin expansion of the foreign war – including declaration of war on Spain – incited resistance to taxation and conscription, which in turn led to tightening of revolutionary surveillance and discipline. The autonomist movement peaked in commercial cities that had enjoyed extensive liberties under the old regime, notably Marseille, Bordeaux, Lyon, and Caen. Sustained rural counterrevolution, on the other hand, broke out chiefly in regions the revolutionary capitals of which had occupied relatively low ranks in the old regime's administrative, fiscal, and demographic hierarchies and the bourgeois of which therefore had relatively weak influence in surrounding regions (Lepetit 1988: 222). In those two kinds of cities and their hinterlands, France fractured into bloody civil war.

In the west, guerrilla raids against republican strongholds and personnel unsettled Brittany, Maine, and Normandy from 1792 to 1799, while open armed rebellion flared south of the Loire in parts of Brittany, Anjou, and Poitou beginning in the fall of 1792 and likewise continuing intermittently until Napoleon pacified the region in 1799 (Bois 1981; Le Goff and Sutherland 1984; Martin 1987). The western counterrevolution reached its high point in the spring of 1793, when the Republic's call for troops precipitated armed resistance through much of the west. That phase saw massacres of "patriots" and "aristocrats," invasion and temporary occupation of such major cities as Angers, and pitched battles between armies of Blues and Whites (as the armed elements of the two parties were known).

The west's counterrevolution grew directly from efforts of revolutionary officials to install a particular kind of direct rule in the region, a rule that

- practically eliminated nobles and priests from their positions as partly autonomous intermediaries
- brought the government's demands for taxes, manpower, and deference to the level of individual communities, neighborhoods, and households, and
- gave the region's bourgeois political power they had never before wielded.

Bourgeois consolidated their power through struggle. On 12 October 1790, at la Chapelle de Belle-Croix, Vendée, a number of people from neighboring parishes arrived for mass and vespers armed with clubs. "Seeing the local National Guard with their regular uniforms and arms, the strangers came up to them and said they had no right to wear the national uniform, that they were going to strip it from them, that they supported the cause of clergy and nobility and wanted to crush the bourgeois who, they said, were taking bread from priests and nobles." The armed men then attacked the National Guards and the Maréchaussée of Palluau, who fought them off only with difficulty (Chassin 1892: II, 220).

In the mouths of Vendeans, to be sure, the word *bourgeois* conflated class and urban residence. Nevertheless, the people of that counterrevolutionary region saw clearly enough that the two connected intimately. In seeking to extend the government's rule to every locality and to dislodge all enemies of that rule, French revolutionaries started a process that did not cease for twenty-five years. In some ways, it has not yet ceased today. Even now, opponents of France's secular, centralized, interventionist government point to the Vendée as a symbol of righteous resistance and as proof of revolutionary evil (see, e.g., Gérard 1999).

In these regards, for all its counterrevolutionary ferocity, the west conformed to France's general experience. Everywhere in France, bourgeois – not owners of large industrial establishments, for the most part, but merchants, lawyers, notaries, and others who made their livings from the possession, protection, and manipulation of capital – were gaining strength during the 18th century. Throughout France, the mobilization of 1789 brought disproportionate numbers of bourgeois into political action. As the revolutionaries of Paris and their provincial allies displaced nobles and priests from their critical positions as agents of indirect rule, existing networks of bourgeois served as alternate connections between the government and thousands of communities across the land. For a while, those connections rested on vast popular mobilization through clubs, militias, and committees. Gradually, however, revolutionary leaders contained or even suppressed their turbulent partners. Through trial, error, and struggle, the ruling bourgeoisie worked out the system of rule that reached directly into local communities and passed chiefly through administrators who served under scrutiny and budgetary control of their superiors.

This process of state expansion encountered three huge obstacles. First, many people saw opportunities to forward their own interests and settle old scores open up in the crisis of 1789. They either managed to capitalize on the opportunity or found their hopes blocked by competition from other actors; members of both categories lacked incentives to support further revolutionary changes. Second, the immense effort of warring with most other European powers strained the government's capacity at least as gravely as had the wars of old regime kings. Third, in some regions the political bases of newly empowered bourgeois proved too fragile to support the work of cajoling, containing, inspiring, threatening, extracting, and mobilizing that revolutionary agents carried on everywhere; resistance to demands for taxes, conscripts, and compliance with moralizing legislation occurred widely in France, but where preexisting rivalries placed a well-connected bloc in opposition to the revolutionary bourgeoisie, civil war frequently developed. In these senses, the revolutionary transition from indirect to direct rule embodied a bourgeois revolution and engendered a series of antibourgeois counterrevolutions.

Revolution and Citizenship

By 1793 France's revolutionary regime had abolished most old regime titles of distinction in favor of calling all the former monarchy's adult male subjects *citoyens*, but many putative citizens were contesting the terms of their relations to the government. The construction of a state church whose

116

priests (the "constitutionals") were civil servants had divided the population sharply between the church's adherents and enemies. "Refractory" priests – those who had refused to swear the oath accepting the Civil Constitution of the Clergy and had thereby rejected incorporation into the government's new religious bureaucracy – disappeared underground or into exile but frequently maintained contact with faithful followers. More generally revolutionary, counterrevolutionary, and in-between French people disputed furiously what it meant to be French, patriotic, Catholic, and/or a citizen.

How did citizenship come into being anyway? And what was it? Political identities in general comprise public, collective answers to the questions "Who are you?," "Who are we?," and "Who are they?" The answer "citizens" specifies a general, political identity that cuts across local and particular circumstances. If citizenship is a tie entailing mutual obligations between categorically defined persons and agents of a government, the identity "citizen" describes the experience and public representation of that tie. In the simplest version, citizenship establishes a quintessential detached pair of identities: citizen versus noncitizen.

Such identities do not spring whole from a deliberate invention or a general principle's ineluctable implications. They emerge from the historical accumulation of continual negotiation. In April 1793 young, unmarried French men held the identity citizen to the extent that they and agents of the revolutionary government mutually recognized and represented rights or obligations stemming categorically from the collective attachment of such young men to the state. In fact, as we have seen, the tie and the identity that grew from it were then undergoing contestation because of other competing ties many young men held simultaneously – ties to friends, co-workers, families, villages, or the old Catholic Church – and because the exemption of republican officials from conscription in order to do their revolutionary work at home made the demand for military service seem all the more unjust to nonofficials.

In old regime France, citizenship had not existed, at least not at a national scale covering any substantial share of the population. To be sure, one might follow Max Weber in arguing that European cities had created small-scale versions of citizenship long before 1789; old regime French cities did typically recognize classes of members who enjoyed political and economic rights that the rest of the population lacked. One might also claim that nobles and priests exercised categorical rights and obligations vis-à-vis the monarchy, even that the Estates General, on the rare occasions that they met, constituted a kind of national citizenry. A rump of the Estates General convened in 1789, after all, converted itself into a national representative assembly and established categorically based rights for large numbers of adult French males. In those senses, the revolutionaries who created citizenship after 1789 borrowed from old regime institutions. Still, only in these thin, equivocal ways could we say that the old regime maintained a system of citizenship.

From its outset, the Revolution enormously increased the scope of citizenship. "The spread of citizenship," notes Pierre Rosanvallon, "arose from the equation of civil and political rights in the new principle of popular sovereignty" (Rosanvallon 1992: 71). According to that radical principle, all worthy and responsible persons should not only enjoy state protection, but also participate directly in governing the nation; the only question was how to identify the worthy and responsible and how to exclude the rest. From the Revolution onward, French citizenship fluctuated in scope, but over the long run expanded greatly. Although women did not vote in French national elections until 1946, among native-born males adult suffrage and eligibility for office reappeared in 1848 to survive with only minor infringements from then onward.

With the Revolution, furthermore, virtually all French people (both male and female) acquired access to government-run courts. During the 19th century, rights to assemble, to associate, to strike, or to campaign for elections expanded in company with obligations to attend school, to serve in the military, to reply to censuses, to pay individually assessed taxes, and to fulfill other now-standard duties of citizens. During the 20th century, finally, a series of welfare benefits including unemployment insurance, guaranteed pensions, and family allowances joined the citizenship package. If to this day French politicians still dispute which persons born to parents who are not themselves citizens are eligible for the rights and obligations of citizenship, on the whole citizenship has acquired a scope France's old regime population would have found incredible. France has created a strong version of citizenship. As compared with old regime rights and obligations, it embodies extensively protected consultation.

Strong citizenship depends on direct rule: imposition throughout a unified territory of a relatively standard system in which an effective hierarchy of government officials reaches from the national center into individual localities or even households, thence back to the center. The Revolution dissolved indirect rule and installed a highly standardized administrative hierarchy from national legislature to local commune, with communication and power running in both directions. Although in the early years France's revolutionaries bypassed old webs of nobles, priests, and royal officials by relying heavily on pre existing networks of merchants, lawyers, other professionals, and their clienteles, by the time of Napoleon the national bureaucracy had acquired a weight of its own. With the creation of an effective, pervasive national police system after 1799 under Fouché's ruthless leadership, the administrative structure that governed France for the next century fell into place.

Seen in historical and comparative perspective, however, the creation of direct rule in France and elsewhere did not depend so much on the genius of a Robespierre, a Fouché, or a Napoleon as on massive struggles of would-be rulers with recalcitrant populations. The lines of force in the process ran something like this:

expanding military activity → state expansion → direct rule
    ↓   ↓   ↑   ↑
popular resistance → struggle → bargaining → citizenship

In a typical Western European scenario, the massive growth of armies and navies after 1750 or so made mercenaries decreasingly attractive to rulers, who turned more and more to drawing troops from their domestic populations and to the extraction of new taxes to pay those troops.

In a wonderful irony, military buildup generally had the side-effect of reducing the military's autonomous political power. That happened because military organizations of which the personnel came from the domestic population could live less easily by preying on their fellow countrymen and therefore created segregated systems of housing and supply; because they came to depend increasingly on appropriations from legislatures that had minds of their own; and because civilian bureaucracies devoted to finance, supply, administration, and long-range planning hedged them in.

Ordinary people, to be sure, bore the costs of these new, expensive military systems. But both ordinary people and their patrons fought war-impelled taxation, conscription, seizures of goods, and restrictions on trade by means ranging from passive resistance to outright rebellion, put down with varying combinations of repression, persuasion, and bargaining. The very acts of intervening, repressing, persuading, and bargaining formed willy-nilly the institutions of direct rule. Out of struggle emerged citizenship, a continuing series of transactions between persons and agents of a given government in which each has enforceable rights and obligations uniquely by virtue of the persons' membership in an exclusive category, a category of native-born or naturalized people. As the Napoleonic and Vichy regimes show, citizenship did not guarantee democracy. But under the right conditions it promoted democratization – movement not only toward relative breadth and equality of political participation but also toward binding consultation of the citizenry and protection of citizens from arbitrary action by governmental agents.

What conditions? First, without some minimum of governmental capacity neither citizenship nor democracy survives; it takes substantial governmental control over persons, activities, and resources to enforce mutual rights and obligations, including democratic rights and obligations. But citizenship takes democratic forms especially when social changes are insulating public politics from existing categorical inequalities, when public politics and governmental agents are becoming significant guarantors of trust networks, and when privileged particular ties between governmental agents and political intermediaries are dissolving. Chapter 1 inventoried specific mechanisms that produce these effects: formation of politically active coalitions that cross-cut categorical inequality, disintegration of existing segregated trust networks, bureaucratic containment of previously autonomous military forces, and so on.

In the case of 17th- to 19th-century France, the Revolution of 1789–99 produced the largest single surge of such mechanisms; it more or less simultaneously eliminated priests and nobles as partly autonomous intermediaries, subordinated military forces to centralized governmental control, dissolved privileged corporate bodies of all sorts, and imposed uniform administrative structures on the whole country. It disrupted the extensive private credit networks that had prevailed under the old regime and initiated a long-term transition toward government-monitored and government-backed lending (Hoffman, Postel-Vinay, and Rosenthal 2000: chapters 8–10). Extensive democracy did not survive the early Revolution. But because these changes had already occurred, each successive reimposition of authoritarian control after Napoleon's fall generated more concerted and effective opposition. The very existence of the first revolutionary democratization provided a model and a warrant for subsequent revolutionary mobilizations. The mobilizations of 1830, 1848, and 1870–71 all receded temporarily, yet produced net movements toward protected consultation.

120

Revolution, Confrontation, Conquest, and Democratization, 1830–2000

As measured by the frequency and coordination of public contention, France's major regime crises after the Restoration of 1815 centered on seven peaks (Lees and Tilly 1974; Rule and Tilly 1972; Shorter and Tilly 1973, 1974; Tilly 1986; Tilly, Tilly, and Tilly 1975):

1830–32: bourgeois-worker coalitions in Paris and other major cities overthrow the regime of Charles X, bringing Louis-Philippe d'Orléans to power; workers continue to bid for their share, but the new regime beats them down

1848–51: a bourgeois-worker-peasant coalition overturns the Orleanist regime, establishing the Second Republic; workers continue to struggle with the regime; Louis Napoleon wins national election as president and begins installing repressive regime, then engineers a coup d'état in December 1851; massive republican resistance to the coup fails

1870–71: military losses to Prussian forces lead to the collapse of Second Empire, German occupation, and moderate republican revolution; citizens of Paris and other cities declare revolutionary Communes but succumb to governmental force by May 1871

1905–7: disestablishment of the Catholic Church, general strikes of industrial workers, and mass mobilization by southern wine growers converge in nation-wide struggles

1935–37: deep polarization between organized workers and socialists, on one side, and right-wing organizations, on the other, centering on the temporary installation of a Popular Front regime after huge strikes

1944–47: liberation of France by Allied forces, resistance against German occupiers, followed by struggles for control of the French state and Communist-led opposition to American influence

1968: extensive mobilizations of students and workers against the de Gaulle government, dissipating in a landslide reelection of Gaullists

To complete the roster of regime crises and transitions, we might want to add the later 1870s (implantation of a secular Third Republic), 1896–1906 (public struggles over the trumped-up conviction for espionage of Captain Alfred Dreyfus, the conviction itself having occurred in 1894), 1940 (German victory and occupation), and 1958 (Charles de Gaulle's return to power amid the Algerian civil war). But none of those crises produced the breadth of public mobilization within metropolitan France that arose in 1830–32, 1848–51, 1870–71, 1905–7, 1935–37, 1944–47, and 1968. Cumulatively, those revolutions, confrontations, and conquests nudged France toward democracy.

The changing place of organized workers in the crucial mobilizations marks the path to democratization. Artisans' mutual aid societies, producers' associations, and conspiratorial organizations joining workers with bourgeois did yeoman work in the struggles of 1830–32, but they never acquired legal public standing. In 1848, similar organizations emerged from the shadows, then multiplied, as workers crowded into units of a revived National Guard. Soon, however, Louis Napoleon's agents were banning workers' organizations, arresting their leaders, and driving them back into shadows; repression that followed the 1851 coup only accelerated those processes. Despite disenfranchising many workers by manipulating requirements for residence and registration, nevertheless, the regime did not dare to abolish the manhood suffrage that had arrived in 1848. Workers began mobilizing, furthermore, as Napoleon III relaxed central controls during the later 1860s.

After the Second Empire's legalization of strikes (1864) and considerable relaxation of restrictions on assembly and association (1868), French workers and radicals greatly expanded their publicly visible contention. (Private-sector labor unions did not become fully legal, however, until 1884, and public-sector unions inhabited a legal twilight zone until the 1950s.) Widespread webs of association with much sending of delegates and addresses from place to place provided bases of coordination for collective action at larger than local scales. They also underlay a popular program of federalism that occupied a middle ground between the radical decentralizing programs of anarchists and the hierarchical structures of many revolutionary organizations.

The war with Prussia that began in July 1870 raised the political stakes and sharpened divisions within the republican opposition. Especially when Prussia gained a massive military advantage and began to fight on French soil, activists divided between those who supported the war effort and those who gave priority to internationalist, autonomist, or anarchist programs. As French national military forces lurched from disaster to disaster, however, temporary alliances formed between those who criticized the government for incompetence and those who complained about its oppression. In parallel with many other revolutionary movements in France and elsewhere, radical programs gained support as a function of the central government's war-driven vulnerability.

Parisian declaration of a Commune on 28 March 1871 followed months of campaigning by Parisian radicals for such a move and numerous attempts – some successful – to establish radical autonomous governments in smaller French cities. Arrondissement-based National Guard units doubled by local committees formed the structure of Parisian government. At the top stood a municipal government consisting of delegates from arrondissements and a National Guard central committee likewise formed by election. These twinned organizations overhauled municipal administration, created public services, and coordinated the city's defense against encircling German and French troops. A third kind of structure – the popular club – played no formal part in government but beginning in the fall of 1870 became a central forum for discussion of public affairs and mobilization of collective claim making.

As the Third Republic stabilized after 1877 or so, workers not only continued to organize at the level of craft and factory, but also started to form worker-based political parties, especially socialist parties. (After having banned socialist organizations in response to the Commune, the government legalized them again in 1879.) Although socialist leader Jean Jaurès spoke out in defense of Alfred Dreyfus during 1898, the struggles of 1905–7 were the first in which socialists participated visibly and actively at a national scale. Their successors – socialists and communists alike – took sides in every subsequent peak mobilization. They came closest to seizing national power in 1935–37, as socialist Léon Blum took the prime ministry in the Popular Front government. German occupiers and their Vichy collaborators shut down all public associations that did not help them implement their rule. Yet skeletons of workers' organizations – especially those of the Communists – survived the war years and returned to vigorous action after World War II. Despite the undemocratic interlude of 1940–43, organized workers had clearly integrated themselves into French public politics.

Signs of Democratization

We can also find signs of 19th-century French democratization in three disparate areas: compulsory military service, the incorporation of private associations into public politics, and changing relations of Jews to the state. First, *military conscription*. By tying (male) citizenship to military service, 18th-century revolutionaries opened a path toward democratization.

Equalization of liability for military service during the 19th century reflected a more general equalization of political rights and obligations. Readiness of young men, their families, and their communities to collaborate with military conscription resulted from a combination of governmental coercion, alternative career opportunities, and commitment to the government itself. In 19th-century France, increasing compliance probably reflects both the insulation of public politics from existing categorical inequalities and the integration of previously shielded trust networks into public politics.

Under the old regime, despite occasional resort to impressment and incorporation of convicts, France's regular army generally drew its troops from volunteers. The royal militia, however, forced local communities to deliver recruits, most often by lot, from among local unmarried, fit, sufficiently tall males; militia service and exemptions from it became a major bone of contention during the 18th century. (Nevertheless, in the flood of petitions to the royal regime generated for the Estates General of spring 1789, complaints against militia service figured far less prominently than condemnations of taxes and noble privileges; Shapiro and Markoff 1998: 386). The first military expansion of 1791 to 1794 divided the country between those segments of the population that supported the draft and those that opposed it. During the early Revolution, region-by-region military service continued to excite resistance in rough proportion to more general political opposition. In the south, for example, Protestants and city-dwellers (the two categories overlapped considerably) more often supported the revolutionary regime.

Even among urbanites, however, draft resistance flourished. "However old their incorporation into the French royal domain," remarks Gérard Cholvy, "from 1792 onward between the banks of the Rhone and the base of Canigou southern populations seem to have felt a powerful repugnance to defending the national soil" (Cholvy 1974: 305; Mount Canigou marks the eastern end of the Pyrenees, at the Mediterranean). During the revolutionary years VII to XIII, for example, almost every department south of a line from La Rochelle to Lyon listed 30 percent or more of its conscripts as missing through desertion or failure to report, while above that line only Morbihan, Vendée, Vienne, and Nièvre reached those proportions (Forrest 1989: 2). For those who collaborated, nevertheless, military service created commitments to the regime as it forged strong bonds across the country (Lynn 1984). By 1806, the government was successfully drafting thousands of young men into the largest, most effective popular army Europe had ever seen.

Resistance to military service rose and fell with more general opposition to 19th-century regimes. Opposition itself depended in part on the extent to which the government showed signs of capacity and intent to meet its commitments and to enforce the obligations of citizenship evenhandedly across the population (Levi 1997: 44–51; more generally, see Levi and Stoker 2000). Resistance to conscription swelled as Napoleon's regime began to falter, but compliance then increased (despite persistent regional variation) across subsequent regimes. By the early 1820s, the median departmental proportion of eligible young men who failed to report for selection had fallen to 1.9 percent, with higher levels of absenteeism still heavily concentrated in southern France (Aron, Dumont, and Le Roy Ladurie 1972: 80–81).

From that point on, equalization of military obligations among social classes became a major demand of French democrats. Although educational and religious exemptions survived the 19th century, compared with their European neighbors the French installed a relatively egalitarian system of male military service. They thereby integrated trust networks into public politics and inhibited the translation of categorical inequalities into public politics. To be sure, the process tilted citizenship and political participation strongly toward males; even the tardy enactment of female suffrage in 1945 did not eliminate that masculine bias.

In the process, shared military service became a basis of male solidarity cutting across boundaries of class, religion, and region. Veterans' groups (e.g., survivors of Napoleonic armies) became political forces from early in the 19th century. Veterans figured significantly in coalitions from right to left as parliamentary politics and elections gained importance under the Third Republic. Uniting their constituents across class boundaries, they connected villages and towns to the central government. In the Angevin village of Chanzeaux during the 1960s, the organization of World War II veterans was practically the only one to bring together men from different classes, political tendencies, and religious persuasions. A parallel unification occurred within *classes*, sets of men who became eligible for military service in the same year:

Prior to entering the service, they meet frequently on Saturday night, Sunday afternoon, or weekends at different houses throughout the commune to "raise the roof" and enjoy their precious moments of freedom. The class allegiance endures even after military service is over through a yearly banquet, honoring all the people born in years ending in the same number as the current year. (Wylie 1966: 205)

The institution of the *classe* bears some kinship with old regime institutions such as brotherhoods and youth abbeys, which frequently organized holidays, shamed rule-breaking couples, and fought with youths from neighboring communes. But it displays one crucial difference from those institutions: whereas the old brotherhoods protected local trust networks from the authorities, shared military service connects them directly with the central government. Thus it promotes democratization.

Popular Associations

Not all French associations served democracy at a national scale. Although recent theorists of democracy (e.g., Putnam 2000) have sometimes seen associational life as a bulwark of democratization, the widespread associations of old regime France generally worked in the opposite direction: they segregated interpersonal trust networks from national public politics, and they translated categorical social inequality into public politics at both the local and the national scale (Bermeo and Nord 2000). Since Maurice Agulhon has painstakingly reconstructed the changing character of associational life in Provence from the 18th century to the late 19th century, let us take advantage of his reconstruction (Agulhon 1966, 1970a, 1970b, 1977, 1993).

In villages and towns of 18th-century Provence, Agulhon documents the central parts played in public life by religious confraternities, youth abbeys, militias, and similar organizations. Despite overlapping personnel, they organized around different activities, rights, and obligations – conducting saints' day processions, shaming immoral persons, providing military escorts for processions, collecting taxes on women's exogamous unions, and (literally) fueling celebrations. In the village of Aups, for example, military organization followed a common Provençal model:

The First Consul of the previous year commands the Watch and the first militia company. The second is led by a young man with the title Youth Abbot. The ensign or flag-bearer leads the artisans who form the third company; and the fourth, composed of peasants and agricultural workers, is chosen from that class of residents. (Agulhon 1966: 102–3, quoting Paul Achard)

The First Consul was often a noble and always a notable. Carrying this sort of division even further, each organized trade typically formed a separate confraternity that occupied its own niche in local public life. While coordinating community-wide activities, then, 18th-century organizations actually wrote community divisions into public politics.

Through the mediation of priests and nobles, such old regime associations served as instruments of indirect rule. The Revolution swept them from public life, substituting patriotic clubs, National Guard units, revolutionary committees, and officially constituted municipalities. The Jacobins closed down or co-opted autonomous organizations as best they could. Popular societies revived temporarily under the Directory in 1799, but again lost autonomy with Napoleon's rise to power (Woloch 1970). The Napoleonic Code decreed: "No association of more than twenty people whose aim is to meet each day or on certain set days to take up religious, literary, political, or other subjects may form except without governmental authorization, under such conditions as public authorities may choose to impose" (Agulhon 1977: 21). Although Masonic lodges thrived as connectors under Napoleon, they faded badly with the Restoration of 1815. A temporary resurgence of church-based organizations under the same Restoration did not stem the long-term decline of the old regime's associational forms.

At the same time, however, the forms of elite association called clubs, circles, casinos, chambers, or societies were proliferating. Devoted to shared intellectual, artistic, and/or political interests, they spread throughout France under the July Monarchy (Agulhon 1977: chapter 4). At a similar rate, workers were forming mutual aid societies – publicly oriented toward the provision of death benefits, sick benefits, unemployment assistance, help in job-finding, and sociability, but often underlying joint action against employers as well. For Lille, an industrial city of about 60,000 people in 1834, royal officials counted no fewer than 106 publicly known mutual aid societies (Archives Nationales BB[3] 167). In Provence, working-class associations commonly carried on the same sorts of activities, but more often went by the name *chambrée*. They commonly served simultaneously as private drinking clubs, especially in wine-growing villages (Agulhon 1970a: 207–45). With the Revolution of 1848, they plunged immediately into public politics, most often on the left end of the political spectrum.

Authorities kept close watch on both bourgeois and working-class associations, looking in the first case especially for political alignments against the current regime and in the second case particularly for "coalitions" against employers. In both cases, associations promoted the integration of trust networks into public politics. They created political actors with a presence on the public scene and a stake in the outcomes of political deliberations. In the short run, they counteracted such democratizing effects with their translation of categorical inequality directly into public politics. With the Revolution of 1848, however, the formation of bourgeois-worker republican coalitions began mitigating that antidemocratic effect as well (see Aminzade 1993). At the installation of manhood suffrage in the Revolution of 1848, explicitly political clubs sprang up throughout Provence; they brought bourgeois, workers, and peasants together into republican politics.

Aware of the crucial part played by newly formed (or at least newly public) associations in nationwide popular mobilization, the government soon began clamping down on a wide range of organizations (Merriman 1978: chapter 3). As Napoleon III stepped up his repression, many public associations mutated into secret societies, still pursuing republican programs in a time of empire (Agulhon 1970a: 389–91; Margadant 1979: chapter 6). By this time, a broad cross-class coalition had formed on behalf of republican programs. The coalition not only promoted democracy by blunting the impact of categorical inequalities on public politics and integrating trust networks into public politics, but also actively fostered programs of democratization.

Despite the nominal founding of the Third Republic in 1870, to be sure, self-styled republicans did not really start running the government until 1879. Under the Third Republic, furthermore, politics seesawed between sharp class divisions and broad left versus right coalitions. Yet on the whole associational life promoted moves toward broad, equal, protected, binding popular consultation, toward democracy. Early in the Third Republic (1881), the National Assembly repealed the Napoleonic requirement of governmental authorization for any public meeting, although it still required organizers to notify police in advance. The law of 1901 that enacted full freedom of association – except for significant restrictions on religious congregations – ratified a century-long evolution.

Jews and the State

Like the development of military service and the mutations of associational life, changing relations between Jews and the French state provide a barometer of democratization (Birnbaum 1992, 1994, 1995, 1998, 2002; Leff 2002). In this case, heavy weather occurred repeatedly; although most French Jews eventually committed themselves strongly to the state and its democratic institutions, organized anti-Semites repeatedly threatened that conjunction.

As in most of Europe, France imposed severe economic and political restrictions on Jews up to the late 18th century. A broad distinction separated the south (where "court Jews" occupied relatively protected positions) from Alsace-Lorraine (where the majority of France's Jews, many of them poor, lived in segregated communities). During the 18th century, their destiny began to concern French reformers. In 1788, future Jacobin the Abbé Grégoire shared the Academy of Metz's essay prize for his *Essay on the Physical, Moral, and Political Regeneration of the Jews*. Following his dream of universal citizenship, Grégoire became a tireless advocate of Jewish citizenship and assimilation. The revolutionary assembly, however, divided on the issue; Alsatian deputies in particular resisted emancipation of their Jewish constituents. Only in September 1791 did the national legislature grant full citizenship to adult Jewish males. Although Napoleon set up new Consistories for Jewish religious self-government and established controversial special taxes to support Jewish institutions that lasted until 1830 (Leff 2002: 37–42), with minor exceptions, Jews thenceforth enjoyed full eligibility for participation in public politics.

Many Jews responded to their new public standing with strong commitment to public service. Before 1870, only a trickle of Jewish migrants left the segregated communities of Alsace-Lorraine to enter the secular world of France at large. But Jews from the south soon took advantage of their citizenship to play significant parts in public finance and government. James de Rothschild, for example, managed Louis-Philippe's personal wealth. Nevertheless, the great movement of Jews into government service began only with the German annexation of Alsace-Lorraine in 1870; at that point, large numbers of Jews emigrated to Great Britain and North America, but many also moved into what remained of France.

The deliberately secularizing Third Republic opened new opportunities. Pierre Birnbaum sums up:

As some members of old Catholic ruling elites rejected the triumphant Third Republic and withdrew from state service, Jews (along with Protestants) reached the highest levels of the civil service: thousands of them became captains, colonels, and even generals, others entered the Council of State, the High Court, and appeal courts, while some became prefects or sub-prefects, and still others became university professors or occasionally entered the Collège de France. Some, furthermore, joined city councils, were elected mayor, deputy, or senator, or now and then even entered the Cabinet. (Birnbaum 2002: 271–72; for more detail, see Birnbaum 1992, 1995: chapters 2 and 3)

By no means did the increasing presence of Jews in public life eradicate anti-Semitism. On the contrary, as royalists and clericals turned against the secularizing Third Republic, political anti-Semitism took on new virulence and currency. In French Algeria (where Jews acquired citizenship only in 1870), anti-Semitic action produced bloody confrontations through much of the Third Republic. In Metropolitan France, the Dreyfus Case brought the first great surge of organized action on that front. Not only did an explicitly named Anti-Semitic League form, but also anti-Semites produced a stream of vitriolic publications, anti-Semitism became a program in electoral campaigns, and an anti-Semitic bloc formed in the national assembly, as widespread meetings, demonstrations, and sermons displayed opposition to the "Jewish state" (Birnbaum 1994, 1998). In Angers, for example, priests and seminarians spearheaded three days of uproarious anti-Semitic demonstrations during the anti-Dreyfus mobilization of 1895. The day's cry was "Death to Jews!"

Anti-Jewish actions multiplied again in the right-wing and fascist movements of the 1930s. But they became government policy only in 1940, after the German occupation and the establishment of the Vichy regime. Far from simply succumbing to German pressure, however, Vichy authorities actually took the initiative in enacting anti-Semitic measures (Jackson 2001: 355–60). In occupied France, French officials likewise cooperated widely with German anti-Semitic policies (Gildea 2002). Democracy reversed rapidly, as Jews lost all citizenship rights and eventually all rights to exist. Michael Marrus and Robert Paxton begin their path-breaking book on the subject with these wrenching words:

During the four years it ruled from Vichy, in the shadow of Nazism, the French government energetically persecuted Jews living in France. Persecution began in the summer of 1940 when the Vichy regime, born of defeat at the hands of the Nazis and of a policy of collaboration urged by many Frenchmen, introduced a series of antisemitic measures. After defining who was by law a Jew, and excluding Jews from various private and public spheres of life, Vichy imposed specifically discriminatory measures: confiscating property belonging to Jews, restricting their movements, and interning many Jews in special camps. Then, during the summer of 1942, the Germans, on their side, began to implement the "final solution" of the Jewish problem in France. Arrests, internments, and deportations to Auschwitz in Poland occurred with increasing frequency, often with the direct complicity of the French government and administration. Ultimately, close to seventy-six thousand Jews left France in cattle cars – "to the East," the Germans said; of these Jews only about 3 percent returned at the end of the war. (Marrus and Paxton 1995: xv)

For those that survived, the postwar settlement restored Jews' rights and drove organized anti-Semitism underground. During the 1980s and 1990s, however, the right-wing National Front brought a muffled anti-Semitism back into France's public politics, as clandestine activists (some of them leaving behind neo-Nazi slogans and markers) toppled gravestones of Jews, burned synagogues, and repeatedly attacked Jewish establishments in Paris, Alsace, Provence, and elsewhere. As Arab-Israeli conflict heated up, furthermore, Muslim activists joined the attacks (*Le Monde* 2002). Official France usually responded quickly with condemnations of intolerance. Still, two centuries of Jewish citizenship had not obliterated anti-Semitism's recurrent threats to French democracy.

Three and a Half Centuries

Over most of the period between 1650 and 2000, French regimes operated undemocratically. Relative to their contemporaries (although not by 20th-century standards), 17th- and 18th-century French regimes imposed authoritarian controls on their subjects: the government itself acquired impressive command of the resources, activities, and people within its jurisdiction, while narrow, unequal, uncertain popular consultation prevailed on the national scale, with few legal protections for minorities or dissidents. The Revolution and the Napoleonic regime laid the ground for democratization. The French actually installed elements of democratic rule between 1789 and 1793, only to reimpose authoritarian controls from then until Napoleon's defeat.

Revolutionary reorganization activated a number of democracy-promoting mechanisms – sweeping aside the institutions of indirect control that gave such power to nobles and priests, facilitating and even coercing popular political participation, establishing elections and legislative assemblies as standard governmental devices, absorption or destruction of existing patron-client networks, formation of cross-class political coalitions, and more. We have seen these mechanisms at work in the experiences of organized workers, military conscription, popular associations, and (more uncertainly) relations between Jews and the state. Democracy rose and fell with regimes; it flourished temporarily in 1848, receded with the Second Empire, recovered through tremendous strife under the Third Republic, and shut down almost entirely during the German occupation, only to burst into riotous bloom after 1944. When de-democratization occurred, it did so through reversals of the standard causal processes: insertion of categorical inequalities directly into public politics, detachment of trust networks from public politics, and so on.

During the immediate postwar years, the victorious Allies (who, after all, stationed troops on French territory into the 1950s) simultaneously backed

131

the government and set limits to gains of the large French Communist Party. The Allied presence did not, however, prevent thousands of summary executions during the Liberation or the handing of essentially dictatorial power to Charles de Gaulle in 1944–45. De Gaulle again came to power with dictatorial controls in 1958, moreover, as he seemed the only one who could end a disastrous civil war in Algeria.

French history after 1650 dramatizes the close connection between contention and democratization. French regimes democratized, when they did, not despite popular contention but because of it. Not that the masses always demanded democracy while the current ruling classes always opposed it. On the contrary, only rarely did protected consultation increase essentially because a bloc of people espousing a democratic program gained control over the state and deliberately steered the regime toward broad, equal, binding consultation and protection. We might claim 1789–93, 1848, 1879, and 1946–48 as moments of that sort, only to recognize that they also stand among the high points of conflict over the entire period we have surveyed. In France, both democratization and de-democratization occurred as partly contingent outcomes of popular contention, of widespread struggles over state power.

5

The British Isles

But the confederates, affrighted with the news that the Rump was sending over an army thither, desired the Prince by letters, to send back my Lord of Ormond, engaging themselves to submit absolutely to the King's authority, and to obey my Lord of Ormond as his lieutenant. And hereupon he was sent back. This was about a year before the going over of Cromwell.

   In which time, by the dissension in Ireland between the confederate party and the Nuntio's party, and discontents about command, this otherwise sufficient power effected nothing; and was at last defeated, August the 2nd, by a sally out of Dublin, which they were besieging. Within a few days after arrived Cromwell, who with extraordinary diligence and horrid executions, in less than a twelvemonth that he stayed there, subdued in the manner the whole nation; having killed or exterminated a great part of them, and leaving his son-in-law Ireton to subdue the rest. But Ireton died there (before the business was quite done) of the plague. This was one step more toward Cromwell's exaltation to the throne. (Hobbes 1990: 162–63).

The Irish events that Thomas Hobbes here recounted in his *Behemoth* took place from 1648 to 1650. Hobbes himself spent most of the 1640s in French exile from the civil wars that were devastating his native England. Shortly after returning to England, he published *Leviathan*, with its famous declaration that without a sovereign to establish order the life of humanity is "solitary, poor, nasty, brutish, and short." Of *Leviathan*, Hobbes's admiring friend John Aubrey reported:

'Twas written in behalfe of the faithfull subjects of his Majestie, that had taken his part in the War, or otherwise donne their utmost to defend his Majestie's Right and Person against the Rebells; wherby, having no other meanes of Protection, nor (for the most part) of subsistence, were forced to compound with your Masters, and to promise obedience for the saving of their Lives and Fortunes, which in his booke he hath affirmed, they might lawfully doe, and consequently not bear Arms against the Victors. They had done their utmost endeavour to perform their obligation to the

King, had done all they could be obliged unto; and were, consequently at liberty to seeke the safety of their Lives and Livelihood wheresoever, and without Treachery. (Aubrey 2000: 429–30)

Hobbes published *Leviathan* in 1651, when he and his royalist friends lived in the midst of a civil war during which parliamentary forces led by Oliver Cromwell were gaining visibly. Although couched as a general philosophical disquisition, the book also provided a rationale for conforming to the hated new regime.

By the time eighty-year-old Hobbes wrote his *Behemoth* during the late 1660s, his former pupil Charles II ("his Majestie," in Aubrey's gloss of Hobbes) had reigned for almost a decade, since the Restoration of 1660. But Hobbes had not forgotten the vivid lessons of civil war. In the Irish episodes that Hobbes described in the passages above, the ascendant military forces of Parliament beat back both the king's Protestant lieutenant in Ireland (the earl of Ormond, or Ormonde) and the Irish armies of the Catholic Confederacy (confederates). Impending defeat prompted papal nuncio Giovanni Rinuccini, who had arrived in 1645, to flee Ireland.

England's Parliament had King Charles I (the Prince, in Hobbes's account) decapitated on 30 January 1649. After insistently negotiating political and financial support for the Irish expedition, Oliver Cromwell himself arrived in Dublin as parliamentary commander in chief (August 1649). Cromwell sacked confederate strongholds Drogheda and Wexford with some 5,000 deaths among the garrisons and inhabitants, then subdued most of Ireland before his return to England in May 1650. His son-in-law Henry Ireton followed up with a scorched-earth campaign; Ireton's policy of crop-burning and starvation may have killed 40 percent of Ireland's people (Russell 1971: 386).

By July of the same year, Cromwell was invading Scotland to dislodge forces that had rallied around the late king's son, also named Charles. The son's followers in Scotland did not give up easily; they crowned the eighteen-year-old king, as Charles II, on New Year's Day 1651. Charles invaded England later that year, only to be routed in the Battle of Worcester (September 1651); self-righteous Cromwell dubbed that victory "The Crowning Mercy" (Maclean 2000: 132).

After six weeks on the run, Charles escaped to the Continent, where he remained in exile until 1660. Famous diarist Samuel Pepys served as secretary to Edward Mountagu, who commanded the fleet that brought Charles back to Dover from the Hague in 1660. During that voyage, the king told Pepys about his pilgrimage of 1651:

Where it made me ready to weep to hear the stories that he told of his difficulties that he had passed through. As his travelling four days and three nights on foot, every step up to the knees in dirt, with nothing but a green coat and a pair of country breeches on and a pair of country shoes, that made him so sore all over his feet that he could scarce stir. His sitting at table at one place, where the master of the house, that had not seen him in eight years, did know him but kept it private; when at the same table there was one that had been of his own Regiment at Worcester, could not know him but made him drink the Kings health and said that the King was at least four fingers higher than he. (Pepys 1985: 49–50)

As Hobbes knew well when he wrote in 1668, Charles survived and eventually thrived as King Charles II. But in 1651 the future of English royalty had looked dim indeed.

Probably spread by military units, not only the plague that Hobbes mentioned, but also smallpox and dysentery ravaged Ireland from 1648 to 1650. (Ireton, however, actually seems to have died not of plague, as Hobbes reported, but of a terrible cold; Gentles 1992: 379–80.) Cromwell became Lord Protector in 1654, but (contrary to Hobbes's innuendo) refused the crown in 1657 before dying in 1658. His son Richard lasted only a few months in office. Neither Parliament nor the multiple armies loosely affiliated with Parliament could then establish simultaneous control over England, Scotland, Ireland, and that semi-independent power London. Coerced by General George Monck and his army, a newly elected and reorganized Parliament called Charles II back to rule in 1660. For another half century, Ireland, Scotland, and England returned to their older standing as formally distinct kingdoms.

From the perspective of London, the Restoration of 1660 closed almost twenty years of civil war and revolution (Harris 1987: chapter 3). Within England, about 85,000 people died in combat between 1642 and 1660 (Outram 2002: 248). During the 1650s, Cromwell's regime had made such revolutionary changes as declaring incest and adultery capital offenses, substituting English for French and Latin in court proceedings, even trying to ban public drinking and dancing. From the perspective of Dublin or Belfast, however, the twenty years of turmoil looked more like a continuation of Ireland's failed but righteous resistance to alien power. During the 1630s, Charles I's lieutenant Thomas Wentworth had made himself unpopular by confiscating estates of uncooperative Irish lords, settling English Protestants in Ireland, reducing the power of the Catholic Church there, converting the nominally autonomous Irish Parliament into an instrument of English rule, aligning the (Protestant) Church of Ireland with Anglican doctrine, and more generally subordinating Ireland to English power. Little of the religious enthusiasm that swept England and Scotland after 1630, furthermore, affected Irish believers. Instead, Irish struggles centered on fierce resistance to increasing English controls.

After Wentworth's recall, trial, and execution, Ulster gentry spearheaded a major rebellion against recent English settlers in 1641 and 1642. The rebellion soon gained allies elsewhere in Ireland. Dispatch of a Scottish army to Ulster, with claims on Irish land, incited further resistance across the country. Both sides attacked with cruelty. In his superb family memoir, Joseph O'Neill reports of his native West Cork:

At Bandon, the old British garrison town of which it used to be said that even its pigs were Protestant, the [Bandon] river passes under Bandon Bridge. It is still remembered that in 1641 English troops tied 88 Irishmen of the town back to back and threw them off the bridge into the water, where all were drowned. (O'Neill 2001: 57–58)

With its new invasion of 1650, Cromwell's regime exacerbated the struggle by pledging Irish land as security for war loans and as rewards to soldiers who took part in subduing Irish rebels. (By and large, soldiers paid in land-backed bonds quickly resold their titles at a discount, which facilitated the concentration of ownership in a few Protestant hands.) In flight from Cromwell's conquest, more than 30,000 Irish warriors emigrated to the Continent (Clarke 2001: 162).

The 1660 Restoration brought partial withdrawal of a conquering power, leaving no more than small minorities of Puritans and parliamentarians in Ireland (Kelly 1991: 163–64). Nevertheless, the twenty-year struggle devastated Catholic property; Catholics owned 60 percent of the land in 1641, 9 percent in 1660, and returned to only 20 percent in the post-Restoration settlement (Foster 1989: 115–16). Ireland endured the reimposition of royal rule as a battered, defeated colony, with clients of the colonizing power in command.

Irish suffering had not ended. Debt-ridden Charles II racked impoverished Ireland for revenues. When Charles's Catholic brother James II succeeded him 1685, James's Irish representatives began ejecting Protestants from law, the army, and local government. Birth of a Catholic heir to James II in June 1688 precipitated Protestant mobilization in both England and Ireland. The calling in of Protestant William of Orange (cousin and husband of James II's Protestant daughter Mary) as king produced quick acceptance in England but initiated another civil war in Ireland: James first fled to France, but soon sailed to Ireland for armed resistance. Although James left Ireland again immediately after his decisive defeat by William at the Battle of the Boyne (1 July 1690), fighting continued in Ireland, with intermittent French support, until 1692. By then, armies had been ravaging one part of Ireland or another much of the time for half a century.

Ireland operated as a colony, or rather as two colonies, through most of the time between 1650 and 2000. With heavy rain and poor soil, most of Ireland yields little agricultural surplus. The chief exception is the Pale, the region including Dublin, which early supported grain-growing agriculture (Crotty 2001: 161–204). Areas of English and Scottish settlement in Ulster long served as adjuncts to the English economy, for example, with extensive textile exports from Belfast between the late 17th century and the early 19th century. The rest of Ireland, however, generally engaged in subsistence agriculture, shipping cattle, beef, pork, and butter to England and England's Caribbean colonies. Although at first smallholders predominated, 17th-century land expropriation and the 18th-century introduction of the potato spurred growth of the landless and land-poor laboring population after 1740 (Mjøset 1992: 195–312). Dependence of the poor on potatoes made the Irish population acutely vulnerable to the potato blight of 1845 to 1850, which spurred mass emigration from the island.

Partition of Ireland in 1922 into a British-held north and what eventually became the Irish Republic reduced connections between the one important center of capitalist industry – Ulster – and the largely agricultural remainder. Up to that point, the history of Ireland resembled that of many other European colonies, with the two crucial exceptions that no racial boundary separated rulers from ruled and that a religious division – between Protestants and Catholics – long served as the major distinction between those who held power and those who did not. As a consequence, rebellion and civil war continued in Ireland long after they had disappeared from the rest of the British Isles.

As Table 5.1 shows, a revolutionary situation – an armed split in which each faction simultaneously controlled some substantial territory and/or institutions as well as commanding significant popular support for at least a month – prevailed somewhere in the British Isles during twenty-seven different years of the century beginning in 1600. By that crude measure, Britain experienced even more revolutionary activity during the 17th century than

137

Table 5.1 *Revolutionary Situations Within the British Isles, 1600–2000*

1595–1603	Rebellion of Hugh O'Neill in Ireland, Spanish intervention (1601)
1608	Irish rebellion of Cahir O'Doherty
1639–40	Scottish rebellion: Bishops' Wars
1641–42	Ulster rising, spreading to other parts of Ireland
1642–47	Civil war in Ireland, Scotland, England (England pacified 1646–47)
1648–51	Second civil war in Ireland, Scotland, England (Cromwell conquest of Ireland, 1649–50)
1660	Monck's coup, Restoration of Charles II
1666	Rebellion of Scottish Covenanters
1679	Second rebellion of Scottish Covenanters
1685	Monmouth rebellion; Argyll rebellion
1688–92	Glorious Revolution in England, Scotland, Ireland; French support for James II
1715–16	Jacobite rebellion, Scotland, under earl of Mar
1745–46	Scottish rising and invasion of England under Young Pretender
1798–1803	Insurrections of United Irishmen; French interventions (1798)
1916	Easter Rebellion, Ireland
1919–23	Civil war in Ireland, Irish independence
1969–94	Intermittent guerrilla warfare, Northern Ireland

did France, with its twenty-three years of revolutionary situations. Then revolution became rarer in the British Isles. The last such split in Scotland occurred with the Young Pretender's rising of 1745–46. Despite much talk and fear of revolution at various times, no revolutionary situation worthy of the name developed in England or Wales after 1689. (Scottish forces did invade England during the Jacobite risings of 1715–16 and 1745–46, but they gained almost no English support.) Ireland, however, remained a trouble spot, as essentially anticolonial struggles persisted into the late 20th century. The last revolutionary transfer of power occurred with the struggle for Irish independence in 1919–23. If (as seems likely at this writing) a substantially new structure of power emerges in Northern Ireland during the early 21st century, that struggle will no doubt also qualify as revolutionary.

Perversely but usefully, this chapter follows the ups and downs of democratization in the British Isles by focusing on what happened in Ireland. Ireland's repeated revolutionary situations help clarify connections not only between struggle and democratization in Ireland itself, but also between Irish conflicts and democratization elsewhere in the British Isles. Such a perspective makes it easier to identify the contentious origins of democracy in Ireland, Scotland, Wales, and England alike. It also shows how momentous alterations in trust networks, in categorical inequality, in public politics, and in relations among them underlay the formation of relatively democratic regimes after 1850.

With respect to coercion, capital, and commitment, the 17th-century British Isles as a whole occupied a distinctive position relative to the rest of Europe. Tudor monarchs Henry VII, Henry VIII, Mary, and Elizabeth I had already reduced the coercive power of autonomous lords and put substantial military force under royal control – although not enough, as we have seen, to prevent rebellion and civil war. London was rapidly becoming a major center of European capital, although its influence extended very unevenly throughout the isles. London's merchants interacted intensively with their continental counterparts, especially those of the prosperous Low Countries. When it comes to commitment, we must distinguish between top-down and bottom-up. By the 17th century, a well-connected ruling class spanned the British Isles, but among ordinary people networks of trust and mutual aid remained regionally fragmented.

As of 1650, Ireland looked quite different in all three regards. Despite nominal subjection to English authority, it featured extensive but regionally segmented top-down coercive power, with great lords still deploying considerable autonomous armed force. (The Catholic Confederacy of 1650, for example, brought together a contingent coalition of well-armed regional leaders.) Few concentrations of significant capital appeared anywhere, especially outside Dublin and Belfast. But the Catholic Church provided extensive commitments among the bulk of Irish people, as did lineage-based patronage networks within different regions.

In the British Isles as a whole, the two centuries following 1650 brought enormous concentration of coercive power in the British government, even greater expansion and concentration of capital, moderate increases, and major transformations of commitment. Within Ireland between 1650 and 1850, coercion also concentrated in governmental hands, but not nearly to the extent of England, Wales, and Scotland. Capital did accumulate and concentrate, especially in the industrial-commercial region of Ulster. And (as we shall see abundantly) political mobilization around Catholic rights intensified commitments within the separate competing communities of Irish Catholics and Protestants. Long-term alterations in coercion, capital, and commitment play important parts in our story.

Glimmers of Democracy

Like France, we see, the British Isles arrived at 1650 deep in civil war. As in France, furthermore, democratic ideas surfaced temporarily during the struggle (Zaret 2000). More so than in France, however, both British political divisions and British democratic ideas took on religious patinas. Although neither Catholics nor Anglicans much warmed themselves at democratic fires, a variety of dissenting Protestants, including Quakers and Congregationalists, pressed for egalitarian programs. Some called for rule by a parliament elected through manhood suffrage. Quakers went a step beyond by instituting rough equality of women and men within their congregations.

Inside Cromwell's New Model Army, radicals established representation by elected men tellingly called Agitators. During the great Putney debates of the army's General Council (October-November 1647), Colonel Thomas Rainborough replied to Ireton's challenge in strikingly democratic, if still very masculine, terms:

Really I think that the poorest he that is in England hath a life to live as the greatest he; and therefore truly, sir, I think it's clear, that every man that is to live under a government ought first by his own consent to put himself under that government; and I do think that the poorest man in England is not at all bound in a strict sense to that government that he hath not had a voice to put himself under. And I . . . doubt whether he was an Englishman or no that should doubt of these things. (Gentles 1992: 209)

At the same time, Levellers in the army and in London were circulating a radical call for a written constitution, an Agreement of the People, including electoral redistribution of parliamentary seats in proportion to population, biennial parliamentary elections and supremacy of the Commons (Gentles 2001: 150). They claimed to speak for the English people. Cromwell's and Ireton's more authoritarian claim to speak with God's inspiration nevertheless prevailed over the next few years. During later debates about parliamentary representation, moreover, Cromwell argued persuasively that manhood suffrage would enable masters and landlords to direct their dependents' votes, hence that only independent propertied men should have the suffrage. For a while, nevertheless, British leaders seriously discussed establishing forms of protected consultation previously unknown in European national regimes – even in the Dutch republican regime from which many British theorists took their lead.

Britain's 17th-century crises anticipate three points of great importance to our analysis. First, despite later British self-congratulation for accommodation and compromise, democratization emerged from bitter contention in the British Isles as it did elsewhere. Second, democratization accelerated in different parts of Britain only when distinct categories of citizenship according to religious affiliation began to crumble. Third, the timing and character of democratization look dramatically different depending on whether we consider England alone or include Wales, Scotland, and (especially) Ireland as well. Neither simultaneous democratization of the whole territory nor gradual diffusion of democratic culture from a few advanced centers comes close to describing the actual process of change. Over the British Isles as a whole, bitter conflict in Northern Ireland reminds us that even today democratization remains contested and incomplete.

Figure 5.1 schematizes the third point. It contrasts movement within our capacity-protection space for Ireland, Scotland, England-Wales, and the British Isles as a whole from 1600 to 2000. In each case, it defines capacity and protection with respect to the government actually operating within the region – the government of Ireland, Scotland, England-Wales, and the British Isles as such. Earlier, Wales too had followed a distinctive trajectory, formally terminated by Henry VIII's Act of Union in 1536. By 1600, however, the satellite region was locking firmly into an English-dominated orbit. My mother, who grew up in Pontycymmr, Wales, sensitized me to differences between English and Welsh ways of life. They certainly exist. But recent devolution of power to Welsh authorities has not so far greatly differentiated the Welsh political regime from the English. While recognizing significant social differences between Wales and England, therefore, this analysis treats them as a single political unit.

For Ireland, the figure portrays much of the 17th century as a time of declining governmental capacity and relatively little protected consultation, followed by an 18th century of increasing capacity and declining protection that preceded a 19th century (from the 1790s onward) in which struggle and concessions extended protections while moderating central controls. The sketch indicates that the 20th century brought some democratization and increased capacity before the split between the North and the rest of Ireland bifurcated Irish trajectories. Thereafter, we see declining protection and rising capacity in the North and modest increases in both regards within the Irish Republic. A more refined picture would of course distinguish at least among Ulster, the Dublin region, and the rest of Ireland, but the scheme would then begin to lose its value in contrasting major segments of the British Isles.

Ireland

Scotland

England and Wales

British Isles

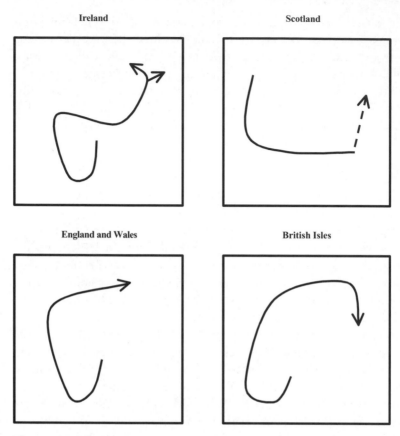

Figure 5.1: Fluctuations in British national regimes, 1600–2000.

For Scotland, the figure portrays a dramatic loss of capacity in the regional government as the Stuarts expanded their political base across the British Isles, some gains in protection over the same process, subordination to English rule during the 18th century, and further democratization and subjection to external rule during the 19th. It then risks a dotted upward line to speculate about the substantial increase in autonomous domestic powers and the modest expansion of democratic access that arrived in principle with the reopening of a distinct Scottish Parliament in May 1999. At a minimum, a more differentiated portrayal would distinguish the mainly Presbyterian lowlands from the religiously mixed (and more landlord-dominated) highlands, but again such distinctions would defeat the scheme's comparative purpose.

In its 17th-century phase, the story for England and Wales resembles that for Ireland. After the 17th century, however, it involves a much greater rise in capacity, coupled with continuing declines in protected consultation, up to the Napoleonic Wars, with more or less continuous, if struggle-ridden, democratization thereafter. A subtler historical sketch would differentiate rule at least among the highly commercialized London region, industrializing northern areas, Welsh mining and farming sections, and agricultural regions elsewhere (Tilly and Wood 2003; Garrard 2002). Even the simplified version, however, brings out how much more the tale of continuous democratization and rising governmental capacity applies to England and Wales than to Scotland or, especially, Ireland.

The diagram for the British Isles as a whole, finally, takes the perspective of the central governmental organization within the isles. With a few interruptions such as the radical centralization under Cromwell, the regime consisted of a triple crown until the formation of a British Union (1707), of distinctly dual power (with Ireland formally quite subordinate) from then until the creation of the United Kingdom (1801). The Union of 1707 dissolved Scotland's Parliament, integrating forty-five Scottish MPs into Westminster's Parliament. The new United Kingdom of 1801, which incorporated one hundred Irish Protestants into the House of Commons and integrated the Church of Ireland into the Church of England, constituted William Pitt's response to the Irish rebellions of 1798 and thereafter. The regime soon began to fragment again, however, with the step-by-step separation of Ireland from 1922 onward.

Any such portrayal commits caricature; the point is not to specify the precise path of change but to identify crucial differences. These resolutely top-down caricatures, furthermore, fail to signal the prevalence of indirect rule through much of the British Isles over much of the time since 1600 (Braddick 2000: chapter 8). Nominal central authorities often conceded great autonomy to warlords, landlords, religious officials, and commissioned representatives of the crown such as sheriffs and Justices of the Peace. The balance of power, furthermore, began shifting visibly from the crown to the British parliament during the 18th century as war grew more expensive and Parliament's revenue-granting powers increased the legislature's leverage.

In France from Louis XIV onward, we saw the crown squeezing out regional autonomies and deactivating religious categories as bases of political rights by direct attacks on Protestants. Britain took a different tack, at first inscribing political rights and obligations into religious categories. As Hugh Kearney sums up the earlier phase:

When the political and religious map of the British Isles was stabilized in 1690 religious unity had not in fact been achieved. In England bitter hostility existed between the Established Church and the dissenting sects, each of which had its own version of the events of the civil war. In Scotland Presbyterians of various persuasions contended for control of the Established Church and were often united only in their hatred of episcopalianism and Popery. In Ireland, the population was divided into "Protestants" (sc. Members of the Established Church), Catholics and Presbyterians. In Wales the Established Church confronted the dissenters. What seems to have occurred during these two centuries was that for many the sense of belonging to a particular Church replaced an earlier cultural identity. The divisiveness of the feudal period gave way to a new form of divisiveness based on religion. (Kearney 1989: 126–27)

Paradoxically, the organization of politics around religious *categories* reduced the tendency to provide religious *justifications* for existing or recommended political arrangements (Zaret 2000: 274). Religious creeds gave way to religiously defined political divisions. But only as the mapping of political rights into religious categories diminished from the later 18th century onward did democratization have much chance anywhere in the British Isles.

How Glorious the Revolution?

The Glorious Revolution that brought William and Mary to power wrought enduring effects, but at a price. Considering the British Isles as a whole, the settlement of 1690 produced a higher capacity government than had ever existed before. It did so, for the time being, at the expense of protected consultation. To be sure, Parliament gained substantial power from its negotiations with William and Mary over the terms of succession – assumption of responsibility (and hence control) for royal income and expenditure, restriction of military appropriations to a year at a time, and establishment of royal prerogative by an Act of Succession conceived of as a contract between Parliament and the crown (for disagreement concerning the extent of Parliament's gains, however, cf. Beddard 1991 with Price 1999: 234–39). The passage of a Bill of Rights (1689) confirmed Parliament's imposition of limits on royal power.

John Locke, in exile since 1683, sailed from Holland to England on the same ship that carried Princess Mary back to become queen. Challenging

Hobbes's apology for absolutism, Locke's second *Treatise of Civil Government* (1689) postulated a state of nature involving free, equal, rational, peaceful men – he did say *men* – abiding by natural law alone. In order to protect their property, Locke argued, men may delegate power to a legislature, which retains its right to rule only so long as it fulfills its end of the bargain. In those circumstances:

> In all cases whilst the government subsists, the legislative is the supreme power; for what can give laws to another must needs be superior to him, and since the legislative is no [*sic*] otherwise legislative of the society but by the right it has to make laws for all the parts and for every member of the society, prescribing rules to their actions, and giving power of execution where they are transgressed, the legislative must needs be the supreme, and all other powers in any members of parts of the society derived from and subordinate to it. (Locke 1937: 101)

Locke explicitly distinguished legislative from executive power, while conceding that the same persons might exercise both. Yet he clearly subordinated executive (read royal) to legislative (read parliamentary) power. He captured the Glorious Revolution's political genius.

The new regime likewise brought the rise of party politics and Dutch-inspired fortification of public finances (Braun 1975: 290–94, 't Hart 1991; Kishlansky 1996: 290; Scott 2000: chapter 21). Creation of a Bank of England (1694) coupled with parliamentary control over governmental indebtedness to produce a relatively secure national debt, heavy involvement of London financiers in the funding of that debt, and widespread investment of the wealthy in government securities (Armitage 1994; Muldrew 1998: 328–29). In the long run, these changes laid the basis for democratization through expansion of parliamentary representation. But in the short run the accession of William and Mary actually restricted political participation in the British Isles.

How so? The Glorious Revolution's settlement barred Catholics from public politics throughout the triple kingdom. It seated an Anglican church firmly in England and Wales, excluding a substantial minority of Protestant dissenters from public life. In overwhelmingly Catholic Ireland (and despite a strong Presbyterian presence in Ulster), it backed the thin hegemony of a Protestant Church of Ireland. From that point on, no Catholic could serve in Ireland's Parliament. The new order strengthened the Presbyterian establishment in religiously divided Scotland. In each case, it doubled the inscription of religious differences into politics with stringent property qualifications for voting and holding office.

145

Within the realm of public politics, these changes reduced the share of the population exercising binding consultation over government and reduced the protection of a significant population segment – especially Catholics – from arbitrary action by governmental agents, while exacerbating inequality in the rights and obligations connecting citizens to governmental agents. They inscribed existing categorical inequalities even more decisively into public politics. Across all three kingdoms, they gave the bulk of the population strong incentives for shielding their trust networks from governmental intervention and public politics. With respect to intersections between categorical inequality and public politics, integration of trust networks into public politics, and internal changes of public politics itself, the settlement inhibited democratization. It solidified religiously organized oligarchy as the basis of rule across the British Isles. Across the British Isles, then, the broad revolutionary crises of 1640 to 1690 ended up reducing levels of protected consultation for the population as a whole.

Despite inhibiting democratization in the short run, however, the Glorious Revolution and political adjustments that soon followed shaped the conditions for subsequent democratization in the British Isles. Precisely because the postrevolutionary settlement tied national political participation to religious membership and property holding, it made exclusions on those grounds matters of contestation in public politics. They did remain contested. In 1711, for example, Queen Anne's regime enacted laws setting property requirements for membership in Parliament that would exclude prosperous merchants and disqualifying the votes of Protestant Dissenters who only occasionally took Anglican communion in order to qualify for the suffrage. After Anne's death in 1714, furthermore, an important faction sought to bring in Catholic James III as king. Jacobites (as supporters of the successive James Stuarts came to be known) soon initiated an invasion and civil war on behalf of their candidate.

By expanding the powers of Parliament, the Glorious Revolution increased the centrality of parliamentary membership, national elections, and legislative activity in public politics. Within the restricted electorate, competition for votes, patronage politics, and influence buying became more extensive and more salient in national politics than they had ever been before (Price 1999: 251–53). With passage of the crown to a German Protestant prince (George I) at Anne's death, power shifted from Tories to Whigs, but the play of party and patronage only intensified.

As military forces exploded during the 18th century, moreover, Parliament's authorization of taxation and expenditure added weight to parliamentary decisions, beginning a decisive shift of power from the royal administration to Parliament (Brewer 1989; Stone 1994; Tilly 1997). Thus voting rights and parliamentary membership became prizes whose withholding called forth challenges from the excluded and their advocates. The House of Commons had long since established a set of geographically distinct constituencies covering the whole of Great Britain in a process of top-down elite control (Morgan 1988: 43). Yet as the Commons acquired weight in national affairs, that more or less accidental arrangement provided a template for popular representation.

The program of Catholic Emancipation illustrates the channeling of democratizing struggles by religious exclusion. The Glorious Revolution pointedly barred Catholics from public office. New laws capped their exclusion with an officeholder's oath that denied tenets of the Catholic religion and (in the case of MPs) explicitly rejected the pope's authority:

Members of Parliament were required to subscribe to: (1) an oath of allegiance; (2) an oath abjuring any Stuart title to the throne; (3) an oath of supremacy ("I, A.B., do swear that I do . . . abjure as impious and heretical that damnable doctrine and position that princes excommunicated or deprived by the Pope . . . may be deposed or murdered by their subjects. . . . And I do declare that no foreign Prince, Person, Prelate, State or Potentate hath, or ought to have, any jurisdiction . . . or authority, ecclesiastical or spiritual within this realm"); (4) a declaration against the doctrine of transubstantiation, the invocation of the saints and the sacrifice of the Mass. (Hinde 1992: 161n.)

As the political overtones of these requirements suggest, Britain's and Ireland's Catholics fell under the double suspicion of subservience to a foreign authority, the pope, and collaboration with Britain's historic enemy, France. In 1689, of course, a Catholic and French-backed Stuart claimant to the throne – the just-deposed James II – loomed as a serious menace to the new regime. Jacobite threats continued to affect religious policies through the defeated rebellion of 1745–46. Although non-Anglican Protestants also suffered political disabilities under the settlement of 1689, in practice subsequent regimes shut Catholics out of Parliament and public life much more effectively than they excluded Dissenters (Clark 1985: 315–24; Colley 1992: chapter 1; Langford 1991: 71–138).

Catholic exclusion had serious political consequences. When the British won Québec from France in the Seven Years' War (1756–63), the British empire not only gained jurisdiction over an almost unanimously Catholic population, but also pacified resistance to British control by large concessions to Québecois, hence to Catholic, self-rule. That settlement inserted a twin to Ireland into the British realm, but granted its Catholics more favorable conditions than their Irish coreligionists enjoyed. To the extent that the British incorporated Catholic Ireland into their economy and polity, furthermore, the Irish Protestant establishment became a less effective instrument of indirect rule, and the demands of Catholic Irish on both sides of the Irish Sea for either autonomy or representation swelled. The enlargement of armed forces during the American war, finally, rendered military recruiters increasingly eager to enroll Irish warriors, already reputed as mercenaries elsewhere in Europe but barred from British military service by the required anti-Catholic oath.

Militarily inspired exemptions of Catholic soldiers from oath-taking during the later 1770s raised strident objections among defenders of Anglican supremacy. The exemptions directly incited formation of a nationwide Protestant Association to petition, agitate, and resist. Scottish MP Lord George Gordon, whose vociferous opposition to Catholic claims made him head of the association in 1780, led an anti-Catholic campaign that concentrated on meetings and parliamentary petitions, but during June 1780 ramified into attacks on Catholic persons and (especially) property in London. A full 275 people died during those bloody struggles, chiefly at the hands of troops who were retaking control over London's streets (Tilly 1995: 160–61). Among Britain's ruling classes, those so-called Gordon Riots gave popular anti-Catholicism an aura of violent unreason. By negation, advocacy of Catholics' political rights acquired the cachet of enlightenment. The word "emancipation" itself stressed the analogy between Catholics and slaves.

In the wake of American rebels' victories over British forces, the British government conceded extensive powers to Ireland's Parliament (1782). The crown could still veto Irish bills, but could not remove Irish judges, while the Westminster Parliament lost almost all power to legislate for Ireland's internal affairs. Ireland was soon establishing its own post office, national bank, and customs service. In 1792, as the French Revolution rolled on and war with France began, Irish Catholics finally regained the right to serve as barristers. In 1793, propertied Catholics could vote again. But the Irish Parliament still seated only Protestants. As a country whose population was roughly 85 percent Catholic continued to live with a constitution excluding Catholics from national public office, anomalies heightened.

Catholic Emancipation as Contentious Democratization

From that time onward an important fusion occurred within Great Britain. Catholic Emancipation became a standard (although by no means universal) demand of reformers and radicals who campaigned for parliamentary reform. By "reform" its advocates generally meant something like elimination of parliamentary seats controlled by patrons, more uniform qualifications for voting across the country, enlargement of the electorate, and frequent parliamentary elections. (Demands for universal suffrage, for manhood suffrage, or even for equal individual-by-individual representation among the propertied rarely gained much of a following before well into the 19th century.) Catholic Emancipation dovetailed neatly with such proposals, since it likewise called for granting a more equal and effective voice in public affairs to currently excluded people.

Both parliamentary reform and Catholic Emancipation surged, then collapsed as national political issues in Great Britain several times between the 1780s and the 1820s. But Emancipation became more urgent during the Revolutionary and Napoleonic wars, when William Pitt the Younger sought to still the Irish revolutionary movement that was undermining the British government's titanic war effort against France. Pitt helped create a (dubiously) United Kingdom of Great Britain and Ireland in 1801, which meant dissolving the separate Irish Parliament and incorporating one hundred Irish Protestant members into what had been Britain's Parliament.

As he engineered the change, Pitt virtually promised major political concessions for Catholics. King George III's hostility to compromising the Anglican establishment (and thereby a crown that was already suffering from the war-driven rise of parliamentary power) made that commitment impossible to keep. The fact that Catholics had to pay tithes supporting the comfortable Anglican clergy in addition to payments for their own less prosperous priests aggravated the pains of Catholic exclusion from public office. Pitt's subsequent resignation by no means stifled Catholic demands. On the contrary, from 1801 to 1829, Catholic Emancipation remained one of the United Kingdom's thorniest political issues. The 1807 wartime resignation of the coalition "Ministry of All the Talents," for example, pivoted on the king's refusal to endorse admission of Catholics to the rank of colonel in England, despite his already having accepted that concession in Ireland.

Much more than a king's attachment to Anglican privilege, however, made the issue contentious. Anti-Catholicism continued to enjoy wide popular appeal in Great Britain, the more so as Irish immigration to England and Scotland (responding to industrial expansion in Britain and consequent industrial contraction in Ireland) accelerated. On the other side, Irish Catholic elites resisted the even greater separation from great decisions affecting their island's fate that had resulted from the transfer of the old Dublin Parliament's powers – however Protestant it had been – to an English-dominated Parliament in distant Westminster. Repeatedly during the 1820s two movements coincided: an increasingly popular campaign for Catholic political rights led by lawyers, priests, and other elites in Ireland, and a coalition of radicals, reformers, and organized Catholics in support of Emancipation within Great Britain. Eventually, a countermovement of Protestant resistance to Catholic claims mobilized as well.

The interweaving movements reached their denouement in 1829. During the previous six years Irish Catholic barrister Daniel O'Connell and his allies had organized successive versions of a mass-membership Catholic Association in Ireland, with some following in Great Britain. They perfected a form of organization (drawn initially, ironically, and significantly from Methodist models) with which radicals and reformers had experimented during the great mobilizations of 1816 to 1819. They enlisted Catholic clergy in a nationwide effort. In 1825 and 1826, they successfully ran sympathetic Protestants to displace members of the Irish Protestant establishment from their seats in Parliament. By these means and through nationwide agitation they sought to move Parliament toward granting of political rights to Catholics. The association collected a monthly penny – the "Catholic rent" – from thousands of peasants and workers. With the proceeds it conducted an incessant, effective campaign of propaganda, coalition-formation, lobbying, and public claim making. Each time the British government outlawed their association, O'Connell and friends fashioned a slightly reorganized (and renamed) successor to replace it.

Efforts by Protestant supporters of Emancipation to get a bill through Parliament failed in 1812, repeatedly from 1816 to 1822, and again in 1825. But in 1828 a related campaign to restore political rights of Protestant Dissenters (e.g., the Baptists, Quakers, and Presbyterians who had figured so prominently in the revolutions of 1640–60) by repealing the 17th-century Test and Corporation Acts gained parliamentary and royal assent. Although it had the effect of removing important allies from the same side of the barrier, on balance such an opening made the moment auspicious for Catholic

150

Emancipation. The regime that had defended Anglican supremacy by excluding non-Anglicans from office in principle (despite frequent exceptions in practice for Dissenters) lost some of its rationale for excluding Catholics.

The House of Lords and the king presented larger obstacles than the Commons, which by the 1820s had on the whole reconciled itself to some expansion of Catholic rights. The Lords included, of course, not only peers of the realm but also bishops of the Anglican church, most of whom would not lightly sacrifice their organization's privileged political position. At their coronations, furthermore, British monarchs swore to defend Anglican primacy; in 1828, King George IV still feared that to approve Catholic Emancipation would violate his coronation oath.

When the House of Lords again forestalled Emancipation in 1828, both Irish organizers and their British allies redoubled the Emancipation campaign, not only expanding the Catholic Association but also staging massive meetings, marches, and petition drives. The election of Catholic O'Connell to Parliament from a seat in County Clare during the fall of 1828 directly challenged national authorities, especially when O'Connell proposed to take his place in Westminster at the new Parliament's opening early in 1829.

This formidable mobilization, in turn, stimulated a large countermobilization by defenders of the Protestant Constitution, as they called it. In Great Britain and to a lesser extent in Ireland itself they organized Brunswick Clubs to produce meetings, marches, petitions, propaganda, and solidarity on behalf of the royal house of Brunswick. In Ireland, Protestant mobilization spurred further Catholic mobilization. A German prince who traveled in Ireland during 1828 reported that he had met a young man in Cork who told him that in Tipperary

they know how to stand against the Orangemen. O'Connell and the Association have organized us there, like regular troops: I belong to them, and I have a uniform at home; if you saw me in it, you'd hardly know me; three weeks ago we all met there, above 40,000 men, to be reviewed. We had all green jackets ... with an inscription on the arm – King George and O'Connell. We have chosen our own officers; they drill us, and we can march and wheel already like the redcoats. We had no arms to be sure, but they could be had too if O'Connell chose. We had flags, and whoever deserted them or got drunk we threw into the water until he was sober again; but that very seldom happened. (Hinde 1992: 114)

That the Commons, the Lords, and the king finally conceded major political rights – although far from perfect equality – to Catholics during the spring of 1829 resulted from an otherwise unresolvable crisis in both Ireland and Great Britain. It by no means represented a general conversion of Britons to religious toleration. Jews, for example, did not receive similar concessions until 1858. Nor did unofficial discrimination against Jews or Irish Catholics ever disappear from British life. We are speaking here of legal exclusion from political rights on the basis of religious identity. We are speaking of a campaign to reduce inscription of religious categories directly into public politics.

British authorities played a double game, dealing with a predominantly anti-Catholic political mobilization in Great Britain and a massive, near-insurrectionary pro-Catholic mobilization in Ireland. A catalog of "contentious gatherings" (CGs, occasions on which ten or more people assembled publicly and somehow made collective claims) reported in one or more of seven British periodicals during March 1829 provides evidence on the British side, although, alas, it does not tell us the comparable story for Ireland (Tilly 1995). During that turbulent month, the Commons finally passed its Emancipation bills and sent them on to the Lords. Altogether the month's catalog yields 153 CGs explicitly centering on support for or opposition to Catholic rights, plus another half-dozen in which public responses to officials clearly resulted from the positions they had taken on Catholic Emancipation. (Because many reports come from parliamentary debates in which MPs reporting petition meetings took pains to mention places but neglected dates, some events in the March catalog surely happened in February, but they just as certainly belonged to the same wave of mobilization.)

A selection of about a twentieth of all events from the month's catalog conveys its contentious flavor:

London: The minister and congregation of Crown Street Chapel assembled to sign a petition declaring, among other things, that "the engine of Romanism, with all its machinery, is still preserved entire, and ready to be brought into action as soon as opportunity and policy shall concur to set it in motion, and should the barriers of our happy Constitution, which now restrain its operation, be once removed, its influence would gradually increase, and from the nature of the very principle it imbibes and inculcates, its overbearing progress must terminate in the complete subjugation of Protestant liberties. . . ." (*Votes and Proceedings of Parliament*, 2 March 1829, pp. 336–37)

Coventry: A public meeting issued an anti-Catholic petition signed by 3915 persons, which generated a pro-Catholic counter-petition signed by 905 others. (*Hansards, Parliamentary Debates*, 3 March 1829, p. 699)

Rothsay: After speeches emphasizing the Catholic threat, a meeting in Mr. M'Bryde's chapel dispersed, "some of the most unruly of them, thinking they would best show their admiration of the opinions of their pastor by a persecution of Catholics, proceeded to the house of the only Irishman in the place (a poor itinerant dealer in earthenware) and demolished every article on his premises." (*Times*, 10 March 1829, p. 4)

Inverness: A number of "boys and disorderly lads" burned an effigy representing Popery, paraded through town hoisting another effigy, then broke doors and windows at both the Catholic chapel and the police office. (*Times*, 17 March 1829, p. 3)

Edinburgh: At a public meeting called in reaction to a pro-Catholic assembly, the provost and inhabitants started an anti-Catholic petition that eventually acquired 13,000 signatures. (*Times*, 19 March 1829, p. 1)

London: After the Commons' second-reading debate on Emancipation, supporters unhitched the horses from the hackney-coach into which Daniel O'Connell had retreated and attempted to draw him in triumph, but he forced his way out, and walked to his lodgings in the midst of thousands "shouting all the way 'Huzza for O'Connell, the man of the people, the champion of religious liberty'; 'George the Fourth for ever'; 'The Duke of Wellington, and long life to him'; 'Mr. Peel and the Parliament.'" (*Times*, 19 March 1829, p. 4)

London: Two days later, several hundred people surrounded the duke of Wellington as he left the House of Lords, "and assailed him with the most opprobrious epithets, and every sort of discordant yelling." (*Times*, 21 March 1829, p. 2)

Chesterfield: An Anti-Catholic public meeting resulted in a petition signed by 4000 people, which stimulated a counter-petition signed by 500 supporters of Catholic claims, "amongst whom were the whole of the magistrates resident in the district." (*Hansards, Parliamentary Debates*, 25 March 1829, pp. 1444–45)

Although such actions as effigy-burning and unhitching a hero's carriage to draw it through the streets conformed to well-established 18th-century antecedents, on the whole these events followed the newly emerging logic of social movements: meetings, marches, demonstrations, petitions, and similar collective displays of worthiness, unity, numbers, and commitment. They conformed to the cosmopolitan, modular, autonomous performances of Europe's democratic repertoires.

Notice the report from Edinburgh. Sir R. H. Inglis, who presented Edinburgh's anti-Catholic petition to Parliament, reported that the local authorities' original plan had been to hold a sort of referendum, a public meeting at which people could vote for or against Catholic relief and "if no public meeting of those favourable to concession was held, none would be convened of those opposed to it" (*Times*, 19 March 1829,

p. 1). But since pro-Catholic forces (no doubt aware that by sheer numbers Edinburgh's anti-Catholic legions would carry any general public assembly) had broken the agreement, held a meeting, and sent Parliament a petition, the anti-Catholic organizers insisted on having their own say.

Supporters of Emancipation put it differently: at a meeting of the Friends of Religious Liberty, "Brunswickers" had attempted to break up the proceedings. If the anti-Catholics had collected 13,000 signatures on their Edinburgh petition, MP James Macintosh (or Mackintosh) reported on presenting the pro-Catholic petition to Parliament that its 8,000 signatures began with an unprecedentedly large meeting involving four-fifths or even nine-tenths

of what, until such a levelling spirit seized the Honourable Gentlemen on the Bench below me, used without objection or exception to be called the respectable classes of the community in the ancient capital of the most Protestant part of this Protestant Empire, which, in my opinion, will perform one of the noblest duties of its high office of guardian to the Protestant interest of Europe by passing this Bill into a law. (*Morning Chronicle*, 27 March 1829, p. 2)

Macintosh echoed the ingenious arguments of several speakers at the Edinburgh meeting. They claimed that political disabilities segregated Catholics, drove them to defend their identities, and therefore made them less susceptible to cool reason. Full membership in the polity and full engagement in public discussion would, if permitted, eventually make them more skeptical of Catholic doctrine and papal authority. Macintosh went on to impugn Edinburgh Brunswickers for having padded their petition with nonresidents, for having circulated libelous tracts, and by implication for having appealed to the city's plebeians. Thus he challenged their numbers, unity, and worthiness, if not their commitment to the anti-Catholic cause.

Both advocates and opponents of the Catholic cause in 1829 used a wide variety of techniques to forward their programs, but the central mechanism connected local political action directly to Parliament. By the thousands, organizers drafted petitions, held local public meetings to publicize them, collected signatures, validated those signatures as best they could, and arranged for MPs to present them during parliamentary sessions. As the intensity of parliamentary debate increased, meetings and petitions multiplied. Each side tried to discredit the other's tactics and support, not only decrying false signatures (e.g., of women, boys, nonresidents, and other persons

outside the political arena), but also complaining about "inflammatory plac-
ards" and incendiary speeches.

If Britons had enjoyed a limited right to petition for centuries, if Britain's
17th-century revolutions set a precedent of widespread popular mobilization, and if such 18th-century political entrepreneurs as John Wilkes and
George Gordon had used public meetings, marches, and petitions quite
effectively, never before had the full panoply of social-movement organization, complete with mass-membership associations, come into play at a
national scale (Tilly 1982). While recognizing 18th-century revolutions as
possible challengers for the title and understanding that in Great Britain
itself the distinctive elements of social-movement practice coalesced in fits
and starts from the time of Lord George Gordon's Protestant Association
onward, we might even be able to call the Catholic Emancipation campaign the world's first national social movement. In the British Isles, only
antislavery (whose national organization of 1787 marks it as an early riser)
competes for the title.

Campaigns both for and against Catholic Emancipation expanded
greatly from 1828 to 1829. By my counts of CGs and of parliamentary
petitions, the scorecards over 1828 and 1829 as a whole ran as the following (see also Jupp 1998: 374):

	CGs, 1828	Petitions, 1828	CGs, 1829	Petitions, 1829
For Emancipation	16	732	99	1,001
Against Emancipation	21	333	141	2,169
Divided	4	0	2	0

The figures refer to Great Britain (England, Scotland, and Wales) alone.
If these had been binding votes and Great Britain the only relevant arena of
political action, Catholic Emancipation would clearly have failed as a political program. Comparable information from Ireland, on the other hand,
would show overwhelming support for the Catholic cause (Hinde 1992:
chapter 4; O'Ferrall 1985: 188–257). Only the virtual ungovernability of
Ireland itself under the impact of Catholic Association mobilization moved
the Duke of Wellington and Robert Peel, reluctant parliamentary midwives
of Emancipation, to persuade an even more reluctant king that he had to
keep the peace by making concessions.

Concessions, not capitulations. The very settlement reveals the sort of
mixed bargain that Emancipation entailed. While removing most barriers

to Catholic officeholding in the United Kingdom, it included the following restrictions:

1. No Catholic could serve as Regent, Lord Lieutenant of Ireland, Lord Chancellor of England or Ireland, or hold any position in Anglican Church establishments, ecclesiastical courts, universities, or public schools.
2. Office-holding Catholics had to swear a new oath of loyalty to the king and the Hanoverian succession, denying the right of foreign princes including the Pope to exercise civil jurisdiction within the United Kingdom, and denying any intention to subvert the Anglican establishment or the Protestant religion.
3. Forty-shilling freeholders (owners of property whose annual rent would be worth at least two pounds per year, who had previously voted in Ireland, and who had provided strong support for O'Connell) lost their franchise in favor of a ten-pound minimum with stronger guarantees against inflation of estimated property values.
4. The government dissolved the Catholic Association and barred successors from forming.

Cautious concession describes the bargain better than Catholic conquest or liberal largesse.

In conjunction with the earlier and less turbulent campaign over repeal of the Test and Corporation Acts, the partially successful social movement for Catholic Emancipation left a large dent in national politics. Those two rounds of legislation broke the hold of Anglicans over public office and Parliament (Clark 1985). The Catholic Association made ordinary Irish people a formidable presence in British politics. Despite all the restrictions on Irish mobilization laid down by Wellington and Peel, their settlement ratified the legitimacy of mass-membership political associations and social-movement tactics.

Almost immediately, advocates of parliamentary reform self-consciously took up the model and precedent to organize political unions and to initiate a campaign of meetings and petitions. This time, after more than half a century of striving, reformers gained a substantial victory; if the Reform Act of 1832 still excluded the majority of adult males (to say nothing of females) from suffrage, it enfranchised the commercial bourgeoisie, gave MPs to fast-growing industrial towns, eliminated parliamentary seats that had lain within the gift of a single patron, and forwarded the principle of representation according to (propertied) numbers rather than chartered privilege (Brock 1974; Cannon 1973; Garrard 2002; Phillips 1992; Phillips and Wetherell 1991; Vernon 1993). Catholic Emancipation did not cause the Reform Act, but it facilitated and channeled the political mobilization that led to reform.

Emancipation thus forwarded citizenship and democracy in Great Britain, directly through its dissolution of barriers to political participation, indirectly through its impact on parliamentary reform. Citizenship refers to a certain kind of tie: a continuing series of transactions between persons and agents of a given government in which each has enforceable rights and obligations uniquely by virtue of the persons' membership in an exclusive category, the native-born plus the naturalized. To the extent that the British government dissolved particular ties to its subject population based on local history and/or membership in locally embedded political identities while installing generalized classifications on the basis of political performance, it gave increasing weight to citizenship. Reducing barriers to the political participation of Dissenters and Catholics clearly moved in that direction.

This does not mean, of course, that Ireland instantly democratized. Great Irish landlords, both Protestant and Catholic, had long benefited from the disfranchisement of their tenants; in that sense, the inscription of unequal religious divisions into public politics had benefited the ruling classes. When Alexis de Tocqueville traveled through Ireland in 1835, he learned with fascination and fear that while the vast bulk of the Irish agriculturalists had become dirt poor, most Irish land remained in the hands of wealthy families. Landlords almost always leased out their holdings to middlemen, who in turn recruited, controlled, and discharged tenants.

Cultivators themselves consisted almost entirely of small tenants and landless laborers. Catholic Emancipation actually threatened landlords, since the vast popular mobilization signaled the possibility of political action for land reform. It also weakened the political leverage that Protestant landlords and middlemen wielded over their Catholic tenants and laborers. In July 1835 Alexander Fitzgerald, head of the Catholic College of Carlow, told Tocqueville:

So long as the ruling classes saw Catholics as slaves who bore their lots submissively, they did not use violence to deal with [the Catholics]. But since the Catholic population has gained political rights and the will to use them, [the ruling classes] persecute [the Catholics] as much as possible, and are trying to uproot them from their land and to replace them with Protestant farmers. (Tocqueville 1991: 529)

157

In fact, far too few Protestant farmers existed in Ireland to make that re-placement possible. But struggles over land soon became the pivots of vio-lent conflict in Ireland. Catholic Emancipation facilitated the politicization of that conflict.

Democratization at Large

The struggle for Catholic Emancipation nicely illustrates a more general set of changes that occurred in the British Isles during the critical century after 1750. In quick summary, they ran like this:

- Britain's enormous increase of military expenditure from the Seven Years' War (1756–63) onward significantly enhanced tax-authorizing Parliament's leverage in national politics.
- Parliament used its enhanced powers by acting more decisively and ef-fectively on matters that directly affected the welfare of ordinary people, even in the face of royal and noble opposition.
- The crown and royal patronage became less central to most forms of national politics, especially those directly involving popular interests.
- Despite a narrow parliamentary electorate, as a consequence, parlia-mentary debates, legislation, and election both more frequently took up issues of concern to ordinary people and incited popular responses.
- Meanwhile, expansion of the middle class produced increasing participa-tion in local forms of government despite (sometimes successful) efforts of local power holders to limit popular participation in such entities as vestries.
- Because propertied males affiliated with the state church wielded dispro-portionate weight in Parliament and in national politics at large, people outside that small category more often faced threats than benefits to their interests from governmental actions.
- Yet some members of Parliament sought popular support as a counter-weight to factions based on landed wealth, and therefore made alliances (intermittent or long-term) with popular political leaders.
- Organized popular forces therefore discovered that they could gain po-litical weight through a combination of (1) displaying support for advo-cates of their interests and (2) threatening to disrupt the routines of elite politics.
- Populist political entrepreneurs experimented incessantly, probing the existing political system for soft spots, adapting established forms of

claim making to new participants, occasions, or issues, and devising new tactics as opportunities presented themselves.

- Repeated interactions among popular claimants, objects of claims, authorities, and Parliament (especially the House of Commons) established the social movement as a standard way of making sustained claims at a national scale in Great Britain.
- Although the process was well under way by 1828, the major national campaigns of 1820 to 1832 – notably the vast mobilization that preceded and produced 1832's Reform Act – consolidated both social movement politics and the position of the Commons at the center of popular claim making.
- In Ireland, however, later social movement mobilizations worked against integration of most Catholics into national politics at the level of the United Kingdom, instead mobilizing resistance against British rule.

To be sure, no necessary connection exists between social movements and democracy (Tilly 2003a); European fascists of the 1920s and 1930s, after all, used social movement tactics quite effectively as they came to power. But in the British Isles between 1750 and 1850 the coordinated establishment of voluntary associations, public meetings, petitions, marches, demonstrations, and pamphleteering – the apparatus of social movement activism – as standard means of popular politics both resulted from and promoted democratization.

Even in beleaguered Ireland, activists commonly used social movement forms both during and after the Emancipation campaign. As Daniel O'Connell lost hope of justice from the Westminster Parliament and began campaigning for Irish home rule, he founded a Repeal Association (1840), collected a "repeal rent" in direct imitation of the earlier Catholic rent, and began a series of mass meetings to press the campaign. During the meetings of 1843, for example, at least 1.5 million people gathered in Ireland to back repeal (Cronin 2000: 141). Although the effort failed utterly, it helped create the national connections that underlay later efforts – some through social movement claim making, some through insurrection – to secure justice for Irish tenants and to seek Irish autonomy.

The intellectual movement called Young Ireland, for example, formed among O'Connell's collaborators during the 1840s, turned toward armed revolution during the terrible famine years of 1845–50, launched a hopeless insurrection in 1848, but reappeared among veterans of that rising as the Irish Republican Brotherhood (Fenians). From that point on, Irish emigres and exiles – especially those based in North America – provided refuge, financial support, and occasional manpower to their allies back home (Hanagan 1998). Fenians themselves organized simultaneously in New York and Dublin (1858) and raised another unsuccessful insurrection in 1867. From 1873 onward, the Fenians foreswore armed rebellion until mass support became available. But during the 1870s and 1880s, Jeremiah O'Donovan Rossa's Skirmishers, the Clan na Gael, and the Irish National Invincibles continued to pursue Irish independence through armed attacks on the English enemy and their collaborators (Townshend 1995: 322–23). Meanwhile an Irish Tenant League (founded in 1850) agitated for land reform that would benefit smallholders. After the Fenian rising of 1867, British Liberal parliamentary leader W. E. Gladstone strove mightily to enact Irish home rule, but failed in the face of repeated opposition from the House of Lords. That failure discredited programs of constitutional devolution in Ireland as it consolidated nationalist demands for independence.

Ireland followed a nationalist path to revolution and thence to further democratization. World War I provided the catalyst. At first most Irish people collaborated with the war effort. Predictably, Ulster's Protestants collaborated much more enthusiastically than the rest of the Irish population. The prewar Ulster Volunteer Force, a Protestant paramilitary unit opposed to Irish home rule established in 1913, joined the British army en masse. Meanwhile, the British maintained 20,000 troops and police in the rest of the island to contain popular militias of Irish Catholics that started forming in 1914. By that time Ireland contained five distinct armed forces: not only the British army and the Ulster Volunteers, but also their opponents the Irish Volunteers, the Citizen Army, and the Irish Republican Brotherhood.

Still, serious opposition to the British cause did not crystallize until the war had been going on for almost two years. The abortive Easter Rebellion of 1916, planned with the help of exiles in New York, supported by German agents, backed by German bombardment of the English coast, and suppressed brutally by British troops, slowed the cause of Irish independence temporarily. Nevertheless, Irish nationalists began regrouping in 1917. Six years of violent conflict began. Over the period from January 1917 to June 1923, over 7,500 people were killed or wounded in the deadliest Irish conflict since 1798 (Hart 1997: 142).

Except for the Protestant representatives of Ulster, Irish MPs withdrew from the United Kingdom Parliament in reaction to the adoption of military conscription for Ireland in April 1918. Returned MPs led the opposition back home. In December 1918, Irish nationalists won Southern Ireland's votes in a parliamentary election handily, with 34 of the 69 successful candidates elected while in prison. The newly elected MPs decided to form their own Irish Parliament instead of joining the U.K. assembly. On meeting in January 1919, they chose Eamon De Valera, then still in prison, as their parliamentary president. De Valera escaped from prison, but after four months of activity in Ireland left for the United States.

Soon the British government was actively suppressing Irish nationalist organizations. Nationalists themselves mobilized for resistance and attacked representatives of British authority. By the end of 1919, Ireland reached a state of civil war. The British painfully established military control, but also began negotiating with Irish representatives. Within two years, the negotiations led to an agreement: partition of Northern Ireland from the rest and dominion status similar to that of Canada and South Africa for a newly created Irish Free State outside Ulster. Although hard-line Irish republicans refused to accept the settlement and raised a new insurrection in 1922, the arrangement lasted in roughly the same form until the 1930s. New divisions arose within the Irish population from 1931 to 1935, as the so-called Blueshirt movement sought to protect small farmers who failed to pay the Irish government quitrents from dispossession and prosecution. In 1937, Ireland (less the North) declared itself a republic without quite withdrawing from the Commonwealth. Under De Valera, the country remained neutral during World War II, and formally cut any remaining ties with the British Commonwealth in 1948.

During the postwar years, southern Ireland settled into its own distinctive form of democratic politics, in which members of the Dail (national parliament) provided crucial links between local-level patronage and national-level policies. Rural Irish people came to treat national politics largely as a matter of pulling strings. "When the statue of the English queen was removed from the square of Leinster House (the building where the Dail meets)," reports political ethnographer Mart Bax,

people discussed which national emblem should be put in its place. It was widely joked that there was no need for another emblem. The word PULL was written in large capital letters on the entrance doors to Leinster House. (Bax 1976: 46)

Even more so than in the average democratic regime, southern Irish politicians spent a good deal of their energy serving as brokers between local constituencies and the national government.

Within Northern Ireland, anti-British forces never gave up. Although the Catholic third of the region's population remained somewhat more rural, more segregated, and more concentrated toward the south than the Protestant population, it constituted a formidable force. A whole new round of conflicts began with Catholic civil rights marches in 1968, violent confrontations with police, struggles with Protestant counterdemonstrators, and more scattered attacks of each side on the other's persons and property. In 1972, British paratroopers trying to break up an unarmed but illegal march through Derry by the Northern Ireland Civil Rights Association fired on the demonstrators, killing thirteen of them. The uproar following that "Bloody Sunday" induced a worried British government to take back direct rule of the province.

After a bilateral ceasefire declared in 1994, raids and confrontations (including some quite outside Ireland) actually accelerated. A further treaty in 1998 (the so-called Good Friday agreement) initiated serious talks among the major parties and terminated most public standoffs between the sides, but did not end guerrilla action by all paramilitary units or produce full disarmament of those units. Despite rough agreement between the governments of Ireland and the United Kingdom, as negotiations proceeded paramilitary fractions on both sides repeatedly broke the peace. Support of Catholic militants by the well-armed Irish Republican Army, based in independent Ireland and extensively supported by Irish overseas migrants, certainly sustained the conflict. But militant Catholics native to Ulster repeatedly challenged equally militant Ulster Protestants. One of Europe's longest runs of large-scale intergroup violence continues.

Although the intensity of violence waxed and waned with the more general rhythms of intergroup struggle in Northern Ireland, mutual attacks continued into the 1990s. Even the tentative settlement of 1998 did not end them:

In the year of the Good Friday Agreement – 1998 – fifty-five people died in violence in Northern Ireland. Three Catholic brothers, aged between eight and ten, died on 12 July when loyalists petrol-bombed their home in a predominantly Protestant area of Ballymoney. On 15 August – a traditional Catholic holiday – twenty-eight people were killed in a car-bomb blast in Omagh. The attack also claimed another victim, who died a few days later. A republican splinter group, the Real IRA, had placed a 500-pound bomb in a parked car in a crowded shopping street on a sunny summer Saturday. It was one of the worst outrages of the Troubles. (Keogh 2001: 332–33)

Repeatedly, groups on the flanks of the two militant movements broke away when peace agreements were crystallizing, using scattered attacks in defiance of national leaders on both sides.

Conventional portraits of British democratization (e.g., Collier 1999: 96–101; Garrard 2002) concentrate on the reform bills that altered the franchise in 1832, 1867, 1884, and 1918. The 1918 legislation, for instance, expanded the electorate to all men twenty-one or older having six months' residence in their constituencies and all women thirty or older living in established households while installing the principle of equal constituency size. (U.K. women did not receive equal voting rights until 1928.) Some accounts add the year 1872, when Britons began to vote with secret ballots. Those landmark acts did, indeed, broaden and equalize public political participation in the United Kingdom. But they worked rather differently in the major segments of the British Isles. In England and Wales, the 1832 reform expanded the franchise modestly overall, bringing a significant portion of the property-holding bourgeoisie into the polity. But in many boroughs, it actually reduced the widespread participation of workers that had grown up after 1750.

Most of the many workers who mobilized in the reform movement of 1830–32, furthermore, found themselves excluded by the final legislation. The exclusion of workers in 1832 helped stimulate the surprising working-class mobilization of Chartists (1838–48) around an almost exclusively political program: manhood suffrage, annual parliaments, vote by ballot, abolition of the property requirement for MPs, salaries for MPs, and equal electoral districts. It took nearly another century before the Chartist program became legal reality. In the meantime, the combination of Test and Corporation repeal, Catholic Emancipation, and the Reform Act redrew the English-Welsh lines of political inclusion and exclusion from religion to class: the propertied taxpayer now exercised national political rights, while workers in general did not.

Scotland and Ireland did not simply follow the lead of England and Wales. In Scotland, a separate reform bill of 1832 increased the number of MPs from forty-five to fifty-three, partially equalized constituencies, more than dectupled the number of eligible voters, and promoted widespread participation in public politics. At the same time, capitalist industrialization rapidly formed a Scottish national bourgeoisie and an active working class. On that basis, Liberals soon acquired hegemony in Scotland, holding power until Labor finally gained strength during the 20th century. Consolidation of many British regional bureaucracies under a semi-autonomous Scottish

Office in 1886 conceded a measure of self-government, long before the more decisive devolution of 1999.

In Ireland, as we have seen, Catholic Emancipation and Reform combined in an enormous expansion of political participation but soon generated an opposition to English power far more tenacious than in Scotland. For another century after 1832, Irish politics proceeded in a colonial mode: increasing, if conflict-filled, political participation within Ireland and deepening struggle among Dublin, Belfast, and London. Even the acquisition of partial independence in 1922 did not resolve the struggle, since it left both Northern Ireland and the Irish Free State internally divided over their relations to Great Britain.

Seen from Ireland, long-run processes of democratization in the British Isles clearly stemmed from continuous struggle. Rarely did the struggles pit zealous advocates of democracy as such against tenacious defenders of privilege. Much more often the parties aligned along competing definitions of just deserts. We might allow rough distinctions among revolutionary change in Ireland, top-down conquest in Scotland, and confrontation followed by accommodation in England. Even those distinctions, however, dissolve as we move back before 1750. Properly compared, the three histories show us the enormous weight of religious and class categories in British democratization; their insulation from public politics constituted a great, struggle-ridden consequence of the century following 1820.

We also see the earlier and more extensive integration of trust networks into public politics in Scotland, England, and Wales than in Ireland. Everywhere landlords, merchants, and professionals invested in government or in organizations linking them to government earlier than did industrial or agricultural workers. But in Ireland significant segments of the dominant classes always sought chiefly to escape British rule, the temporary reconciliation of Catholic Emancipation soon shifted to mass opposition, and the bulk of the working population entered public politics through anti-British nationalism. The British Isles as a whole therefore constitute a remarkable laboratory for the emergence of democracy from strenuous struggle.

France versus Britain

In some respects, the histories of democratization and de-democratization we have reviewed confirm old stereotypes of France and the British Isles. France did indeed make repeated revolutionary breakthroughs in a democratic direction (1789, 1830, 1848, and 1871 being the most prominent dates) and did also generate repeated democratic reversals in revolutions from above (1799, 1851, and 1940 being the most salient years). The British Isles did, on the whole, democratize through grudging step-by-step expansion of political rights that elites had long enjoyed.

On balance, furthermore, France's old regime centralization had indeed produced a more uniform, centralized, and powerful national state structure than formed in the British Isles before the 19th century. France moved to a relatively direct system of rule between 1789 and 1793, never fully reversing that elimination of indirect rule. Britain stuck with indirect rule through clergy and magistrates well into the 19th century. Universal military service in France connected citizens – both the males who served and their families – more firmly with the central government. These differences mean that in France both democratization and de-democratization occurred more abruptly, and more often as the direct outcome of crises in which the whole regime's future lay at risk, than was the case in Britain.

Both stereotypes, however, understate the importance of conquest and colonization in these national histories. In France, the external military conquests of 1815, 1870, 1940, and 1944 all shaped democratic institutions, 1815 and 1940 by pushing the country toward authoritarianism, 1870 and 1944 by (eventually) pushing the country toward democratic citizenship. In Britain, failed military conquests precipitated major alterations of national power repeatedly between 1650 and 1746, while foreign military power continued to figure in Irish transitions up to 1916. British colonization eventually established more or less democratic institutions in Australia, New Zealand, North America, and (more uncertainly) South Asia and South Africa. Within the British Isles, however, colonization de-democratized Ireland by installing a client Protestant minority in that largely Catholic country.

Whether revolution, confrontation, conquest, and colonization de-democratized or democratized, they did so by accelerating the activation of mechanisms in our three portfolios: those affecting insulation of categorical inequality from public politics, those affecting integration of trust networks into public politics, and those acting directly on the breadth, equality, consequentiality, and protection of popular political participation. We have seen, for example, how governmental containment and reduction of privately controlled armed force made it more difficult for magnates and landlords to translate class inequalities directly into public politics. Ireland, where multiple militias continue to operate today, encounters stubborn obstacles to democratization on precisely that account.

Again, we have seen how shattering the patronage networks that had grown up around nobles and clergy in old regime France provided an opportunity for bourgeois-centered trust networks to integrate French citizens into public politics; 19th-century cross-class coalitions – notably those aligning workers with bourgeois – magnified that effect. As a consequence, after 1815 French democratizing coalitions typically brought bourgeois, workers, and some segments of the peasantry together against landlords, churchmen, and beneficiaries of royal power. By the time democratization began in earnest, agricultural capitalism had long since squeezed out the peasantry from all but a few enclaves in the British Isles. English agricultural laborers mobilized vigorously during the 19th century, making temporary alliances with organized workers toward the end of the century, but playing a significantly smaller part in English class struggles than did French agricultural workers. In Ireland, however, agricultural workers regularly doubled their anti-British nationalism with attacks on (predominantly Protestant) landlords and middlemen. In all these cases, cross-class coalitions became more prominent and effective during the 19th century.

The processes we have been following in France and Britain produced decisive shifts in political identities. On balance, embedded identities such as being a member of a local congregation, craft, or lineage gave way to memberships in associations, unions, parties, federations, and movement-style fronts. Correspondingly, performances within the prevailing repertoires of contention shifted from the parochial, particular, bifurcated forms characteristic of undemocratic Europe to the cosmopolitan, modular, autonomous forms so familiar in democratic polities. Meetings, marches, petitions, specialized associations, lobbying, strikes, pamphleteering, election campaigns, and appeals to mass media crowded out shaming ceremonies, local seizures of food, attacks on residences, and other once common varieties of direct action. These general transformations occurred in both France and the British Isles, but on very different schedules and in distinctive regional patterns corresponding to their differences in democratization.

Not every feature of French and British political change, however, conformed precisely to the models I laid out in this book's introduction. Organized religion played a larger part in democratization and (especially) de-democratization on both sides of the channel than my earlier formulations suggested. In the British Isles, 17th-century struggles ended with the Anglican Church ensconced as an integral part of rule in England, Wales, and Ireland, if not in Scotland, where an establishment Presbyterian Church likewise represented the central power. Exclusion of Catholics defined a boundary of struggle in the British Isles until the 19th century.

In France, a similar struggle in reverse ended in 1710 with a shrunken, cowed, contained Protestant minority. But revolutionary attacks on the French Catholic Church produced a long-term alignment of clericals against anticlericals, with the clericals usually favoring de-democratization of one variety or another when they got their way. Above all, the troubled experience of Ireland displays the limits and consequences of churches as instruments of rule. Exclusion of whole categories of people from public politics on the ground of religious affiliation simultaneously increases those people's incentives to shield their trust networks from public politics and inscribes categorical inequality directly into public politics. The two mechanisms together constitute serious obstacles to democratization.

Despite their differences, France and Britain both followed relatively strong state paths to democracy. Their old regime governments never reached the extremes of Prussia and Russia, but in general they achieved higher capacity than the governments of Iberia and the Low Countries. In both the French and British cases, the buildup of central military power in the course of foreign war making fortified the government's fiscal and administrative apparatus. Ironically and consequentially, the increased dependence of bulky military establishments on parliamentary funding and administrative support reduced direct military intervention in public politics far earlier and more effectively than in most of Europe. That process, in turn, gave civilian rulers the means of extending their power over the population at large. It also made control of the government worth fighting for, and hence helped set the stakes of struggles over democracy.

Relative to Europe as a whole, moreover, French and British democratization processes took place in regions featuring moderately high concentrations of coercion and capital in the company of extensive connections of commitment among people in different parts of their states' territory. The comparison of France and Britain therefore immediately sets the challenge of determining whether democratization occurred very differently where weak state paths prevailed, military force remained fragmented, capital accumulation lagged, and/or great segmentation of interpersonal ties marked the world of commitment. To determine how generally the mechanisms that promoted democratization in France and Britain exercised similar effects elsewhere, we can take an even closer look at Switzerland during a crucial transition from undemocratic to democratic politics.

6

Switzerland as a Special Case

As we have seen repeatedly, 350 years go quickly at the national and international scales. Our overflights of European history afford virtual views of important trends and variations in democratization, but they do not display crucial change mechanisms close up. To see the mechanisms at work more clearly, let us turn up the magnification. Switzerland over the nineteen years from 1830 to 1848 offers a marvelous microcosm for the study of de-democratization and democratization. It also allows us to watch Europe's oldest continuously functioning democratic regime undergo a formative set of transitions. Contrary to Switzerland's reputation as a stodgy, stuffy, but civil political backwater, we witness bitter division and armed conflict. Far from easing into democracy as a consequence of age-old habits and culture, we see Switzerland fashioning democratic institutions as a contested and improvised compromise solution to a revolutionary crisis (for general historical background, see Bonjour 1948; Bonjour, Offler, and Potter 1952; de Capitani 1986; Gilliard 1955; Gossman 2000; Kohn 1956).

Long a scattering of belligerent fiefs within successive German empires, most Swiss areas acquired de facto independence at the Peace of Basel (1499) and de jure recognition as a federation at the Peace of Westphalia (1648). Their control of major transalpine routes for trade, travel, and troop movements gave Switzerland's segments the means of political and commercial survival, but also made them objects of incessant intervention by neighboring powers. "The peculiarity of Switzerland's former social order," observed Karl Deutsch,

expressed itself in the singularity of its mountain cantons. A mountain canton such as Uri is a peasant canton with moneyed, armed, superbly informed peasants; it is a natural city with mountains instead of city walls and mountain passes instead of city gates. It is also an agricultural region that hosts an urban style of government that conceives of itself as a self-governing city. Below, in the Midlands exists the league of burghers of city-states such as Bern and Zurich with the peasants of their own canton, hence another relation between urban citizens and rural residents. Thus the rights of small towns were well established and the self-government of those towns all the more respected. (Deutsch 1976: 34–35)

Until the 18th century's very end, the federation remained no more than a loose alliance of thirteen cantons with strong ties to allied territories of Geneva, Grisons, and Valais, plus subject territories (e.g., Vaud, Lugano, Bellinzona, and Valtellina) of their component units or of the federation as a whole.

Linguistic and religious fault lines crisscrossed the highlands. Multiple versions of Romance and Germanic languages mingled and varied from valley to valley. Well before the Reformation, the high Alps nurtured beliefs and practices that the Catholic Church regarded as heresies; the adjacent mountains of Savoy became the heartland of Waldensian belief. The 16th-century Reformation swept much of the Alpine region, although the Catholic Church won back compliance from a majority of its population by word and sword. Religious struggles of the 16th and 17th centuries, furthermore, left behind not a simple Catholic-Protestant split but multiple sects, with Geneva (pried loose from Savoy in the course of intense conflict) ending up Calvinist and Basel Zwinglian. With the cantons' tight controls over residence, citizenship, and religious expression, linguistic and religious fragmentation persisted into the 19th century.

From the 16th to 18th centuries, Switzerland withdrew almost entirely from international war on its own account, but provided crack mercenary troops to much of Europe (Casparis 1982). Cantonal elites drew substantial revenues both from the trade in mercenaries and from rents or fees supplied by rural populations that lay under their control. During that period, Switzerland's politics operated chiefly at the local and cantonal levels: outward-looking efforts to hold off other powers, inward-looking efforts to deal with enormous disparities and particularities of privilege. Of the roughly 1.6 million people who lived in the territory of today's Switzerland toward the end of the 18th century, fewer than 200,000 had rights to participate in public politics (Böning 1998: 6–7). Over this entire era, nevertheless, qualified citizens of individual cantons engaged in a degree of democratic deliberation that stood out from almost all of Europe.

The union as a whole exercised only limited governmental capacity. "The old Confederation in its last decades," remarks Jonathan Steinberg,

> was a marvellous thing, a patchwork of overlapping jurisdictions, ancient customs, worm-eaten privileges and ceremonies, irregularities of custom, law, weights and measures. On the shores of Lake Luzern, the independent republic of Gersau flourished with all of 2,000 inhabitants and enjoyed much prestige among political theorists of the time as the smallest free state in Europe. The famous Göttingen Professor Friedrich Christoph Schlosser seriously toyed with the idea of writing a multi-volume history of the republic under "a universal-historical" aspect as a microcosm of all of European history. (Steinberg 1996: 39–40)

Although the federation had a Diet of its own, it operated essentially as a meeting place for strictly instructed ambassadors from sovereign cantons. Within each canton, furthermore, sharp inequalities typically separated comfortable burghers of the principal town, workers within the same town, members of constituted hinterland communities, and inhabitants of dependent territories who lacked any political representation. In Bern, for example, 3,600 qualified citizens ruled 400,000 people who lacked rights of citizenship, while in Zurich 5,700 official burghers governed 150,000 country dwellers (Böning 1998: 8). Within the ranks of citizens, furthermore, a small – and narrowing – number of families typically dominated public office from one generation to the next.

Both the countryside's great 18th-century expansion of cottage industry and the mechanized urban industrial concentration that took off after 1800 increased discrepancies among the distributions of population, wealth, and political privilege. Cantonal power holders controlled the press tightly and felt free to exile, imprison, or even execute their critics. From the outside, the federation as a whole therefore resembled less a zone of freedom than a conglomerate of petty tyrannies. The majority of the population who lacked full citizenship, or any at all, smarted under the rule of proud oligarchs. Meanwhile, politically excluded intellectuals and bourgeois formed numerous associations – notably the Helvetic Society – to criticize existing regimes, revitalize rural economies, promote major reforms, and advance Swiss national patriotism as an alternative to locally and religiously circumscribed parochialism.

The French Revolution shook Switzerland's economic and political ties to its great westward neighbor while exposing Swiss people to new French models and doctrines. From 1789 onward, revolutionary movements formed in several parts of Switzerland. In 1793 Geneva (not a federation member, but closely tied to Switzerland) underwent a revolution on the French model. As the threat of French invasion mounted in early 1798, Basel, Vaud, Lucerne, Zurich, and other Swiss regions followed the revolutionary path. Basel, for example, turned from a constitution in which only citizens of the town chose their canton's senators to another giving urban and rural populations equal representation.

Conquered by France in collaboration with Swiss revolutionaries in 1798, then receiving a new constitution that year, the Swiss regime as a whole adopted a much more centralized form of government with significantly expanded citizenship. The new regime incorporated the territories of cantons St. Gallen, Grisons, Thurgau, Ticino, Aargau, and Vaud on equal terms with the older cantons, but followed French revolutionary practice by reducing the cantons to administrative and electoral units. The central government remained fragile, however; four coups occurred between 1800 and 1802 alone. At the withdrawal of French troops in 1802, multiple rebellions broke out. Switzerland then rushed to the brink of civil war. Only Napoleon's intervention and imposition of a new constitution in 1803 kept the country together.

The 1803 regime, known in Swiss history as the Mediation, restored considerable powers to cantons, but by no means reestablished the Old Regime. Switzerland's recast federation operated with a national assembly, official multilingualism, relative equality among cantons, and freedom for citizens to move from canton to canton. Despite some territorial adjustments, a weak central legislature, judiciary, and executive survived Napoleon's defeat. Survival occurred, however, only after another close brush with civil war, this time averted by Great Power intervention, in 1813–15. In the war settlement of 1815, Austria, France, Great Britain, Portugal, Prussia, Russia, Spain, and Sweden accepted a treaty among twenty-two cantons called the Federal Pact (now adding Valais, Neuchâtel, and Geneva) as they guaranteed Switzerland's perpetual neutrality and the inviolability of its frontiers.

Switzerland arrived in 1815 with a regime very different from the one that first faced French revolutionary might. Not only did it now include twenty-two cantons, not only had each canton undergone significant internal change, but also Swiss internal and external boundaries shifted between 1792 and 1815. Take just one example: the canton of Bern lost territories on one side but acquired most of the predominantly Catholic and French-speaking Jura on the other. From 999 to 1792, the Jura had belonged to the autonomous Bishopric of Basel, which in turn formed one of the Holy Roman Empire's many principalities (Wiegandt 1992). French forces conquered much of the northern Jura in 1792, declared its conquests the République rauracienne, annexed the south in 1797, established the whole region as the French department Mont Terrible, merged it into the adjacent department of Haut-Rhin in 1800, but lost the entire territory at the settlement of 1815. Despite the region's francophone Catholic majority, the conquering powers attached it to mainly Protestant and German-speaking Bern. Thus they added complexity to the already variegated linguistic-religious map of Switzerland. (In 1979, that francophone region finally became a separate canton under the old name Jura.)

Perhaps with malice aforethought, the victors of 1815 did not give Swiss central authorities adequate means for managing their country's complexity. Switzerland of the Federal Pact operated without a permanent bureaucracy, a standing army, common coinage, standard measures, or a national flag, but with multiple internal customs barriers, a rotating capital, and incessant bickering among cantonal representatives who had no right to deviate from their home constituents' instructions. At the national scale, the Swiss lived with a system better disposed to vetoes than to concerted change.

Another Revolutionary Era

At France's July 1830 revolution, anticlericalism became more salient in Swiss radicalism. After 1830, Switzerland became a temporary home for many exiled revolutionaries (e.g., Giuseppe Mazzini, Wilhelm Weitling, and, more surprisingly, Louis Napoleon), who collaborated with Swiss radicals in calling for reform. Historians of Switzerland in the 1830s speak of a Regeneration Movement pursued by means of "publicity, clubs, and mass marches" (Nabholz et al. 1938: II, 406). A great spurt of new periodicals and pamphlets accompanied the political turmoil of 1830–31 (Andrey 1986: 551–52). Within individual cantons, empowered liberals began enacting standard 19th-century reforms such as limitation of child labor and expansion of public schools. Nevertheless, the new cantonal constitutions installed during that mobilization stressed liberty and fraternity much more than they did equality.

Between 1830 and 1848, Switzerland underwent a contradictory set of political processes. Although the era's struggles unquestionably activated many convinced democrats, they pitted competing conceptions of democracy against each other. They played out, furthermore, over a substratum of competition for control of the Swiss federation as a whole. The country's richer, more Protestant cantons struggled their way toward democracy.

172

Those cantons installed representative institutions instead of the direct democracy of male citizens that had long prevailed in highland communities and cantons. Activists based in reformed cantons then used armed force to drive their unreformed neighbors toward representative democracy. They did so first in raids across cantonal boundaries, then in open, if short-lived, civil war. During the crisis, furthermore, confessional qualifications for citizenship became even more salient. As astute observer Alexis de Tocqueville put it shortly after the civil war:

> Nowhere else has the democratic revolution that is now stirring the world occurred in such complicated, bizarre circumstances. One people composed of multiple races, speaking multiple languages, adhering to multiple faiths and various dissident sects, two equally established and privileged churches, every political question soon pivoting on religious questions and every religious question leading to political questions, really two societies, one very old and the other very young, married to each other despite the difference in their ages. That is Switzerland. (Tocqueville 1983: 635–36)

Considering the effects of these conflicts on breadth, equality, consultation, and protection, Switzerland as a whole actually de-democratized between 1830 and 1847. Yet the settlement of 1848 clearly advanced democracy at a national scale beyond the level it had reached in 1798, 1803, 1815, or even 1830.

Figure 6.1 provides a rough sketch of the regime changes that Tocqueville was describing. It imagines that we could arrive at estimates of governmental capacity and of protected consultation for the whole of the Swiss federation at different points from 1790, locating them in comparison with other 19th-century European regimes. It shows Switzerland of 1790 as having a low-capacity central government but still providing more protected consultation at the national scale than most of its neighbors. It follows the rise of both capacity and consultation with the French-backed regime of 1798, the recession of both in the 1803 regime, the mild recovery of capacity in 1815, the fairly extensive expansion of protected consultation around 1830, the subsequent descent into civil war at the expense of both central capacity and protected consultation, finally the startling increase of both capacity and consultation with the peace settlement of 1848.

How and why could that happen? With a Protestant majority concentrated in the richer, more industrial and urban cantons, an approximate political split Protestant-liberal-radical versus Catholic-conservative became salient in Swiss politics. In regions dominated by conservative cities such as Basel, the countryside (widely industrialized during the 18th century, but

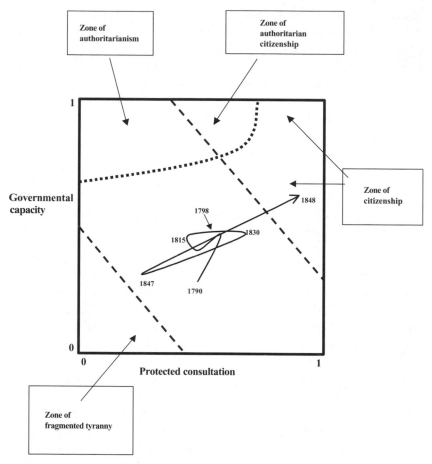

Figure 6.1: Fluctuations in Swiss national regimes, 1790–1848.

suffering contraction in cottage industry during the early 19th) often supported liberal or radical programs. In centers of growing capital-intensive production such as Zurich, conflict pitted a bourgeoisie much attached to oligarchic political privilege against an expanding working class that bid increasingly for voice in public politics and allied increasingly with dissident radicals among the bourgeoisie. In these regards, political divisions within Switzerland resembled those prevailing elsewhere in Western Europe.

The political problem became acute because national alignments of the mid-1840s pitted twelve richer and predominantly liberal-Protestant cantons against ten poorer, predominantly conservative-Catholic cantons in a

Diet where each canton had a single vote. (Strictly speaking, some units on each side, products themselves of earlier splits, qualified as half-cantons casting half a vote each, but the 12:10 balance of votes held.) Thus liberals deployed the rhetoric of national patriotism and majority rule while conservatives countered with cantonal rights and defense of religious traditions. Three levels of citizenship – municipal, cantonal, and national – competed with each other.

Contention occurred incessantly, and often with vitriolic violence, from 1830 to 1848. Reform movements were already under way in Vaud and Ticino as 1830 began – indeed, Ticino preceded France by adopting a new constitution on 4 July 1830 (Sauter 1972). Nevertheless, France's July Revolution of 1830 and its Belgian echo later in the year encouraged Swiss reformers and revolutionaries. As the French and Belgian revolutions rolled on, smaller scale revolutions took place in the Swiss towns and cantons of Aargau, Lucerne, St. Gallen, Schaffhausen, Solothurn, Thurgau, Vaud, and Zurich. Thereafter, republicans and radicals repeatedly formed military bands (often called free corps, or *Freischärler*) and attempted to take over particular cantonal capitals by force of arms. Such bands failed in Lucerne (1841), but succeeded in bringing new administrations to power in Lausanne (1847), Geneva (1847), and Neuchâtel (1848).

The largest military engagement took place in 1847. Switzerland's federal Diet ordered dissolution of the mutual defense league (Sonderbund) formed by Catholic cantons two years earlier; when the Catholic cantons refused, the Diet sent an army to Fribourg and Zug (whose forces capitulated without serious fighting), then Lucerne (where a short battle occurred). The Sonderbund had about 79,000 men under arms, the federation some 99,000. The Sonderbund War itself produced fewer casualties than the smaller-scale struggles that preceded it. The war ended with thirty-three dead among Catholic forces and sixty dead among the attackers. Its defeat consolidated the dominance of liberals in Switzerland as a whole and led to the adoption of a cautiously liberal constitution, on something like an American model, in 1848.

The subsequent period resembled America's Reconstruction, the troubled time that followed the United States's own civil war – grudging coexistence, persistent testing, but no more approaches to a definitive split. The "patriots" of 1848 led the country for years. General Guillaume Dufour, who led the federal troops that defeated the Sonderbund (and who had once taught Louis Napoleon at the Thun military school), for example, commanded the Swiss army for much of the first postwar decade.

175

A last ricochet of the 1847–48 military struggles occurred in 1856. The coup of 1848 had effectively, but not formally, displaced the King of Prussia from shared sovereignty in Neuchâtel. Forces loyal to the king seized military control over part of Neuchâtel's cantonal capital, only to be defeated almost immediately by the cantonal militia. Prussia's threats to invade Switzerland incited other European powers to hold Prussia in check. From that point on, the liberal constitution applied to all of the Swiss Federation. Between 1849 and 1870, furthermore, all Swiss cantons terminated their profitable centuries-old export of mercenary units for military service outside Switzerland. Thereafter, only papal guards and a few ceremonial military units elsewhere represented Swiss soldiery outside Switzerland itself. From that point onward, Switzerland's image of tidy villages and orderly cities displaced the memory of incessant, bitter military strife.

Despite definitive installation of a limited democratic regime in 1848, Switzerland remained an exception among Europe's democracies. In general, European countries homogenized internally during the 19th and 20th centuries: demographic, economic, religious, linguistic, and cultural differences among regions declined within countries (Caramani 2003; Rokkan and Urwin 1982; Watkins 1990). On the whole, political homogeneity likewise increased, as regional concentrations of parties declined (Caramani 1997: 110). In Switzerland, however, extreme geographic segmentation of language, religion, and party persisted into the 20th century. In fact, most of Switzerland's major parties *de*-nationalized during the 19th century and never gained anything approaching equal geographic strength across cantons during the 20th (Caramani 1997: 242–48).

The post-1848 system displayed remarkable stability and an impressive capacity to meet challenges by co-opting challengers. Although they created a formal party only in 1858, for example, Switzerland's Radicals held ministries in every government from 1848 to 2000. They finally allocated a single seat to the Conservative Catholic opposition in 1891. The agrarian Swiss People's Party gained a place for itself in 1929. Starting in 1943, Socialists also joined the government, remaining until 1953 and rejoining in 1959. After that, they never left. From 1959 to 2000, every cabinet consisted of two Radicals, two Socialists, two Christian Democrats, and one member of the Swiss People's Party. (Characteristically, the seven ministers had to come from seven different cantons.) Only at the century's very end did anti-immigrant support for the increasingly nativist Swiss People's Party begin threatening a shift in the 2-2-2-1 balance the Swiss had called their "magic formula."

After 1848, Switzerland adopted democratic procedures with a vengeance. At the federal level, the country voted on referenda and initiatives an impressive 451 times – almost exactly three times per year – between 1848 and 1997 (Trechsel 2000: 16). Almost half of the proposals passed and became law. Although federal referenda greatly accelerated after 1960, they already ran at one or two per year during the 19th century (Trechsel 2000: 11). Between 1900 and 1993, Switzerland staged almost half of all the national referenda conducted anywhere in the entire world (Frey and Stutzer 2002: 424). By the 1970s, furthermore, individual cantons were holding more than 100 referenda and initiatives of their own during the average year (Trechsel 2000: 23). This happened despite the fact that Appenzell, Glarus, and Unterwalden retained their general assemblies, and therefore avoided cantonal referenda. Referenda made a difference. National referenda, for example, finally authorized women to vote in national elections (1971), rejected the Diet's proposal of full membership in the United Nations (1986), and reduced the national voting age from twenty to eighteen (1991).

Voting did not exhaust Switzerland's democratic activities. By the 1970s, Swiss social movement activists were organizing about fifty visible public events – demonstrations, marches, and the like – per year (Giugni and Passy 1997: 20–22). Although Switzerland did not fully legalize labor unions until 1864 and strikes until 1885, the inscription of freedom to associate into the 1848 constitution gave not only social movement participants, but also workers warrants for organizing. Like party and reform activists, 19th-century Swiss workers organized unions and strikes resembling those of their French and German counterparts (Gruner 1968: 908–53). On the whole, the Swiss fulfilled their smug international image by being quite satisfied with themselves and with their government; within Switzerland, furthermore, the more extensive a locality's direct democracy, the greater the residents' expression of satisfaction with their lives and governments (Frey and Stutzer 2002: 425).

Not long after 1848, in short, Switzerland had switched from violent militia-based politics to the standard democratic repertoire of social movements, strikes, and election campaigns. But it did so with a distinctive Swiss twist. As Hanspeter Kriesi and his collaborators put it for the 20th century:

The weak, inclusive Swiss state has given rise to a social movement sector characterized by a very high aggregate level of mobilization and a very moderate action repertoire. Formal SMOs [social movement organizations] tend to be strongly developed, as are moderate forms of mobilization such as direct-democratic campaigns, petitioning, and to some extent moderate unconventional forms like demonstrations. (Kriesi et al. 1995: 51–52)

Despite subsequent stability, between 1830 and 1847 Swiss democracy receded into civil war. Only military victory of one side wrenched the federation back toward a democratic settlement. As of 1848, we might call Switzerland as a whole either a weak democracy or a democratic oligarchy. Property owners prevailed and only males could vote, but the federation transacted its business through elections, referenda, and parliamentary deliberations.

Democratic institutions comparable to those that now prevail in Western Europe still took a long time to form in Switzerland, and many vestiges of earlier fragmented regimes remain today. Jews could not acquire Swiss citizenship, for example, until 1866. Women could not vote in Swiss federal elections, as we have seen, until 1971. Even then, two half-cantons rejected female suffrage. Swiss national citizenship still depends on cantonal citizenship, which in turn depends on citizenship in a specific municipality. While twenty cantons today elect two members each to Switzerland's Council of State (Senate), three cantons (Basel, Appenzell, and Unterwalden) divide into separate half-cantons having one senator each. By the middle of the 19th century, nevertheless, Switzerland had formed one of Europe's more durably representative regimes. Switzerland created democracy with a difference.

What Must We Explain?

Swiss experience is all the more remarkable for its transition to representative government in the presence of persistent linguistic differences. Important distinctions have long existed between Switzerland's Germanic-speaking northern and eastern cantons, its French-speaking western border cantons, its Italian-speaking southern rim, and its Romansch-speaking enclaves in the southeast. Complexity extends to the very names of cantons. German speakers, for example, call Waadt the canton I earlier referred to as Vaud. A single canton bears the four names Grisons, Graubünden, Grigioni, and Grischun in French, German, Italian, and Romansch, respectively. Switzerland also features sharp town-to-town differences in the Alemannic dialects known generically as Schwyzerdütsch, which actually serve as languages of choice for spoken communication in nominally germanophone

Switzerland, which these days contains about two-thirds of the total population. With dominant cleavages based on religion and inherited from the Reformation, the Swiss have rarely fought over linguistic distinctions. Separation of francophone Jura from predominantly German-speaking Bern (1979) marks a break with earlier Swiss practices.

Switzerland stands out even more for the vitality of representative institutions in company with fairly weak state structures. Similar regimes elsewhere in Europe generally succumbed to conquest by higher-capacity (and much less democratic) neighbors. Switzerland's topography, its ability to summon up military defense when pressed, and rivalries among its powerful neighbors gave it breathing room similar to that enjoyed by Liechtenstein and Andorra. Switzerland's tough independence likewise inspired Europe's regional politicians, so much so that Basque nationalists of the 19th century proposed that their own land become the "Switzerland of the Pyrenees" (Agirreazkuenaga and Urquijo 1994: 11–12).

Whatever else we say about the Swiss itinerary toward democracy, it certainly passed through intense popular struggle, including extensive military action. The same process that produced a higher-capacity central government, furthermore, also created Switzerland's restricted but genuine democracy: as compared with what came before, relatively broad – if unequal – citizenship, binding consultation of citizens, and substantial protection of citizens from arbitrary action by governmental agents. As compared with late 19th-century French or British models of democracy, however, the Swiss confederal system looks extraordinarily heterogeneous: a distinctive constitution, dominant language, and citizenship for each canton; multiple authorities and compacts; and a remarkable combination of exclusiveness with the capacity to create particular niches for newly accepted political actors. Through all subsequent constitutional changes, those residues of Swiss political history have persisted. They continue to exercise profound effects on contentious politics within Switzerland (Giugni and Passy 1997; Kriesi 1980, 1981; Kriesi et al. 1981, 1995).

Let us concentrate on the critical period from 1830 to 1848. During those nineteen years, Switzerland went from an uneasy federation among cantankerous, unequal, internally oligarchic cantons connected politically by no more than exiguous central institutions to a relatively solid semidemocratic union. On the way, it passed through repeated armed conflicts, multiple small-scale revolutions, and a civil war that could have split the country permanently. This chapter's appendix lays out a chronology of Switzerland's larger-scale contentious events during those turbulent years.

Given Switzerland's subsequent staid reputation, the chronology conveys startling news. During 1831, 1832, 1833, 1834, 1839, 1841, 1844, 1845, 1847, and 1848, armed struggles over forms and prerogatives of government shook one part of Switzerland or another. Hundreds of Swiss men died in military combat. Canton after canton split into armed factions. The settlement of 1847–48 occurred only as a result of outright civil war. Yet that peace settlement initiated a long period of limited but stable democracy at a national scale. What is more, cantons of direct democracy at the local and cantonal scale – Lucerne, Uri, Schwyz, Unterwald, and Zug – formed the heart of resistance to democratic reform at the national scale. Cantons that had set up representative systems instead of direct democracy – Geneva, Fribourg, Vaud, Bern, Solothurn, Aargau, Zurich, Thurgau, Schaffhausen, and Ticino – generally supported the federal cause and representative democracy at the national scale. Predominantly Catholic Fribourg (which had installed representative cantonal institutions) was the major exception. Two paradoxes, then: popular armed struggle that issued in democracy, and fiercest opposition to national democracy from those who practiced direct democracy at home.

On closer examination of Swiss political processes, both paradoxes dissolve. Resolution of the second paradox helps resolve the first. The "direct democracy" of regions that opposed federal reform consisted of government by assembly based on jealously guarded equality within a severely restricted class of qualifying citizens. In direct parallels to those parts of urban Europe where cities enjoyed considerable political autonomy, male citizens of Swiss communes and cantons had rights and obligations to bear arms in civic militias – so much so that well into the 19th century eligible voters commonly carried a sword, dagger, or bayonet as signs of their distinction. For centuries before the 1840s, furthermore, armed assemblies frequently formed on their own initiative to protest actions by one authority or another; sometimes they overturned regimes by force, created temporary assemblies to judge or debate authorities' actions, or coerced authorities themselves to call assemblies of citizenry. (Chapter 2 described Graubünden's version of insurrectionary assembly, the Strafgericht.) Behind public equality stood oligarchy, chauvinism, and coercion. Although an assembly's majority could and sometimes did reject proposals by a commune's or canton's officers, in practice wealthy men generally dominated high public office and rarely let serious opposition to their role reach public expression.

Where the sheer scale of local polities inhibited routine government by direct assembly, cantons commonly adopted the veto (in which only a majority of all qualified voters could overturn a formal proposal, regardless of how many actually voted) or the referendum (in which a majority of those voting on a proposal carried the day, regardless of how many actually voted) as a substitute for face to face, viva voce deliberation. No matter what the procedures, Swiss versions of direct democracy typically involved narrow participation, relatively equal rights within the charmed circle of partici- pants, binding consultation of those participants, and limited protections for anyone outside their number. Swiss direct democracy also coupled with fierce protection of local and cantonal politics from outside interference. The system protected not individual liberty so much as collective autonomy (Barber 1974). Cantons that adopted representative democracy, in contrast, generally expanded popular participation in cantonal politics. Switzerland's armed struggle between 1830 and 1848 resulted largely from efforts of ac- tivists for representative democracy to beat down the oligarchic politics of direct democracy, and thus to increase their own political weight at the national level. In so doing, those activists willy-nilly became advocates of a stronger central government as well.

What have we to explain? In terms of the federal government's trajec- tory within our capacity-protection space, Switzerland arrived at the 1830s with a very low-capacity federal government featuring modest protected consultation; extremely narrow but relatively equal political participation at a national scale, binding consultation not of citizens at large but of the cantons as collective entities, fairly generous protection against arbitrary action by agents of the federal government, and little that we could call either authoritarianism or citizenship at a national scale.

As in many federal systems, defining Switzerland's "national scale" poses problems. Even today, Swiss cantons perform many activities that more centralized systems assign unambiguously to direct agents of a national state structure. The Swiss national army, for example, still lies partly under cantonal control; cantonal authorities can promote officers up to the rank of captain. During the 1830s and 1840s, cantons and smaller units within them provided almost all of Switzerland's effective day-to-day government. When we speak of the national scale or the federal government, then, we are using a shorthand for political activity involving either the federal Diet, its direct agents, or coordinated action among cantons.

By the end of 1848, Switzerland at the national scale had moved significantly toward broadened citizen-agent relations and had arguably extended political equality among groups and individuals, maintaining binding consultation and protections while considerably augmenting the central government's capacity. At that point, we can reasonably speak of nonauthoritarian Swiss federal citizenship. In between, the Swiss federal government had suffered grievous attacks on its capacity, protections had declined, and civil war had torn the country apart. But in the course and aftermath of that civil war, the federal government built its capacity to a level unprecedented except perhaps under French hegemony between 1798 and 1803. Swiss political history from 1830 to 1850 followed a struggle-filled version of the weak state trajectory toward democracy.

Note the weakness of governmental capacity in the 1830s. Writing from Bern to Claude-François de Corcelle on 27 July 1836, Tocqueville declared:

In my quality as an *American* I have already developed proud disdain for the Swiss federal constitution, which I frankly call a league and not a federation; a government of this sort is the softest, most powerless, most awkward, and the least capable of leading people anywhere but to anarchy that one can imagine. The kingdom of England is a hundred times more republican than this so-called Republic. Mignet would attribute it to a difference in race, but that's an argument I'll never accept except as a last resort, when I have absolutely nothing else to say. I prefer to identify its origin in a little known fact, at least unknown to me until recently: that communal liberty is a recent phenomenon in most Swiss cantons. The urban bourgeoisie ruled the countryside as the royal power ruled it in France. It was a small scale bourgeois centralization which like our royal centralization – masterwork of a great man, according to M. Thiers – would not allow anyone to meddle in its work. (Tocqueville 1983: 70–71)

The canton of Bern had recently adopted a nominally republican constitution on the model of representative (rather than direct) democracy. Tocqueville saw clearly in Bern that burghers within hinterland villages enjoyed local hegemony, but only within limits set by the wealthy burghers of Bern itself. As for the federal government, Tocqueville's sharp French eyes detected little capacity at all.

The federal government that Tocqueville then observed had actually lost some power over the previous few years. The pact adopted in 1815 served chiefly as a treaty among nearly sovereign cantons. The federal legislature, the Diet, served principally as a treaty enforcer; it had few powers of its own and could act at all only on a majority vote among instructed delegates, one per canton regardless of the canton's size. Its armed force consisted entirely of militia contingents supplied by cantons on the Diet's request, generally following population-based quotas. So long as those cantons were dealing collectively with external enemies, they lent support to the Diet's efforts on their behalf.

As some cantons adopted reforms in 1830 and thereafter, however, a series of armed struggles broke out between reformers and their enemies within those cantons and in neighboring cantons as well. When federal forces – that is, federalized cantonal militias – intervened in such struggles, they generally supported the reform side. Drawing their troops disproportionately from cantons that had already adopted reforms – which were also, on average, more populous, urban, and industrialized cantons – federal forces supported the familiar logic of representation proportionate to adult male population. In cantons Basel and Schwyz, the Diet went so far as to support secessionist movements and to ratify the formation of new half-cantons dominated by reformers. In reaction, two different groups of cantons formed mutual aid pacts to guarantee the integrity of each other's constitutions. Thus cantons were actually reducing their already low level of collaboration with federal authorities.

This weakening of the Swiss state and its later splintering into civil war make the constitutional reinforcement of 1848 more remarkable. The hard-won Swiss constitution of 1848 established a federal system, not a unitary state on the French model. It split sovereignty between the federal government and the cantons. It created a bicameral representative system in the American style, with equal representation of cantons in the upper house and roughly equal representation of voters in the lower house. It undercut the previous widespread inscription of religious divisions into cantonal and national politics.

Because it occurred in the immediate aftermath of a civil war when European powers were preoccupied with revolutions at home, the Swiss constitutional convention that assembled in February 1848 could proceed in secret as the deliberation of 200 uninstructed delegates rather than as an old fashioned treaty-building session among the previously established cantons. Despite this relative freedom and the Sonderbund's chastening lesson, Swiss constitution makers still had to get their proposals past a majority of cantons, then past a majority of voters in a national referendum. In the process they won the crucial battle for nationalization of customs revenues, but lost proposals for a strongly centralized army, a national public school system, a national road system, and a single national language (Ruffieux 1986: 601–2).

Our problem, then, is to fashion partial explanations for changes in Swiss national governmental capacity and protected consultation between 1830 and 1848, asking whether the mechanisms of change in inequality, networks, and citizen-agent relations enumerated in Tables 1.1–1.3 played a significant part in those changes and whether revolution, confrontation, conquest, and/or colonization worked whatever effects they had on democratization by accelerating the same mechanisms rather than producing sui generis political transformations. Since Swiss historians have posed their questions about the period in rather a different vein, my proposals contain significant elements of interpretation and conjecture. Still, the arguments provide at least a rough fit to the surprising Swiss transformations of 1830 to 1848.

Swiss Inequality

As we trace the influence of changes in inequality, trust networks, and public politics on democratization in Switzerland, we concentrate on effects at the national scale. The temporary democratization of national politics around 1830 resulted in part from local and regional seizures of power by democrats of various stripes, but it did not always entail democratization of local and regional politics. Some cantons actually de-democratized over substantial spans of the 19th century. In the highly industrial half-canton of Appenzell Ausserrhoden, for example, a semi-annual outdoor general assembly (*Landsgemeinde*) of male citizens long held ultimate political authority. But as typical ages of school attendance and work shifted, the canton raised its minimum age for participation from sixteen to eighteen in 1834, and again from eighteen to twenty in 1876 (Tanner 1982: 396); with respect to age, the canton de-democratized. What is more, major cantonal officers, who actually set the agenda for general assemblies, originated overwhelmingly in the leading mercantile and industrial families. When it came to officeholding in parish government, the town of Bühler actually included more poor men in 1810–20 (after French hegemony had extended political participation) than toward 1840 (Tanner 1982: 382–83). Increasing material and political inequality in villages, towns, and cantons could cohabit with increasing political equality in national politics so long as the spheres remained partially insulated from each other.

On the small scale, indeed, Switzerland featured startling combinations of equality and inequality. Fellow citizens of cities or of villages, speakers of the same dialects, and co-members of religious congregations insisted on equal public standing. In the federation as a whole before 1830, equality among obviously disparate cantons ranked as a sacred political principle. Yet outside the crucial arenas of solidarity and of arms'-length public equality, the Swiss combined finely graded material and political inequalities with exquisite protocols of rank and deference.

184

So long as Switzerland relied on agriculture, small crafts, transalpine shipping, and the export of troops for its livelihood, its localized governments fitted forms of rule to patterns of material inequality like glove to hand. During the 18th century, however, the expansion of cottage textile production created new classes of workers and entrepreneurs who escaped the usual relations of urban masters, merchants, and landlords, on one side, with artisans and peasants, on the other. By 1774, for example, in the hinterland of Basel only 18 percent of all household heads were farmers, 27 percent were day laborers, and the remaining 55 percent were industrial producers in homes and shops (Gschwind 1977: 369; for comparable evidence on Zurich, see Braun 1960).

The conquering French and their Swiss revolutionary allies abolished urban guilds, those mainstays of material inequality. After 1800, machine-based urbanization of cotton textile spinning left an increasingly dissident body of handloom weavers in the countryside; mechanization of weaving after 1840 then began to wipe out those weavers in turn. Urban concentration of textile production also shaped a classic, if small-scale, conjunction of industrial bourgeoisie and proletariat in Switzerland's major centers of cloth production (Braun 1965; Gruner 1968). Organized crafts and their masters lost much of their predominance in the politics of those centers. Correspondences among wealth, landowning, and political power declined.

Not that Swiss industrialization reduced material inequality. On the contrary; in the short run, extremes of poverty and wealth increased. But by maintaining landed oligarchies in political power as industrialization generated important populations off the land, the Swiss system of segmented, privileged public politics grew increasingly insulated from prevailing material inequalities. The logics of numbers and of politically established categories contradicted each other ever more sharply. It was precisely against partial exclusion from public politics and against the domination of landed elites that merchants, professionals, and industrial bourgeoisie banded together in favor of political reform. Sometimes they even dared to ally themselves with industrial workers in radical politics. Expansion and nationalization of citizenship promised to increase their power vis-à-vis old landed elites, but only at the expense of giving poorer workers direct access to government. In this way, transformations of inequality – and especially inequality's relation to public politics – gave a small boost to democratization in Switzerland's more industrialized cantons during the 1830s and 1840s.

Although single individuals and invisible networks sometimes accumulate great power, categorical inequality by gender, race, ethnicity, religion trade, wealth, or local membership has the more profound, durable, and direct effects on public politics. Categorical inequality therefore deeply affects prospects for democracy. Categorical inequalities translate easily into differences in political rights and obligations as well as providing bases for collective contention. Four main families of mechanisms create and transform categorical inequalities: exploitation, opportunity hoarding, emulation, and adaptation (Tilly 1998).

Exploitation is the deployment of resources within a collective enterprise in a way that gives a whole category of participants less reward than their effort adds to the enterprise. Opportunity hoarding is exclusion of others from a valuable productive resource in a way that means the excluded get less reward for their effort than they would if included. Old regime Swiss guilds combined exploitation and opportunity hoarding in a classic manner, with masters gaining a disproportionate share of financial return from craft production, but workers still profiting by exclusion of nonguild workers from their trade. Emulation reproduces unequal patterns of social relations by means of imitation or direct transfer of persons from setting to setting. Adaptation, finally, involves integration of existing inequalities into social routines in ways that support those social routines, including routines of people who suffer from exploitation and opportunity hoarding.

Here we focus not on the waxing, waning, and alteration of categorical inequality in general but on its intersection with public politics. Of the checklist in Table 1.1, Switzerland's changing inequality promoted democratization chiefly through two mechanisms: (1) dissolution of coercive controls supporting current relations of exploitation and opportunity hoarding and (2) insulation of existing categorical inequalities from public politics. In the first case, abolition of guilds and expansion of factory production dissolved the previously close connection between Swiss governmental institutions and craft organization.

In the second case – insulation of existing categorical inequalities from public politics – retention of political institutions based on the implicit assumption of fixed local populations organized around relations to landed property in the face of massive commercialization, proletarianization, and migration blocked immediate translations between economic and political power. Mobilization of conflict along religious lines between 1830 and 1847, furthermore, motivated the constitution makers of 1848 to erect barriers against translation of religious into political divisions, most

186

obviously by barring clergymen from national public office. Against these democracy-enabling mechanisms, however, we must weigh the large increases in material inequality generated by Switzerland's industrialization. On balance, Switzerland made its 19th-century moves toward democracy despite, rather than because of, overall alterations in material inequality. That makes the insulation constructed in 1848 all the more impressive.

Trust Networks

Alterations of trust networks probably played a larger part in promoting Swiss democracy. From the late 16th century onward, the Swiss had organized much of their lives within segments defined by trade, language, dialect, and religion. Patron-client ties linked richer and poorer members of those segments. Religion in particular etched sharp boundaries within Swiss social life. Communal and cantonal citizenship often depended on religious affiliation. Up to the French conquest of 1798, for example, "with the exception of most Calvinist refugees, no Catholic or non-Zwinglian Protestant could become a citizen of Basel, whether the city or the countryside" (Gschwind 1977: 423). Although minorities including Jews lived in the interstices, religious affiliation mattered enormously to public standing. At a much smaller scale, 18th-century Switzerland resembled the British Isles and the Netherlands in building religious categories directly and unequally into public politics.

Over the long run of 1750 to 1840, however, Switzerland's two-stage industrialization undermined trust networks built on religion, language, craft, and perhaps those built on older forms of transalpine trade as well. First, the dynamic expansion of cottage industry drove a large increase in rural landless populations. Then, after 1820 or so, concentration of textile production in factories – first for spinning, then for weaving as well – generated a movement of workers to industrial towns as well as a shorter term rise and fall of handloom weaving in the countryside. Both French abolition of guilds and competition from manufacturers operating outside of established crafts undermined the networks of journeymen that had previously organized small-scale production (cf. Rosenband 1999: 457).

Although new workers generally came from old rural families, their altered social situations detached them from established rural networks of reciprocity and patronage. In Zurich's hinterland, for example, incremental effects of industrialization coupled with the struggle of liberal bourgeois to reduce the control of conservative Protestant ministers over family law, charity, schools, Sunday entertainment, and local finances (Joris and Witzig 1992: 26; see also Joris 1994). Most likely, similar processes eroded networks of credit and mutual aid among village women.

Before 1848, these processes proceeded earlier and farther in Switzerland's predominantly Protestant regions than in its regions of Catholic hegemony. Switzerland's early industrialization concentrated in Protestant-dominated cantons such as Bern and Zurich rather than in Catholic cantons such as Lucerne and in high mountain areas. Historians have not so far examined the effect of this difference on trust networks. In addition to the usual difficulties of reconstructing interpersonal networks from historical sources (see, e.g., Bearman 1991, 1993; Gould 1995; Kalb 1997), historians of Switzerland must cut through powerful myths of social disintegration that saturate commentaries of the time (Braun 1965: 41–43). Still, we can plausibly speculate that Catholic networks of kinship, parish membership, friendship, mutual aid, and godparenthood retained greater salience and greater insulation from public political life at the large scale than did their Protestant counterparts. Similar differences seem to have separated liberal Protestants and secularists of industrial cities such as Zurich from conservative Calvinists in their agricultural hinterlands. Liberal Protestants and secularists, that is, integrated their trust networks into public politics more extensively than did Catholics or Protestant conservatives.

My historical reconstruction runs as follows: in large portions of Switzerland, rural industrialization, proletarianization of rural populations, then urban implosion undermined the operation of trust networks that had connected local groups in marriage, credit, mutual aid, gossip, and trade as well as sustaining patron-client ties between richer and poorer households. Those processes activated most of the destructive mechanisms enumerated under the heading of trust networks in Table 1.2:

- disintegration of existing trust networks
- expansion of the population lacking access to effective trust networks for their major long-term risky enterprises
- appearance of new long-term risky opportunities that existing trust networks can't handle

At the same time, continues my conjecture, occurred investment of a prospering bourgeoisie in higher capacity governments that could abolish internal customs barriers, create protections against external competition, establish standard measures, build commercial infrastructure, and expand public education activated mechanisms that attach trust networks to public politics, even to government itself:

- creation of external guarantees for governmental commitments
- governmental incorporation and expansion of existing trust networks
- governmental absorption or destruction of previously autonomous patron-client networks
- substantial increase of government's resources for risk reduction and/or compensation of loss
- visible governmental meeting of commitments to the advantage of substantial new segments of the population

These mechanisms extend from government to institutions of public politics that depend on government – political parties, elections, special interest associations, labor unions, and so on. Incorporation of such institutions into people's trust networks enables and commits the same people to monitor governmental activity and press for collective voice. The shift from government as a shield for existing local privileges and hierarchies to government as an instrument of top-down control – a shift that, to be sure, went much further in France and Prussia than in Switzerland – served as a solvent and transformer of trust networks.

Take just one of these mechanisms, governmental incorporation and expansion of existing trust networks. At the cantonal level, leaders certainly claimed that the mechanism worked. "Our dear God," ran a children's reading book sponsored by Appenzell's cantonal government in 1805, "has put the Authorities [*Obrigkeit*] in place. That is a great blessing for us. If there were no Authorities, neither our lives, nor our property, nor our peace would be secure" (Tanner 1982: 400).

Whether or not God made the mechanism work within cantons, however, the question is whether the federal government incorporated networks on which people regularly relied for risky enterprises. The answer seems to be that before 1848 among Catholic Swiss no such incorporation occurred, but among Protestants and others some movement in that direction began with the Helvetian Republic of 1798 and continued thereafter. The federal government became especially the government of Protestants; the more Catholics in general resisted federal power, the more Protestants clung to it. Detailed evidence of such a tendency would in principle show Protestants investing in federally backed securities, paying federal taxes, reporting for military service, placing children in careers depending on federal support, and demanding federal mediation of disputes more energetically than Catholics.

No one has yet assembled the crucial evidence. In a country where – especially before 1848 – so many public powers remained in the cantons, furthermore, 19th-century Swiss had relatively few opportunities to commit themselves in these regards. Nevertheless, it is at least suggestive that during the Mediation government of 1803–13, the mainly Protestant cantons of Zurich, Bern, Basel, Solothurn, Schaffhausen, Aargau, and Vaud paid higher per capita taxes than their Catholic neighbors (de Capitani 1986: 492). Those cantons were also, to be sure, generally more industrial and commercial than their neighbors. On the whole, capitalism and Protestantism coincided in 19th-century Switzerland. The advance of capitalism fragmented older trust networks and made the state more central to the enterprises of entrepreneurs and workers alike.

Public Politics

Switzerland's sensational alterations of public politics during the 1830s and 1840s have attracted much more historical attention than have transformations of inequality and trust networks. As a result, it is much easier to identify relevant causal mechanisms within public politics. We are looking for evidence and causes of changes in governmental capacity, breadth and equality of political participation, binding consultation of political participants, and protection of political participants from arbitrary actions by governmental agents. We are also looking for evidence and causes of citizenship: the formation of large, uniform, categorical sets of rights and obligations binding governmental agents to people living under the same government's jurisdiction. Switzerland underwent changes of these kinds between 1830 and 1848 at the price of violent struggle.

The transformation operated at two levels. First, coalitions of radicals and reformers self-consciously adopted models of democratic organization and campaigned to implement those models both within cantons and across the federation as a whole. To some extent, they succeeded. Second, unintended by-products of deep, hard fought struggles for preeminence at the cantonal and federal levels fortified governmental capacity, protected consultation, and citizenship in Switzerland.

In the first regard, France's revolution of 1830 and Switzerland's earlier experience under French hegemony provided specific models for mobilization and constitution making. Reform meant creation of a central government having institutions designed to represent popular will, promote commerce, increase enlightenment, dispense justice, comfort the worthy poor, and block the inscription of private privilege into public law. Even there, Swiss reformers of 1830 gave the presentation of proposals a national twist with their mass meetings in the open air and their tumultuous assemblies of armed activists. Thus "... on 22 November 1830 a gathering of 7,000 to 8,000 people, meeting in the open air at Uster under the presidency of Heinrich Gujer, a miller from Bauma, listened to an exposition of the [reformist] Küssnacht proposals and, with enthusiasm and solemnity, accepted them by acclamation" (Craig 1988: 46). Nabholz et al. write of "wilde Tumulte" in Vaud, Schaffhausen, and Basel as well as of a "bloody confrontation [blutige Auseinandersetzung]" in Fribourg, all in the course of public deliberation over explicit proposals for constitutional reform (Nabholz et al. 1938: II, 411).

What is more, radicals and reformers repeatedly sought to impose their programs on reluctant regions by force. In January 1831, for example, anti-oligarchic activists of Basel's hinterland raised a rebellion against the canton's conservative capital, only to be put down by cantonal troops with deaths on both sides. Basel's struggle revived and radicalized later that year, with the characteristic Swiss solution of 1832 being to create two provisional "half cantons," one for the city, another for the countryside. An assembly of the rural half-canton (Baselland) almost immediately adopted a broadly democratic constitution. The old cantonal authorities refused to accept that solution, and sought to reimpose their rule. Struggles between city and countryside continued into August 1833, when lethal military combat in Gelterkinden and Pratteln slowed the cantonal effort and precipitated commitment of previously hostile communes to the new half-canton. At that point, federal authorities recognized the complete separation of the two half-cantons.

Schwyz's divisions resembled Basel's (Wyrsch 1983). Six districts of Outer Schwyz contained a majority of the canton's population but held only a third of its legislative seats. Reformers of Outer Schwyz first demanded a new constitution in 1830, and soon withdrew their representatives from cantonal assemblies dominated by Innerschwyz. Through several stages of negotiation, Outer Schwyz moved toward a declaration of independence and federal recognition as a separate half-canton, suffering two military occupations by Innerschwyz before a large dispatch of federal troops (August 1833) settled the matter. Federal intervention restored the single canton but established representation proportionate to population. This process

191

made authorities of Outer Schwyz more reliant than ever on the federal government, while rendering authorities of Inner Schwyz even more hostile than before. Rural Schwyz then divided sharply between factions of Hooves (small peasants, opting for liberal measures) and Horns (larger peasants, more conservative in their politics). Only intervention of the Diet and the canton of Uri prevented a new split in 1838.

Such struggles edged over into our second category of democracy-promoting causes, unintended consequences of deep, hard-fought struggles for preeminence at the cantonal and federal levels. Struggles over the public standing of religious institutions and affiliations figured centrally in Swiss democratization. Reformers of the 1830s already pursued a program of religious reform. In the Protestant canton of Zurich, for example, a reforming administration deliberately liquidated church tithes and ground rents in 1830 (Braun 1965: 13). Nevertheless, through most of the 1830s, Switzerland's major political divisions cut across confessional lines. If the greatest concentrations of reformers and radicals appeared in predominantly Protestant cantons, both Protestant and Catholic ranks supplied significant supporters for standard liberal reforms. At that point, the deepest political divisions separated defenders of cantonal autonomies against advocates of federally instigated reform.

Starting in the mid-1830s, liberals began pressing harder for action to reduce the clergy's power and to abolish the separate, equal confessional assemblies (*Landsgemeinden*), Protestant and Catholic, that had held ultimate authority in such religiously mixed cantons as Glarus. A series of moves and countermoves raised the stakes, eventually realigning politics along a Catholic/anti-Catholic divide. Switzerland's most intense battles of the period pitted a coalition of radicals, reformers, and secularists against defenders of Catholic privilege. For a few years, political divisions within Switzerland resembled those that had rent the British Isles during the Glorious Revolution.

Within cantons as at the national scale, Catholic/anti-Catholic divisions frequently deepened over issues of representation. The canton of Aargau offers a telling case in point. When a cantonal majority of Protestants, secularists, and liberal Catholics installed a new constitution after a vote of 5 January 1841, they eliminated a system of parity (in which Protestants and Catholics received equal numbers of seats on the governing Grand Council) in favor of combined voting by head. Catholics immediately began demanding a separate canton where they would have a majority. Cantonal authorities arrested leaders of the secessionist movement, violent confrontations began, and in one local skirmish seven secessionists and two members of government forces died. At that point, cantonal authorities decreed military occupation and disarmament of the rebellious districts. On 13 January, they violated provisions of the existing Federal Pact by abruptly closing Aargau's four monasteries and four nunneries, which they deemed centers of rebellion. After a series of protests from elsewhere in Switzerland and from abroad, the federal Diet declared the closings illegal; the issue roiled Aargau and Switzerland until August 1843, when the Diet in effect accepted Aargau's gesture of reopening the nunneries but keeping the monasteries shuttered.

For a while, however, similar differences also separated secularist liberals from *Protestant* conservatives. In 1839, Zurich's government offered a university professorship to Tübingen theologian David Friedrich Strauss, whose demystifying *Life of Jesus* had made him notorious among conservatives. In February 1839 opponents of Strauss's appointment organized meetings in Protestant churches throughout the canton. When the government refused to back down, they held a mass meeting of protest in Kloten, near Zurich, on 2 September. On the 6th, rural Protestants carrying weapons marched to Zurich singing hymns. The liberal government resigned and called elections, which brought conservatives back to power in the canton. The new government revoked Strauss's contract, bought him off with a pension, and sacked the university official who had engineered Strauss's appointment in the first place.

The Strauss affair reverberated. Responding explicitly to Zurich's controversy as well as to Aargau's suppression of its monasteries, the predominantly Catholic canton of Lucerne vigorously debated proposals to recall the long-banned Jesuits. The federal Diet considered a counterproposal to ban the Jesuits, but in August 1844 massively rejected it on the ground of unconstitutionality. Lucerne's own assembly then ended several years of debate on 24 October 1844 by inviting the Jesuits back to run the seminary, staff the theological faculty, and operate their own church. In December, radicals made a botched attempt at armed invasion of Lucerne, whereupon Lucerne's Great Council decreed the death penalty for anyone leading such a rebellion. Refugees from Lucerne joined protest meetings in adjacent cantons Aargau and Bern; in March-April 1845 they played a part in a well-organized but ultimately disastrous invasion of Lucerne from Aargau led by lawyer, politician, and General Staff captain Ulrich Ochsenbein. Ochsenbein's retreating forces left 105 dead and 785 prisoners (Remak 1993: 43).

Catholic rights became increasingly contentious. The Sonderbund of Lucerne, Uri, Schwyz, Unterwald, Zug, Fribourg, and Valais formed in December 1845, after all, precisely to defend its predominantly Catholic members from encroachment by Protestant neighbors. Its members committed themselves unequally:

Lucerne led the Sonderbund, receiving its strongest support from the people and governments of the oldest cantons, although Zug only lined up with the inner regions reluctantly and then only fought half-heartedly. Valais could only be won to the politics of the four forest cantons after a bloody conflict over the radical Young Switzerland, and vulnerable Fribourg finally reconciled itself to joining the other Catholic-conservative cantons. (Bucher 1966: 16)

The appeal of Sonderbund members to Catholic powers Austria, Sardinia, and France for support emphasized the seriousness of their cause and bid fair to split the country permanently. A draft declaration that circulated in the Sonderbund after 1845 proposed redrawing cantonal boundaries to consolidate Catholic populations – including those of Aargau – in largely Catholic cantons; Aargau's Catholic districts Muri, Bremgarten, Baden, Laufenberg, and Rheinfelden were to join Lucerne (Bucher 1966: 20). From the 1830s through the settlement of 1848, conservative Catholic activists sought repeatedly to carve out a protected space for themselves within a Switzerland they portrayed as secularizing rapidly. But the threat of external support for Catholics drove non-Catholic cantons together into a stronger alliance in support of the federal government.

Religious divisions, in short, were politicizing. They were aligning many people who had previously shown little interest in religious organization on one side and the other. Rather than a straightforward victory for anticlerical radicals, however, the struggle eventually generated a series of mutual accommodations that both strengthened the federal government and established respect for difference as a Swiss political principle, but excluded religious divisions from public politics. Surprisingly and crucially, the settlement secularized citizenship by eliminating confessional requirements for voting, confirming the rights of citizens to move from canton to canton regardless of their religious persuasion, and barring clergymen from service in the national legislature. The settlement inhibited the translation of religious and linguistic divisions into public politics while greatly fortifying the principle of national representation by territory and proportionate to population.

Dynamics of Democratization

Even before the Sonderbund formed, the mechanisms of public politics that would produce civil war and its paradoxically democratic consequences were already visibly at work. For the Sonderbund's master historian, Erwin Bucher, the fundamental explanation was straightforward:

As the July Revolution introduced a new movement into Switzerland, its aristocratic constitutions were again set aside. Forces for transformation and strengthening of the federation aligned themselves. In place of the old fashioned model of 1815 the federation was to don new clothes. The Diet worked all year on constitutional reform, but all its effort finally crumbled into sand. The forces seeking renewal were thereby dragged off the legal path. The federation with its virtually unrevisable Pact resembled a boiler without its safety valve – it finally exploded in civil war. Nevertheless the political struggle had to pass through many stages of increasing heat to reach that point. (Bucher 1966: 13–14)

The steam boiler analogy, last resort for many a puzzled analyst of contentious politics, will not withstand critical scrutiny. But Bucher rightly noted that canton-by-canton reforms in Switzerland's mainly Protestant regions altered public politics at the national scale. In fact, Switzerland's turbulent history from 1830 to 1848 shows us most of our hypothetical mechanisms of change in public politics at work:

- *coalition formation between segments of ruling classes and constituted political actors that are currently excluded from power*: cantonal constitution making in regions that adopted representative government relied on and reinforced coalitions of wealthy merchants and manufacturers with previously excluded male workers
- *brokerage of coalitions across unequal categories and/or distinct trust networks*: radical leaders such as Ulrich Ochsenbein and his liberal allies spent much of their effort brokering coalitions across cantons, classes, and religious boundaries
- *central co-optation or elimination of previously autonomous political intermediaries*: as Catholic resistance stiffened, previously autonomous cantonal authorities opted increasingly for the federation
- *bureaucratic containment of previously autonomous military forces*: to a previously unprecedented degree, cantonal military forces fell under federal control, especially after military mobilization of the Sonderbund in September-October 1847

- *imposition of uniform governmental structures and practices through the government's jurisdiction*: although variability in this regard remained greater in Switzerland than in most other countries, the war mobilization of 1847 and (especially) the peace settlement of 1848 produced dramatic increases in uniformity
- *mobilization-repression-bargaining cycles during which currently excluded actors act collectively in ways that threaten survival of the government and/or its ruling classes, governmental repression fails, struggle ensues, and settlements concede political standing and/or rights to mobilized actors*: we can reasonably see the entire period from 1830 to 1848 as cycle after cycle in precisely this form

The only strong exception to our inventory of likely democracy-promoting mechanisms is the absence from Switzerland at the national scale in this period of extraction-resistance-bargaining cycles – sequences during which governmental agents demand resources under control of nongovernmental networks and committed to nongovernmental ends, holders of those resources resist, struggle ensues, and settlements emerge in which people yield resources but receive credible guarantees with respect to constraints on future extraction. Although such cycles occurred later in Swiss history, between 1830 and 1848 Swiss national authorities had their hands full simply keeping the federation together, without imposing new taxes, widespread military service, or confiscation of property.

It goes almost without saying that confrontation, conquest, and revolution, if not colonization, all figured significantly in the democratization of Swiss politics, and created their effects through acceleration of the same causal mechanisms that had been reshaping Switzerland from the late 18th century. Confrontation between various radical-liberal-Protestant coalitions and their chiefly Catholic opponents repeatedly shook the system and eventually led to a settlement in which each side gave up advantages to remain in a larger union. Revolutionary situations of dual power repeatedly opened up within cantons and across the federation as a whole, and the revolutionary split of 1845 to 1847 yielded a substantial transfer of power.

Reviewing a recent book on Swiss democracy in his address to France's Academy of Moral and Political Sciences on 15 January 1848 (hence while negotiations over the Swiss peace settlement were just beginning), Tocqueville declared that the book's true title should have been "on the democratic revolution in Switzerland." Switzerland, Tocqueville continued,

has been undergoing revolution for 15 years. Democracy there is less a regular form of government than a weapon that people have used to destroy, and now and then to defend, the old society. We can certainly discern in Switzerland the special phenomena that attend the revolutionary condition in the present democratic era, but cannot draw from it a portrait of stable, calm democracy. (Tocqueville 1983: 637)

But the Swiss revolution coupled with conquest. The Sonderbund ended with military occupation of Catholic cantons by their mainly Protestant neighbors and a peace settlement in the shadow of military defeat. These shocks promoted democratization by activating the same mechanisms – insulation of categorical inequalities from public politics, integration of previously shielded trust networks into governmental activity, formation of cross-class coalitions, and so on – that had incrementally transformed Swiss political life long before 1847.

One could, of course, tell a tale of Swiss democratization as the outcome of canny negotiation among representatives of the civil war's victorious and defeated powers during the winter and spring of 1848. One could also, in contrast, treat Swiss democratization as an inevitable long-term expression of Swiss civic culture, with only the precise path of institution building open to contingency. One could, finally, press an interpretation of Swiss democratization as a characteristic by-product of advancing capitalism. The troubled history we have reviewed, however, makes clear that the formation of 1848's limited democracy resulted from widespread popular contention.

Military, diplomatic, and popular confrontations from 1830 through 1847 came close to shattering the Swiss federation forever. Switzerland could easily have split into two separate countries, one mainly Protestant, the other almost entirely Catholic. It could also have split into multiple clusters of cantons, some of which would have most likely ended up incorporated into adjacent states as Italy, Germany, Austria, and France all organized or reorganized their territories after 1848. But Switzerland survived as a direct result of its war settlement.

Creation of democratic institutions at a national scale, far from simply adapting smaller scale democratic practices, occurred through partial curtailment of the consultative forms that had governed public life in most cantons. The shock of civil war accelerated transformations of inequality, trust networks, and public politics that had been occurring sporadically for half a century. Swiss citizenship and democracy, with all their limitations, emerged as contingent products of popular struggle.

Switzerland in Perspective

The Swiss experience by itself raises serious doubts about any possibility of a standard sequence by which regimes move from undemocratic to democratic rule. As compared with the Low Countries, Iberia, France, and the British Isles, Switzerland shows that it is possible – if difficult – for democratization to occur along a weak state trajectory. Placed in comparative perspective, the country's history during the 1830s and 1840s makes its own special case for this book's major arguments:

1. *Differing combinations of coercion, capital, and commitment in various regions promote the formation of significantly different kinds of regimes, and different directions of regime change, within those regions.* In Switzerland, we see extensive and fairly even accumulations (but relatively little concentration) of coercion, capital, and commitment. The combination produced highly fragmented political regimes and a weak-state path of democratization.

2. *Trajectories of regimes within a two-dimensional space defined by (a) degree of governmental capacity and (b) extent of protected consultation significantly affect both their prospects for democracy and the character of their democracy if it arrives.* Even today, Swiss decentralization, segmentation, and variability make its democratic institutions unique in the world.

3. *In the long run, increases in governmental capacity and protected consultation reinforce each other, as government expansion generates resistance, bargaining, and provisional settlements, on one side, while on the other side protected consultation encourages demands for expansion of government intervention, which promote increases in capacity.* Although the Swiss national state remained weaker vis-à-vis its component cantons and its citizenry than the great bulk of European states, both French conquest and the Sonderbund's outcome promoted increases in central governmental capacity without which no authority could have enforced democratic rights and obligations at a national scale.

4. *At the extremes, where capacity develops farther and faster than consultation, the path to democracy (if any) passes through authoritarianism; if protected consultation develops farther and faster than capacity and the*

regime survives, the path then passes through a risky zone of capacity-building. Switzerland dramatically illustrates the second case and its dangers.

5. *Although the organizational forms – elections, terms of office, areal representation, deliberative assemblies, and so on – adopted by democratizing regimes often emulate or adapt institutions that have strong precedents in villages, cities, regional jurisdictions, or adjacent national regimes, they almost never evolve directly from those institutions.* In fact, direct democracy survived in some municipalities and cantons, but except for such institutions as initiative and referendum the Swiss installed a strictly limited representative democracy at the national level.

6. *Creation of citizenship – rights and obligations linking whole categories of a regime's subject population to governmental agents – is a necessary but not sufficient condition of democratization.* At a national level, with all its peculiarities, Swiss citizenship only formed in 1848, but it then became utterly essential to democratic functioning.

7. *In high-capacity regimes, nondemocratic citizenship sometimes forms, and with extensive integration of citizens into regimes, even reduces or inhibits democracy.* We see examples at various points in the histories of Iberia, France, and the British Isles, but only at the regional levels in the Low Countries and Switzerland.

8. *Nevertheless, the prior presence of citizenship, other things equal, generally facilitates democratization.* Among the national experiences examined so far, France provides the clearest exemplification of this principle. Switzerland illustrates its corollary, the difficulties of creating national democracy without a prior experience of fairly broad, equal citizenship.

9. *Both creation of citizenship and democratization depend on changes in three arenas – categorical inequality, trust networks, and public politics – as well as on interactions among those changes.* Across those experiences, we have seen these changes working as expected in the Low Countries, France, the British Isles, and (in greater detail) Switzerland. The next chapter displays them at work elsewhere in Europe.

10. *Regularities in democratization consist not of standard general sequences or sufficient conditions, but of recurrent causal mechanisms that in varying combinations and sequences produce changes in categorical inequality, networks of trust, public politics, and their interactions.* Taken together, the national experiences reviewed so far deeply challenge any notion of standard general sequences or generally applicable sufficient

conditions. They offer at least plausible support for the efficacy of the mechanisms in our inventory.

11. *Under specifiable circumstances, revolution, conquest, confrontation, and colonization accelerate and concentrate some of those crucial causal mechanisms.* In the Low Countries, France, the British Isles, and Switzerland, we have clearly seen such crises accelerating standard democracy-promoting mechanisms. The next chapter shows that they had similar accelerating effects in Iberia and elsewhere.

12. *Almost all crucial democracy-promoting causal mechanisms involve popular contention – politically constituted actors' making of public, collective claims on other actors, including agents of government – as correlates, causes, and effects.* Whatever else the histories reviewed here have established, they have certainly demonstrated intimate connections between democratization and popular contention.

13. *In the course of democratization, repertoires of contention (arrays of widely available claim-making performances) shift from predominantly parochial, particular, and bifurcated interactions based largely on embedded identities to predominantly cosmopolitan, modular, and autonomous interactions based largely on detached identities.* Quite rapidly in Switzerland, more irregularly in the other countries, just such a change commonly occurred, with the standard forms of social movements becoming prevalent as democratization advanced.

In all these regards, then, Switzerland's turbulent experience between 1830 and 1848 supports the book's major arguments. Placing Switzerland in comparison with the Low Countries, Iberia, France, and Great Britain, however, adds three further principles to the original set:

14. *So long as military forces retain extensive political autonomy, democratization does not advance.* In very different ways, the Low Countries, Iberia, France, the British Isles, and Switzerland all illustrate the hindrance to democratization set by politically autonomous military units, including both local militias and national armies. Such units provide their members and patrons with almost irresistible means of pursuing advantages by undemocratic means.

15. *Inscription of religious identities into public politics – especially exclusion of whole categories from full citizenship on religious grounds – likewise constitutes an almost impenetrable barrier to democratization.* Although we might interpret the Low Countries and Switzerland as countries that invented compromises and subterfuges to retain a degree of

religious inscription, on the whole our cases strongly support the new generalization.

16. *Relations with other countries and with the international system as a whole repeatedly affect the path and timing of democratization or de-democratization.* Wars and adjacent revolutions make the point most strongly, but every one of our histories displays incessant interaction between domestic political processes and external actors. International concentration of democratization and de-democratization in periods of extensive war and revolution underlines the importance of this set of external effects.

It is therefore time to step back for a larger look at the whole range of democratization and de-democratization in Europe during the 19th and 20th centuries. Chapter 7 takes on that assignment.

Appendix 6.1: A Chronology of Contentious Politics in Switzerland, 1830–1848

1830, 4 July	Reformist constitution in Ticino
1830, July	Revolution in France
1830, fall	Throughout Switzerland, except Neuchâtel (member of federation, but ruled by King of Prussia) and Basel: clubs, local public meetings, pamphleteering, petitions, press campaigns, and marches to cantonal capitals on behalf of cantonal elections for constituent assemblies by manhood suffrage
1830, fall	Elections of constituent assemblies
1831, Jan.	Basel: armed uprising of country people against urban domination, put down by cantonal troops
1831, Jan.–March	Meetings of assemblies, enactments of new cantonal constitutions, generally asserting popular sovereignty and declaring civil liberties but restricting suffrage significantly by property, education, gender, and age
1831, 13 Sept.	Neuchâtel: after overlord king of Prussia grants moderate constitution, republicans attempt to seize power by force of arms, but Swiss federal executive, fearing external intervention, sends troops to put them down
1831–32	Bitter political struggles between radicals and conservatives in Basel, ending in split of Basel into two

	half-cantons, central city vs. rural areas; on 14 May 1832 the rural half-canton adopts a broadly democratic constitution
1832	Schwyz: communes of canton's dependent territories declare themselves an independent half-canton, only to receive military occupation by Innerschwyz; federal authorities broker a new constitution enfranchising outer territories
1832, July	Appointment of commission to revise the federal constitution (strictly speaking, the Pact)
1833, March	After liberal cantons attempt to force revision of the federal pact of 1815 through the Diet, cantonal authorities of Schwyz send troops to repress liberals and radicals in the neighborhood of Küssnacht, Outer Schwyz; Diet calls up 16,000 troops to advance on Küssnacht, Schwyz troops withdraw; separation of Schwyz into two half-cantons becomes definitive
1833, July–Aug.	Basel: rural uprising against city's dominance; battle (3 August) at Pratteln in which country people suffer five deaths and Basel troops fifty-four
1834, Jan.	Armed band including Mazzini raids Carouge (Savoy) and sacks customs post, but is overwhelmed by Geneva police
1834	Liberals from seven cantons meet to plan anticlerical program, then propose to create cantonal councils; liberal clergy stop movement, but "unrest" in Aargau brings in troops from neighboring cantons
1836	Glarus: after new constitution abolishes separate Protestant and Catholic Landsgemeinden, Catholics try to hold their own separate assembly, but federal occupation of communes Näfels and Oberurnen ends Catholic resistance
1838	Half-canton of Outer Schwyz: Landsgemeinde of Rothenthurm breaks up in brawl between supporters of Hooves (small peasant liberals) and Horns (large peasant conservatives)
1839, Feb.–Sept.	Zürich: when by a bare majority the cantonal education council appoints to the university a liberal theologian (David Friedrich Strauss of Tübingen),

	committees of protest form throughout the hinterland, and localities send petitions; Zürich authorities pension off Strauss before he begins teaching
1839	Valais: when liberals (mainly from Lower Valais) try to force a new constitution through the Diet of Sion, conservatives (mainly from Upper Valais) withdraw and form their own separate government at Sierre
1839, 6 Sept.	Zürich: 1,500 armed country people assemble and march to town singing hymns, scuffle with government troops, and finally disperse
1840	Valais: troops from Upper and Lower Valais confront each other before settlement backed by federal Diet reunifies cantonal government
1841, Jan.	Aargau: cantonal authorities decree suppression of convents, Catholics storm the capital under arms and are repelled by government troops; Swiss Diet brokers compromise reopening nunneries, but not houses of male orders
1841	Lucerne: newly elected Legislative Assembly asks Jesuits to take over secondary education; widespread demands in Protestant cantons for expulsion of Jesuits, formation of anti-Jesuit societies
1842, fall	Free corps (*Freischaren*) of volunteers form and attempt military expeditions against Lucerne
1844, May	Valais: after cantonal government asks Lucerne authorities to intervene against adherents of Young Switzerland in Lower Valais, inhabitants of region ambush emissary (Bernhard Meyer) on his way to deliver decree against them
1844	Basel: national shooting festival occasion for manifestations (speeches, cheers, etc.) by Catholics and (especially) radicals
1844, 8 Dec.	Lucerne: a "few hundred" men in armed bands from Zürich and elsewhere head for the city to overthrow the government, but give up en route; in the city, radical anti-Jesuit "riot" is put down by government forces
1845, spring	Musters of free corps in a number of rural locations
1845, March	Skirmishes between free corps and government troops

1845, 31 March	Canton of Lucerne: 3,600 radical volunteers (*Freischärler*) enter from Aargau under command of Bernese Ulrich Ochsenbein (former member of Mazzini's Young Europe) and march to capital, where government troops repel them, killing 105 (or 115) and jailing 1785; Lucerne celebrates with a religious procession
1845, spring	Lucerne: petition campaign to save Jacob Steiger, military leader of the March raid, from Lucerne's death penalty; when Steiger escapes from his prison in Savoy, there are widespread radical celebrations, and honorary citizenship for Steiger in Zürich and Bern
1845	Lausanne: mass march of country people to government building, demanding removal of conservative council; radical leader takes over
1845, Dec.	Catholic cantons (Lucerne, Uri, Schwyz, Unterwald, Zug, Fribourg, Valais) form a mutual defense league (*Sonderbund*) and approach Austrian, Sardinian, and French governments for aid
1846, July	Bern adopts a new constitution strengthening state powers and broadening political participation, thus increasing the radicals' power
1847	Widespread mobilization of Catholics: pilgrimages to saints' tombs, collective attendance at masses
1847, spring	Geneva: popular uprising (radical-led peasants, artisans, and factory workers); after arrest of leaders, streets are barricaded against conservative-liberal militia; radical-dominated provisional government comes to power and enacts more democratic constitution
1847, spring	Radical coup d'état in Lausanne displaces conservative militia and government
1847, spring	Elections favorable to radicals elsewhere
1847, spring	Fribourg: failed radical coup attempt
1847, July	Diet (by 12 votes to 10) demands dissolution of Sonderbund
1847, 10 Oct.	Valais: voters approve canton's adhesion to Sonderbund

1847, 4 Nov.	Diet orders dissolution of Sonderbund by force of arms, mobilizes cantonal troops, and begins military operations under General Dufour, relatively moderate veteran of Bavarian and Dutch armies
1847, 14 Nov.	Fribourg surrenders to Dufour
1847, 22 Nov.	Zug capitulates without a fight; Dufour proceeds to Lucerne, where general exit of authorities begins
1847, 24 Nov.	Dufour attacks Lucerne, which surrenders; Sonderbund collapses after minor skirmishes elsewhere (e.g., Schwyz, 26 Nov.)
1847, 29 Nov.	End of hostilities; within the next few days, federal troops occupy all Sonderbund cantons, including Valais
1847, 7 Dec.	Diet refuses French offer of mediation, rejects all intervention in settlement by external powers
1848	New Swiss constitution approved by referendum establishes federal government (bicameral assembly, Federal Council, Federal Tribunal), divides sovereignty between federal government and cantons, and establishes federal citizenship including rights of mobility and settlement throughout the state
1848, Feb.	On news of February revolution in Paris, democratic force invades Neuchâtel (Neuenburg) from Chaux de Fonds and establishes republican regime on 2 March
1848, April	Referendum in Neuchâtel endorses republican constitution 5,800 to 4,400; rejected by Prussian king
1848, April	Canton of Basel: when Johann Ludwig Becker starts recruiting a German Legion to support revolutionaries in Baden, federal government sends troops to seal borders with Baden and Alsace
1848	As German revolutions begin in March, German workers in Switzerland meet and organize in support, eventually forming military forces to support revolutionary activity in various German territories

7

Democracy and Other Regimes in Europe, 1815–2000

The New York–based monitoring agency Freedom House employs an undemanding definition of democracy: civilian government competitively elected by general adult suffrage. By that standard, Freedom House retrospectively scores none of the world's 55 independent national regimes as democratic in 1900; suffrage restrictions by gender and/or property then applied in every representative regime. It evaluates 22 of 80 regimes as democratic in 1950, and 121 of 192 as democratic in 2001 (Freedom House 2002: charts; Karatnycky 2000: 7–9). For the world as a whole, it thereby claims modest democratization between 1900 and 1950, followed by enormous democratization during the 20th century's second half.

The 121 regimes Freedom House rated democratic in 2001 on the basis of competitive elections, however, included such divided, violent places as Bangladesh, Benin, Colombia, Fiji, Georgia, Haiti, the Kyrgyz Republic, Liberia, Mongolia, Niger, Sierra Leone, and Sri Lanka. None of these regimes then scored very high on our more demanding criteria of broad and equal relations with governmental agents, exercise of collective control over governmental personnel, policies, and resources, and enjoyment of protection from arbitrary action by agents of government. The world still has a long way to go before most regimes install broad, equal, protective, and effective democratic consultation. When it comes to Freedom House ratings, democracy is obviously a matter of degree.

Perhaps recognizing the inadequacy of competitive elections as the litmus test for democracy, Freedom House also makes more refined ratings of political rights and civil liberties. In that dual scheme, countries run from 1 (high) to 7 (low) on each of the two. Table 7.1 lists the questions that raters are supposed to ask about each regime. Although we might quibble with the checklist's neglect of such matters as arbitrary taxation, official

Democracy and Other Regimes in Europe, 1815–2000

Table 7.1 *Freedom House Checklist for Political Rights and Civil Liberties*

Political Rights

1. Is the head of state and/or head of government or other chief authority elected through free and fair elections?
2. Are the legislative representatives elected through free and fair elections?
3. Are there fair electoral laws, equal campaigning opportunities, fair polling, and honest tabulations of ballots?
4. Are the voters able to endow their freely elected representatives with real power?
5. Do the people have the right to organize in different political parties or other competitive political groupings of their choice, and is the system open to the rise and fall of these competing parties or groupings?
6. Is there a significant opposition vote, de facto opposition power, and a realistic possibility for the opposition to increase its support or gain power through elections?
7. Are the people free from domination by the military, foreign powers, totalitarian parties, religious hierarchies, economic oligarchies, or any other powerful group?
8. Do cultural, ethnic, religious, and other minority groups have reasonable self-determination, self-government, autonomy, or participation through informal consensus in the decision-making process?
9. (Discretionary) For traditional monarchies that have no parties or electoral process, does the system provide for consultation with the people, encourage discussion of policy, and allow the right to petition the ruler?
10. (Discretionary) Is the government or occupying power deliberately changing the ethnic composition of a country or territory so as to destroy a culture or tip the political balance in favor of another group?

Civil Liberties

1. Is there freedom of assembly, demonstration, and open public discussion?
2. Is there freedom of political or quasi-political organization, including political parties, civic organizations, ad hoc issue groups, etc.?
3. Are there free trade unions and peasant organizations or equivalents, and is there effective collective bargaining? Are there free professional and other private organizations?
4. Is there an independent judiciary?
5. Does the rule of law prevail in civil and criminal matters? Is the population treated equally under the law? Are police under direct civilian control?
6. Is there protection from political terror, unjustified imprisonment, exile, or torture, whether by groups that support or oppose the system? Is there freedom from war and insurgencies?
7. Is there freedom from extreme government indifference and corruption?
8. Is there open and free private discussion?

(continued)

Table 7.1 *(continued)*

9. Is there personal autonomy? Does the state control travel, choice of residence, or choice of employment? Is there freedom from indoctrination and excessive dependency on the state?
10. Are property rights secure? Do citizens have the right to establish private businesses? Is private business activity unduly influenced by government officials, the security forces, or organized crime?
11. Are there personal social freedoms, including gender equality, choice of marriage partners, and size of family?
12. Is there equality of opportunity, including freedom from exploitation by or dependency on landlords, employers, union leaders, bureaucrats, or other types of obstacles to a share of legitimate economic gains?

Source: Adapted from Karatnycky 2000: 584–85.

corruption, and unequal liability to military service, Freedom House's questions cover the conventional range of democratic rights and liberties. The more emphatically raters can say "yes" to its array of twenty questions, the more extensive the regime's political rights and civil liberties. In the Freedom House procedures, knowledgeable raters assign values from 0 to 4 for each required question, temper the scores with judgments about special circumstances, then combine them into overall assessments.

Our reviews of Ireland and Switzerland have already shown us that even countries receiving a score of 1 on rights and 1 on liberties – as both did in 2001 – fall well short of complete democracy. Implicitly, raters are comparing regimes with each other rather than applying strict absolute standards to individual cases. Take, for example, question 7 under political rights: *Are the people free from domination by the military, foreign powers, totalitarian parties, religious hierarchies, economic oligarchies, or any other powerful group?* Construed strictly, the question would produce a "no" answer for every country in the world; everywhere, after all, "powerful groups" dominate significant segments of the population. Again, question 11 under civil liberties sets a very demanding standard: *Are there personal social freedoms, including gender equality, choice of marriage partners, and size of family?* By a strict reading of the question, no actual country could qualify. We should therefore imagine these ratings as taking place in relation to other really existing regimes. As compared with, say, citizens of tyrannical Burma, citizens of Russia enjoy at least a modicum of political rights and civil liberties. With that understanding, Freedom House rankings of European regimes do resemble those that we might assign for protected consultation if we had reliable, distinct measures of breadth, equality, consultation, and protection.

Ratings for rights emphasize breadth, equality, and consultation, while ratings for liberties emphasize protection. Change in the quantity (rights × liberties) therefore provides a rough measure of democratization (positive) and de-democratization (negative). Thus Freedom House rated Hungary 6 on rights and 6 on liberties in 1973, for a combined score of $6 \times 6 = 36$, while Hungary received 1 and 2 in 2001, for a $1 \times 2 = 2$, scoring an impressive $36 - 2 = 34$ for democratization between 1973 and 2001. Meanwhile, between 1991 and 2001, Russia (not rated separately before 1991) went from $3 \times 3 = 9$ to $5 \times 5 = 25$, for a resounding de-democratization score of -16.

In 2001, Freedom House classified every European country except Belarus, Bosnia-Herzegovina, and Yugoslavia – the three regimes outlined in Figure 7.1 – as democratic. All but the three pariahs featured civilian governments competitively elected by general adult suffrage. But Freedom House's evaluators introduced much more variation into ratings of political rights and civil liberties. Figure 7.1 arrays the ratings for forty-three European political units, from tiny to huge. Sixteen of them received the highest possible rating: 1 on political rights and 1 on civil liberties. Andorra, Austria, Greek Cyprus, Denmark, Finland, Iceland, Ireland, Liechtenstein, Luxembourg, Malta, the Netherlands, Norway, Portugal, San Marino, Sweden, and Switzerland all qualified for the highest possible grades on political rights and civil liberties. Fourteen otherwise democratic countries received ratings of 1, 2. All were experiencing major ethnic conflicts and/or visible political discrimination against minorities. In fact, they included all the larger democracies. In the language of this book, they offered fairly broad, equal, and binding political rights, but faltered somewhat when it came to protection.

No European regime, according to Freedom House evaluations, quite traveled in the company of Afghanistan, Burma, Cuba, Iraq, North Korea, Libya, Saudi Arabia, Sudan, Syria, and Turkmenistan. All those non-European regimes scored at the bottom of the Freedom House scale: a bottom-scraping 7 for political rights, another abysmal 7 for civil liberties. But among European countries Belarus (6, 6) stood close to the bottom, while Moldova, Yugoslavia, Albania, Bosnia-Herzegovina, Macedonia, Ukraine, Turkey, and Russia all remained outside the privileged zone of regimes having extensive political rights and civil liberties.

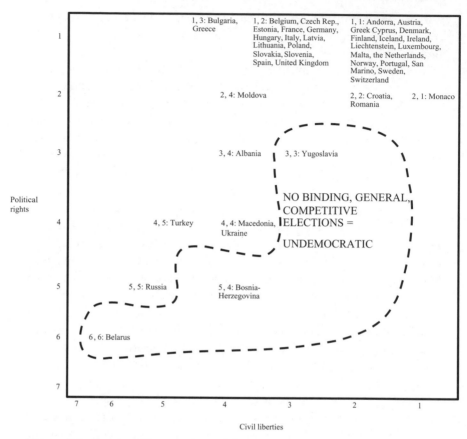

Figure 7.1: Freedom House ratings of European countries on political rights and civil liberties, 2001. *Source:* Compiled from Freedom House 2002.

Except for Turkey, as of 2001 all the low-ranking European countries had recently shed state socialist regimes. Among the regimes that had still styled themselves socialist or communist in 1989, the Czech Republic, Estonia, Hungary, Latvia, Lithuania, Poland, Slovakia, Slovenia, and – more dubiously – Croatia and Romania had as of 2001 moved away from their fellows by installing ostensibly democratic institutions. The political problems of Belarus, Bosnia-Herzegovina, Macedonia, Ukraine, Yugoslavia, Moldova, and Russia did not stem, however, from too much socialism. They had all stuck with, or slid into, locations in our capacity-protection space ranging from petty tyranny to authoritarianism. Tyrants small and large blocked their ways to breadth, equality, protection, and binding consultation. Many of those tyrants had, of course, survived from socialist

210

regimes. Yet their commitment to socialism did not hold back their countries from democratization; their tyrannies did.

Despite the current incompleteness of European democratization, the continent as a whole traveled an impressive distance within the capacity-protection space between 1650 and 2001. With respect to internal governmental capacity – control over resources, activities, and persons within their territories – even the least effective European states today deploy capacity surpassing that of 1650's titans. The bulk of Europe's regimes have also moved well into the terrain of protected consultation. Relative both to the rest of the world and to their own pasts, most European regimes now feature fairly broad, equal, binding consultation and protection. With the European Union, nongovernmental organizations and international agencies all pulling in the same direction, furthermore, we are likely to see more and more European regimes adopting at least the outward ornaments of democracy. What happened? What is now happening?

Previous chapters built an armature for answers to those questions. Analyses of the Low Countries, Iberia, France, Britain, and Switzerland indicated that moves within the capacity-protection space generally occurred as a consequence of contentious politics. They made a general case that broad patterns of struggle varied according to the intersections of coercion, capital, and commitment in different parts of Europe. They suggested that extreme values on any one of the three – coercion, capital, or commitment – hindered democratization. They identified significant shifts in the character of claim-making repertoires over the course of democratization, with the increasing prevalence of cosmopolitan, modular, and autonomous performances corresponding to social movement logics and the expansion of citizenship. They argued a broad shift from embedded to detached identities as the basis of public political claim making, which likewise corresponded to social movement politics and expanding citizenship.

For the histories of France and the British Isles from 1650 to 2000, then more narrowly for Switzerland between 1830 and 1848, earlier chapters also claimed that alterations in the articulation of trust networks with public politics, in the insulation of categorical inequalities from public politics, and in the internal dynamics of public politics promoted democratization and de-democratization in predictable ways. Mechanisms promoting democratization included those that

1. equalized wealth, income, power, and prestige across major categories of the population

2. buffered politics from categorical inequality
3. dissolved trust networks that were insulated from public politics
4. created politically connected trust networks
5. directly broadened political participation
6. equalized political participation
7. enhanced collective control over government by political participants, and/or
8. inhibited the arbitrary exercise of power by governmental agents

More or less symmetrically, inverse mechanisms – for example, proliferation of trust networks outside the realm of public politics – promoted de-democratization. Mechanism clusters 1 and 2 operated on categorical inequality, 3 and 4 on trust networks. Clusters 5 through 8 acted directly on public politics, and thence a bit more indirectly on relations between citizens and governmental agents.

Earlier chapters indicated further that revolution, conquest, confrontation, and colonization produced their effects on democratization and de-democratization through acceleration of the same sorts of changes in trust networks, categorical inequality, and public politics that caused more incremental shifts toward or away from democracy. Close comparison of France, the British Isles, and Switzerland, furthermore, brought out the importance of rearrangements in military and religious institutions as causes of democratization and de-democratization.

By now we know that all of Europe's transitions into democratic territory before 1815 reversed significantly during the Napoleonic Wars. In the short run, war promoted authoritarianism or petty tyranny by reversing mechanisms within bundles 5 through 8 above. At war's end, we might think of the British Isles as hovering on the brink of democracy. Yet even in Britain the Irish experience, a narrow electorate, exclusion of large religious categories from public office, and stringent controls on association and assembly left over from wartime repression should all give us pause. Parts of the Low Countries, France, and some territories conquered by French forces had passed through democratic moments before 1800, but authoritarian rule had returned where petty tyranny or open civil war had not prevailed. By either the weak version (contested elections) or the strong version (political rights × civil liberties) of Freedom House's criteria, no European regime of 1815 qualified as democratic. Let us therefore take 1815 as a baseline for the development of European democracies. How did Europe move from various degrees of authoritarianism and petty tyranny in 1815 to the fairly extensive democratization of 2001?

The current chapter does not take up this question with the detail previously supplied for France, the British Isles, and Switzerland. It asks instead whether broad variations in timing and trajectories of democratization or de-democratization elsewhere in Europe are consistent with the answers proposed in earlier chapters.

A Rough Map of European Democratization

As a first sketch of what we must explain, Daniele Caramani's heroic compilation of European experience with suffrage and elections (2000) disciplines our inquiry. (Caramani describes his scope as Western Europe, but his elastic boundaries for the region include Norway, Italy, Spain, Sweden, Iceland, Finland, Portugal, and Greece while excluding a number of other countries in between.) For eighteen political units (not all of which existed as autonomous states in 1815, and all of which shifted boundaries at least a bit after then), Caramani provides a wealth of information on suffrage. He distinguishes representation of whole classes through estates and similar institutions from general parliamentary representation, which means selection of deputies to a national assembly by an electorate, however large or small. Leaving aside discontinued earlier trials such as the French national assembly of 1789, Figure 7.2 marks with the letter "A" the start of continuous parliamentary representation. The "B" and "C" of Figure 7.2 signpost the establishment of general male suffrage, and general female suffrage, respectively.

We can of course question Caramani's dates. Norway did not gain independence from Sweden – and thereby acquire a truly independent national Parliament – until 1905. Although Finland did, indeed, install a democratic constitution in 1906, it remained part of the Russian Empire until 1917, and did not start operating as an independent democracy until after the civil war of 1917–18 (Alapuro 1988). Louis Napoleon used a wide array of devices to compromise the manhood suffrage a revolutionary assembly had passed in 1848, so we might well date France's effective manhood suffrage in the early Third Republic. Italy as such did not become a unified country until 1870, so that dating continuous parliamentary representation from Piedmont's reforms of 1848 might seem premature. We might also wonder whether 20th-century intervals of authoritarian

Country	1810	1820	1830	1840	1850	1860	1870	1880	1890	1900	1910	1920	1930	1940	1950	1960	1970
United Kingdom		A									B	C					
Switzerland			AB														C
Norway	A									B	C						
Belgium		A							B					C			
Luxembourg				A							BC						
The Netherlands				A							B	C					
Italy				A							B			C			
Denmark				A							BC						
Spain					AB												C
France			B				A							C			
Germany			B				A				C						
Sweden						A					B	C					
Iceland							A				BC						
Austria								B	A			C					
Finland										ABC							
Portugal											AB						C
Ireland											B	AC					
Greece			B								A					C	

Decade beginning in:

Figure 7.2: Representation and suffrage in selected European countries. A: Start of continuous parliamentary representation; B: first manhood suffrage; C: first general female suffrage. *Source:* Compiled from Caramani 2000: 52–53.

regimes in Italy, Germany, Spain, France, and elsewhere interrupted parliamentary rule so thoroughly as to require new starting points after World War II. Nevertheless, Caramani's datings generally mark durable advances in representation as plausibly as any single alternatives we might propose.

The three minority cases where manhood suffrage preceded a continuously functioning representative assembly – France, Germany, and (most dramatically) Greece – all resulted from moments in the revolutions of the 1840s when new regimes temporarily installed both representative legislatures and general male suffrage, but authoritarian regimes then took over, sapping legislative power without eliminating elections. In France, as Chapter 4 reported, Louis Napoleon cut back the National Assembly with his 1851 coup, but did not quite dare to reinstate property qualifications for male suffrage.

In Germany, one might date parliamentary government from as early as 1808, since that is when Prussia established elections to a national assembly through a broad (but still property-restricted) male electorate. During the temporary unification of 1848 a German Union Bundestag adopted suffrage for independent adult males, although individual German states retained the right to define "independent" and "adult." Nevertheless, Caramani reasonably dates continuous parliamentary rule for Germany as a whole from German unification in 1871.

In Greece, the revolutionaries who wrested independence from the Ottoman Empire during the 1820s temporarily established a representative assembly chosen through manhood suffrage via an intermediate body of elite electors. But authoritarian regimes soon removed all pretense of popular representation. Greek revolutionaries of 1843 brought back manhood suffrage and initiated a series of virtually powerless legislatures. Given a rocky history of coups and revolutions thereafter, exactly when we place the beginning of continuous parliamentary rule in Greece remains arbitrary, but Caramani's choice of 1926 plausibly marks the point at which the first legislature after the monarchy's abolition (1924) came to power through popular elections.

The timetables in Figure 7.2 make several important points.

- As the orders of points A, B, and C signal, the great majority of Western European countries began parliamentary representation with restricted electorates.
- Manhood suffrage (points B) commonly arrived decades after the initial establishment of parliamentary representation.
- Although a few countries established full male and female suffrage simultaneously, on the whole women got the vote (points C) decades after men.
- The later the establishment of representative government, the shorter the duration of restricted suffrage.
- Transitions in different countries clustered, notably in the 1840s (the revolutions of 1848 and their reformist counterparts) and the 1910s (World War I and its aftermath).

As charted by landmarks of parliamentary representation and suffrage, then, European democratization occurred in fits and starts, concentrating especially in periods of international turmoil. Similar rhythms governed the establishment of workers' rights to organize and strike; both clustered around the revolutions of 1848 and World War I (Ebbinghaus 1995). Parallel changes also occurred in civil rights – speech, press, assembly, and association (Anderson and Anderson 1967: chapter 6). In all these regards, regime crises and bottom-up mobilization converged to extract concessions from existing holders of power.

Among our four democracy-accelerating processes, colonization did not figure very importantly within Europe between 1815 and 2000. But confrontation, conquest, and revolution all played significant parts in surges of European democratization. Confrontation, conquest, and revolution overlapped intensively, for example, during and immediately after World War I. Among European states, Austria, Belgium, Bulgaria, France, Germany, Greece, Italy, Montenegro, Portugal, Romania, Russia, San Marino, Serbia, Turkey, and the United Kingdom all eventually joined the war on one side or the other. The war and its aftermath brought every one of those regimes significant shifts with respect to breadth, equality, consultation, and protection – not to mention overall governmental capacity. The Austro-Hungarian, Ottoman, and Russian empires collapsed. Germany, Hungary, Ireland, and Russia all broke into revolution and/or civil war. Elsewhere, widespread demands for democratization arose. During the decade following World War I, for example, every country in Figure 7.2 that had not done so earlier installed manhood suffrage, and a majority enacted female suffrage as well.

Caramani's compilation understandably omits six small Western and Southern European political units that appear in Freedom House tabulations: Andorra, Greek Cyprus, Liechtenstein, Malta, Monaco, and San Marino. In general, those small polities followed the democratization rhythms of their colonial masters or their close neighbors. Caramani also omits the other twenty-nine Central and Eastern European units Freedom House now rates in its tabulations. Since almost all of those countries maintained state socialist regimes for substantial periods between 1917 and 1991, dating representation and suffrage in their political histories poses delicate problems. For the most part, Europe's socialist regimes instituted broad voting rights and nominally powerful legislatures, but controlled elections rigorously. They also subordinated parliaments to powerful executives backed by omnipresent state parties and security apparatuses. Yet between the world wars, a number of regimes that later installed socialist governments – notably Czechoslovakia, Estonia, Latvia, Lithuania, and Poland – passed through relatively democratic political phases.

Considering the whole range of experiences from 1815 to 2000, we can expand the list of clustered transitions to four: not only the 1840s and World

War I, but also World War II and the collapse of socialist regimes from 1989 onward. World War II ended with a variety of Central and Eastern European regimes moving into fairly undemocratic forms of socialism. But it also brought Germany, Austria, Italy, and France out of authoritarianism into troubled but durable democracy. In the most recent surge, the Soviet Union's collapse and the subsequent splintering of Yugoslavia precipitated power struggles throughout Central and Eastern Europe.

We have no one-way path toward democracy to trace across Europe between 1815 and 2000. Almost every country that moved significantly toward broad, equal, protected consultation during one period or another veered back toward authoritarianism or petty tyranny during some subsequent periods. Europe as a whole provides plenty of variation for examining whether the sorts of mechanisms I have clustered under the headings categorical inequality, trust networks, and public politics do, indeed, cause democratization, and whether their reversals do, indeed, cause de-democratization.

Russia, 1815–2000

To follow Europe's processes of democratization and de-democratization, let us look quickly at three contrasting regional experiences between 1815 and 2000: those of Russia, the Balkans, and Iberia. At the terminus, Russia had not established a working democracy, the Balkans ranged from shaky democratization to emphatically undemocratic regimes, while after multiple earlier reversals of democratization Iberia had spent a quarter of a century in troubled but unreversed democracy. Comparing the three trajectories will not establish whether the critical mechanisms operated in detail as the analyses of France, Britain, and Switzerland suggest, but it will show us whether the differences among them correspond broadly to the implications of this book's arguments. Did contention drive democratization and de-democratization? Did confrontation, conquest, and revolution produce their effects on democratization and de-democratization through acceleration of the same processes that produced incremental moves in the same directions? Did weak-state, strong-state, and intermediate trajectories toward or away from protected consultation differ significantly? At least roughly, the histories of Russia, the Balkans, and Iberia after 1815 conformed to expectations.

In 1815, Russia was emerging battered but nominally victorious from the Napoleonic Wars. From then until 2000, war played a dual role in Russian political history. Russian (and then Soviet) military power expanded over most of the period, generally increasing governmental capacity as it grew. Precisely because of its investment in war, however, the government remained vulnerable to serious setbacks when its military forces failed. At those points, temporary moves toward protected consultation regularly occurred, only to reverse as rulers again established top-down control. Through most of the 19th century the Russian Empire was expanding aggressively northward, eastward, and toward Ottoman territory near the Black Sea. During the 1820s, the empire took pieces of the Caucasus from both Persia and the Ottoman Empire. It faced down serious revolts in its tributary Poland during 1830–31 and 1863–64, emerging strengthened and more repressive from the crises.

Russia lost ground to France, Britain, and the Ottomans, however, with the Crimean War (1853–56). That revelation of the government's fallibility led to widespread demands for domestic reform, to which Tsar Alexander II soon began concessions: administrative changes, emancipation of serfs, and local representative institutions (*zemstvos*). Russia's partial victory in the Russo-Ottoman war of 1877–78 strengthened the tsar's hand, but did not stem the proliferation of subversive political movements, including the terrorists who planted a bomb in St. Petersburg's Winter Palace (1880) and assassinated Russia's interior minister (1881).

Japan's smashing defeat of Russian forces in the Russo-Japanese war of 1904–5 in the midst of rapid Russian industrialization started another cycle of attacks on the government, hesitant reform, and reaction. In this cycle, the popular claim-making repertoire combined the clandestine attacks of 19th-century conspirators with elements of the social movement already familiar in Western Europe. Assassination of interior minister Vyacheslav Plehve (1904) and the Bloody Sunday attack of troops on St. Petersburg workers who were marching to the Winter Palace for presentation of a petition to the tsar (1905) preceded widespread strikes, demonstrations, and mutinies. St. Petersburg workers organized a soviet (council) to organize their action, as workers elsewhere followed suit. The movement's first wave culminated in a general strike (October 1905). Tsar Nicholas II decreed a constitution and called an election of a national assembly (Duma) for 1906.

When Prime Minister Sergei Witte consolidated his position, called back military forces from the Far East, and arrested 190 members of the St. Petersburg soviet, Moscow workers rushed to the streets and battled imperial troops (December-January 1905–6). By the Duma's meeting of May 1906, however, the government had reestablished its repressive apparatus. The tsar's dissolution of the deadlocked Duma in July generated little reaction across the country. Writing from his Swiss exile later that year, Bolshevik leader V. I. Lenin declared:

The principal forms of the December movement in Moscow were the peaceful strike and demonstrations, and these were the only forms of struggle in which the vast majority of the workers took an active part. Yet, the December action in Moscow vividly demonstrated that the general strike, as an independent and predominant form of struggle, is out of date, that the movement is breaking out of these narrow bounds with elemental and irresistible force and giving rise to the highest form of struggle – an uprising. (Lenin 1967: I, 577)

Another temporary surge toward protected consultation had ended in re-action. Lenin saw the next step as a popular insurrection with revolutionary possibilities.

The next temporary cycle of democratization and reaction made its pre-decessors look like fleeting summer storms. When World War I began, the Russian Empire included the territories we now know as Finland, the Baltic states, Belarus, Ukraine, and eastern Poland. Its long western borders joined those of its enemies, Germany and Austria-Hungary. The Eastern Front's major battles of 1914–16 took place mainly in Polish territory and the Baltic region. Significant defeats in the south (Galicia and Bukovina) during 1915 made Russian military vulnerability more visible. In 1916, German forces promoted uprisings against Russian rule and announced creation of an in-dependent Polish state. As Russian armies retreated, soldiers deserted in growing numbers, workers struck increasingly, and public opposition to the tsarist regime swelled.

Before the war, St. Petersburg served as Russia's capital and major link to Western Europe via the nearby Baltic. At the war's start, the tsar changed his capital's name to Petrograd, which sounded less German than St. Petersburg. Petrograd's ungrateful citizens, however, spearheaded op-position to the tsar's regime. In early 1917, the city's workers mounted huge strikes, which soon led to a general mutiny of the capital's troops. In March, the Duma answered an imperial order to dissolve by establishing a provisional government. Tsar Nicholas abdicated in favor of his brother Michael, who soon abdicated as well. All this happened against a background of strikes, street fighting, and factional maneuvering.

As Leon Trotsky later reconstructed the situation in his brilliant *History of the Russian Revolution*,

The struggle in the capital lasted not an hour, or two hours, but five days. The leaders tried to hold it back; the masses answered with increased pressure and marched forward. They had against them the old state, behind whose traditional façade a mighty power was still assumed to exist, the liberal bourgeoisie with the State Duma, the Land and City Unions, the military-industrial organizations, academies, universities, a highly developed press, and finally the two strong socialist parties who put up a patriotic resistance to the assault from below. In the party of the Bolsheviks the insurrection had its nearest organization, but a headless organization with a scattered staff and with weak illegal nuclei. And nevertheless the revolution, which nobody in those days was expecting, unfolded, and just when it seemed from above as though the movement was already dying down, with an abrupt revival, a mighty convulsion, it seized the victory. (Trotsky 1965: 164)

In Petrograd about 1,500 people died, more than half of them soldiers on one side or the other. The Duma set in place a provisional government of liberals and conservatives, but soon faced determined opposition from another Petrograd soviet of workers' and soldiers' deputies. The soviet organized committees in factories and army units that began to act together as a countergovernment.

Leftist social democrats bulked large in the soviets and the committees, but an earlier split had produced two rival parties within social democracy: the relatively accommodationist Mensheviks (meaning "minority") and the more radical Bolsheviks ("majority"). The Bolsheviks gained strength day by day. A first revolutionary situation (undermining of the tsar) gave way to a second (struggle between the Provisional Government and its soviet-based opposition). All this happened in March 1917. During April and May, Radical leaders such as Lenin and Trotsky began returning to Russia from exile. The revolutionary situation mutated rapidly as Bolsheviks organized opposition to the Provisional Government and the Mensheviks within it. Parallel soviets were organized in Moscow and elsewhere, including army units, factories, and peasant communities across the land. A number of former left Mensheviks, including Trotsky, joined the Bolsheviks. Nevertheless, a Bolshevik bid to seize control of the government by force in July 1917 failed, sending Lenin back into exile and Trotsky to prison.

The surviving government itself split over how to deal with the Bolsheviks. When newly appointed Prime Minister Alexander Kerensky dismissed hard-line Commander-in-Chief Lavr Kornilov, the dismissed commander tried unsuccessfully to execute a coup. Kerensky switched direction, releasing the imprisoned Bolsheviks and calling for Petrograd's workers to save the revolution. From that point onward, the Bolsheviks and their allies the peasant-based Social Revolutionaries gained strength steadily. When Kerensky again tried to shut down the Bolshevik newspaper *Pravda* ("Truth") and arrest Petrograd's radical leaders on 5 November,

Trotsky and the Bolsheviks returned to open resistance. On 6 and 7 November, Bolsheviks and Social Revolutionaries drove out the Provisional Government and seized power. Lenin emerged from hiding in the Petrograd suburbs to join Trotsky in leading the new regime. Kerensky fled to organize resistance at the front, his magnificent touring sedan protected by a car from the American embassy flying an American flag. The events of 6 and 7 November constitute the centerpiece of the Bolshevik Revolution (24–25 October in the old Russian calendar).

Late on 7 November, a turbulent meeting of the national Congress of Soviets in Petrograd endorsed the Bolshevik coup, but with bitter dissent in its midst. The workers' and soldiers' soviets found themselves being cut out from central power, while peasants had hardly any voice at all. American radical journalist John Reed, whose *Ten Days That Shook the World* offered his eyewitness account of the October Revolution, described the scene:

Always the methodical muffled boom of cannon through the windows, and the delegates, screaming at each other.... So, with the crash of artillery, in the dark, with hatred and fear, and reckless daring, new Russia was being born. (Reed 1977: 100)

In power, the Bolsheviks faced serious challenges. The war went on, as independence movements and counterrevolutionary armies began forming across much of the empire. Trotsky led the organization of a Bolshevik-dominated military force, the Red Army. At the same time, the new government was trying to collectivize industry, land, and capital. Peasants themselves were seizing land from large estates or their own communities. In largely peasant Russia, November elections for a constituent assembly produced a large majority for the Social Revolutionaries, not the Bolsheviks. When that assembly met in January 1918, Red troops dissolved it immediately. The Bolsheviks had essentially driven out their Social Revolutionary partners and seized sole control of the central government.

Soon after taking power, Trotsky was bargaining out peace terms with the Central Powers at Brest-Litovsk (now in Belarus, near the Polish border). Between the opening of talks (3 December 1917) and the treaty signing (3 March 1918), Russia lost imperial territories Poland, Ukraine, Estonia, Finland, Moldavia, Latvia, Lithuania, Georgia, Armenia, and Azerbaijan, some to local rebellions, others to pressure from the Central Powers. Forces from the Central Powers, moreover, soon invaded different parts of the Russian periphery. Civil war continued into 1920. But a reorganized Red Army, led by Trotsky, eventually reclaimed most of the empire's old territory. The army did not win back Finland, Poland, or the Baltic states. But it did build up to a mighty force of 5 million men by 1920.

Under Trotsky, in collaboration with Lenin, Bolsheviks (by then known as the Communist Party) penetrated and controlled the armed forces. As the army demobilized during the 1920s, a civilian government emerged. Centered on the Communist Party, it incorporated many military veterans into a system of control far more centralized than the tsars had ever managed. After fitful experiments with democratization, the Communists had created an unprecedentedly authoritarian regime.

Soviet Collapse

Yet another war precipitated the Soviet Union's collapse seventy years later. In 1979, a decade before the collapse, Soviet assistance to Afghanistan's left-leaning military coup seemed like just one more Cold War confrontation. But it proved crucial. As the United States poured in support for a variety of Afghan rebels, the Soviet military suffered a frustrating and humiliating stalemate.

Leonid Brezhnev had become Communist Party leader (and thus effective ruler of the Soviet Union) in 1964. He was still in charge fifteen years later, at the age of seventy-three, when the USSR intervened in Afghanistan. Under Brezhnev, the Soviet Union began efforts to stimulate the economy through various forms of decentralization and devolution of power. Brezhnev died in 1982. After a quick shuffle of leaders, liberalizer Mikhail Gorbachev arrived at the party's head in 1985. Gorbachev soon began promoting *perestroika*, a shift of the economy from military to civilian production, toward better and more abundant consumer goods, and in the direction of higher productivity. He also moved hesitantly into a program of opening up public life *(glasnost)*: releasing political prisoners, accelerating exit visas for Jews, shrinking the military, reducing the Soviet Union's external military involvement, and ending violent repression of demands for political, ethnic, and religious autonomy. In terms of this book's scheme, he concentrated on increasing protection more than on securing breadth, equality, or binding consultation.

Reduction of central controls over production, distribution, and public politics eventually promoted a whole series of strong effects across the Soviet Union. Most of the effects came as surprises to their initiators. In the hard times of previous Soviet regimes, citizens had spun vast webs of barter, contraband, mutual aid, and unauthorized influence – trust networks segregated from public politics – in the regime's shadows. Those networks made survival possible in the presence of shortage and rigid bureaucracy. As the regime collapsed, they emerged into the light, mutated, and often became the bases of new commitments (Humphrey 1999, 2001; Johnson, Kaufman, and Ustenko 1998; Ledeneva 1998; Lonkila 1999; Volkov 2002; Woodruff 1999).

The years after 1985 also brought proliferation of small firms and attempts to set up joint ventures with foreign capitalists. Payments and goods deliveries to central organizations slowed down enormously. Many people began substituting private currencies and systems of exchange for the official system of money and credit. Other people were diverting government-owned stocks and facilities into profit-making or monopoly-maintaining private distribution networks. Substantial benefits went mainly to existing managers, quick-thinking entrepreneurs, and members of organizations that already enjoyed preferential access to desirable goods, facilities, or foreign currencies. Those organizations visibly included the Communist Party.

All this happened as the Soviet government was attempting to generalize and liberate national markets. That meant reducing government involvement in production and distribution of goods and services. As a result, the central government's capacity to deliver rewards to its followers declined visibly from one month to the next. In response, officials and managers engaged in a sort of run on the bank: wherever they could divert fungible assets to their own advantage, they increasingly did so. They started stealing the state (Solnick 1998). The more one person stole, the more reason the next person had to steal before no assets remained. Soon a large share of government resources had moved into private hands.

On the political front, a parallel and interdependent collapse of central authority occurred. The results of Gorbachev's economic program alienated three different groups: (1) producers who had benefited from the previous regime's emphasis on military enterprise, (2) consumers who did not have ready access to one of the new distribution networks, and (3) officials whose previous powers were now under attack. The new political program opened up space for critics and rivals such as Boris Yeltsin. From his base in Moscow, Yeltsin rose to control the Russian federation. Yeltsin promoted Russian nationalism in opposition to the Soviet regime, including Gorbachev. Gorbachev himself tried to check the threatened but still intact military and intelligence establishments through conciliation, caution, and equivocation. That effort, however, alienated reformers without gaining him solid conservative support. Simultaneously, he asked the legislature for emergency powers that would free him to promote economic transformation. His bid for independent authority brought him into conflict with rival reformers, political libertarians, and defenders of the old regime alike.

Opportunism channeled by the old regime's own institutions undid the regime. Russia's Communists had long dealt with non-Russian regions by co-opting regional leaders who were loyal to their cause. The regime had integrated such leaders into the Communist party, recruited their successors among the most promising members of designated nationalities, but trained them in Russia and accustomed them to doing business in Russian. Candidates for regional leadership made long stays in Moscow under close supervision. The ones who proved smart, tough, and reliable went back to run their homelands' Communist parties.

At the same time, the Soviet government had dispatched many Russians to staff new industries, professions, and administrations, promoting Russian language and culture as media of administration and inter-regional communication. In that system of rule, the central government granted regional power holders substantial autonomy and military support within their own territories just so long as they assured supplies of government revenue, goods, and conscripts. The regime struck immediately against any individual or group that called for liberties outside this system. Such a system could operate effectively under two conditions: first, that regional leaders received powerful support from the center, and, second, that their local rivals had no means or hope of appealing for popular backing. Those conditions held most of the time from the 1930s to the early 1980s. The system survived.

The system's strength also proved to be its downfall. Gorbachev and collaborators actively promoted opening of political discussion, reduced military involvement in political control, tolerated alternatives to the Communist connecting structure, and made gestures toward truly contested elections. At the same time, they acknowledged their reduced capacity to reward faithful followers. They asked Soviet citizens to remain loyal through hard times, but provided few guarantees of future rewards for loyalty. Widespread popular demands for guarantees of religious and political liberties arose in 1987. But disintegration really began during the next two years, as nationalist and nationalizing leaders rushed to seize assets and autonomy that would fortify their positions in the new regime. Most of the people who came to power in the Soviet Union's successor states had already held important positions under the Soviet regime. But even politicians who had long served as party functionaries began portraying themselves as independents, reformers, or nationalists. Many of them actually succeeded.

As the USSR disintegrated, accordingly, both regional power holders and their rivals suddenly acquired strong incentives to distance themselves from the center. Most of them started recruiting popular followings. Ambitious regional leaders established credentials as authentic representatives of the local people, urged priority of their own nationalities within territorial subdivisions of the USSR they happened to occupy, and pressed for new forms of autonomy. In the Baltic republics and those along the USSR's western or southern tiers, new nationalists capitalized on the possibility of special relations with kindred states and authorities outside the Soviet Union – Sweden, Finland, Turkey, Iran, the European Community, and NATO. Those relations offered political leverage and economic opportunity the union itself was decreasingly capable of providing.

Time horizons contracted rapidly. On the large scale and the small, people could no longer count on payoffs from long-term investment in the existing system; they reoriented to short-term gains and exit strategies. In a referendum of March 1991, Gorbachev sought a new union treaty, with greater scope for the fifteen republics but preservation of a federal government's military, diplomatic, and economic priority. Six republics (Latvia, Lithuania, Estonia, Moldavia, Armenia, and Georgia) had already started the process of declaring themselves independent. Their leaders boycotted the referendum. Results for the other republics confirmed the division between Russia and non-Russian portions of the tottering federation. From outside, venture capitalists, development economists, world financial institutions, and powers such as the United States, Turkey, Iran, and the European Union all grabbed for their pieces of the action. At the same time, they tried to contain ugly spillover from Soviet turmoil.

Ethnic segmentation, economic collapse, undermining of the old regime's powers, and Gorbachev's principled refusal to engage in the old regime's customary vigorous, violent repression transformed public politics. Among other things, they combined to open opportunities for right-wing movements. Many observers and participants on the Soviet scene feared a bid of the military, intelligence, and party establishment to reverse the flow of events. History proved them right to worry. In August 1991, a self-identified Emergency Committee sequestered Gorbachev. The committee failed to accomplish a coup, however, as Yeltsin led resistance in Moscow. Over the next four months Yeltsin sought to succeed Gorbachev.

He proposed to take power not as party secretary but as chief of a confederation maintaining a measure of economic, military, and diplomatic authority over its component states. Even that effort ended with dissolution of the Soviet Union into an ill-defined and conflict-ridden Commonwealth. The Baltic states absented themselves entirely from the Commonwealth, while other soviet republics began rushing toward exits.

Postsocialism

Once the Soviet regime collapsed, Russian nationalists within Russia (including the opportunistic nationalist Yeltsin) faced a fierce dilemma. On the one hand, they claimed the right of Russians to rule the Russian Federation, which actually included millions of people from non-Russian minorities. Their claim supported the principle that titular nationalities should prevail throughout the former Soviet Union. On the other hand, they vigorously criticized the treatment of Russians outside the Russian federation as second-class minorities. Estonia, Lithuania, Ukraine, and Kazakhstan, for example, all numbered millions of self-identified Russians.

Those numerous Russians had suddenly become members of minorities – sometimes very large minorities – in newly independent countries. They faced choices among assimilation to the titular nationality, lesser forms of citizenship, and emigration. The Russian Federation posed as their protector. Unsurprisingly, newly independent neighbors often accused the Russian federation's authorities of imperialism. Fairly soon, the great western powers lined up together in a program of containing Russia and drawing its former satellites selectively into western political and economic circuits. They tried to secure the enormous resources of former Soviet territories, for example, the huge oil reserves of Kazakhstan under and around the Caspian Sea. Led by the United States, the great powers unilaterally ended the Cold War. Outside the Baltic, economies collapsed across the former Soviet Union, with output dropping about 60 percent across the region as a whole between 1989 and 1998 (Campos and Coricelli 2002: 794). At the same time, what remained of the Soviet Union's economic regulatory system fell to pieces.

Not all postsocialist regimes, by any means, then proceeded to democratize (Fish 2001). Again using Freedom House measures, Figure 7.3 displays trajectories of four postsocialist countries from 1991 to 2001. (Freedom House started treating Belarus, Croatia, Estonia, and Russia separately from the preceding socialist federations only in 1991.) According to these

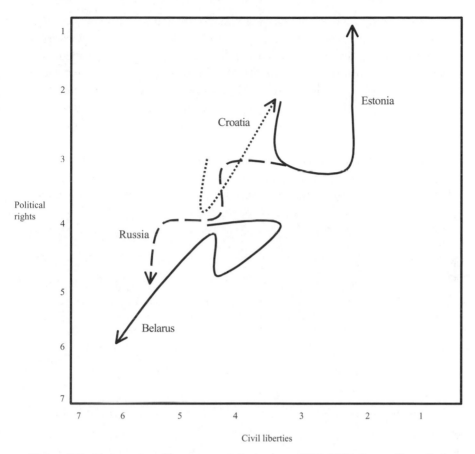

Figure 7.3: Trajectories of four postsocialist regimes, 1991–2001. *Source:* Compiled from Freedom House 2002.

ratings, every one passed through an early decline of political rights and/or civil liberties. But after its civil war ended, the scores indicate, Croatia took significant steps toward democracy. Estonia restricted political rights at first, but made a U-turn as civil liberties increased and then political rights expanded; the regime's discriminatory treatment of its substantial Russian minority accounts for Estonia's 2001 rating of 1, 2 – in the company of France, Germany, and the United Kingdom.

Meanwhile, Russia and (especially) Belarus headed downward toward fewer political rights and diminished civil liberties (Hanson 2000; Tolz 2000). In Russia, the Yeltsin-Putin wars in the Northern Caucasus and their silencing of opposition voices pulled back their country from the partial democratization Gorbachev had initiated. Yeltsin and Putin concentrated their energy on restoring the Russian state's internal capacity and external standing. They sacrificed civil liberties – or, more generally, protected consultation – as they did so. Inequalities of class and ethnicity became more salient in Russian public politics, Russian citizens disconnected their tattered trust networks even more definitively from public politics, and protection, breadth, equality, and bindingness of political participation diminished visibly.

Belarus President Aleksandr Lukashenka won his office in a 1994 popular election as an anticorruption watchdog. But as soon as he had consolidated his hold on office, Lukashenka instituted censorship, smashed independent trade unions, fixed elections, and subjugated the legislature, thus compromising the country's small previous democratic gains. "Less than a year into his presidency," reports Kathleen Mihalisko,

in April 1995, riot police acting on Lukashenka's orders beat up Popular Front deputies on the steps of the Supreme Council, in what was a first manifestation of regime violence. Ever since, the special interior ministry troops (OPMON) have become a most visible reminder of how Lukashenka prefers to deal with critics, being used against peaceful demonstrators with escalating brutality and frequency. In two years, the number of security forces is estimated to have risen to about 180,000, or double the size of the armed forces. (Mihalisko 1997: 237)

The use of specialized military forces to establish political control drew on an old Eastern European repertoire. Postsocialist regimes that dedemocratized after 1991 teetered between dictatorship and civil war.

Figure 7.3 makes a point that was already implicit, but not immediately visible, in Figure 7.1. Regimes crowd along the diagonal, generally receiving broadly similar scores for political rights and civil liberties. When political rights and civil liberties change in any particular regime, furthermore, they tend to change together in the same direction – not in lockstep but in rough synchrony. In this book's terms, the installation of relatively broad, equal, and binding popular consultation promotes the strengthening of protections against arbitrary action by governmental agents, and vice versa. Not perfectly, as the erratic courses of Belarus, Russia, Estonia, and Croatia tell us, but enough so that democratization arrives as a simultaneous increase in political rights and civil liberties. That increase, as we have seen, often occurs with impressive rapidity in the aftermath of intense conflict.

The Balkans

The case of Croatia takes us over into the Balkans, the mountainous south-ern peninsula bounded by the Adriatic, Mediterranean, and Black Seas. Like the Russia of an earlier age, until recently the Balkans suffered re-peated conquests by adjacent (and occasionally domestic) imperial powers, but never fell durably under control of any single empire. The Ottomans came closest, overpowering almost the whole region by the late 17th cen-tury. (In 1529 and 1683, Ottoman forces besieged Vienna, but fell back both times.)

Even the Ottomans ruled indirectly through most of the Balkans, ex-acting tribute and taking slaves, but allowing local strongmen extensive autonomy so long as they collaborated generally with imperial programs. At the limit, for example, the formally independent Republic of Dubrovnik paid the empire massive tribute but retained its freedom to trade around the Adriatic. Over much of the period from 1650 to 2000, in any case, Europe's great powers disputed Ottoman hegemony. By 1815, the Ottomans had lost some territory in the northern Balkans, had experienced repeated re-bellions in the region, had seen regional warlords gain strength in Albania and Bulgaria, but remained the dominant power in the areas we now know as Greece, Bulgaria, Romania, Macedonia, Albania, Serbia, Montenegro, and Bosnia-Herzegovina. At that point, regimes ranged from authoritar-ian near Istanbul to petty tyrannies – low in capacity and belligerently undemocratic – farther away.

For the next century, however, European powers battered the Ottoman Empire mercilessly. They supported the Greek independence war of 1821–30, then intervened to produce increasing autonomy in Romania, Serbia, Montenegro, Bulgaria, Bosnia, and Herzegovina. The Russian-Ottoman war of 1877–78 tipped the balance decisively, first establishing Russia as a looming presence in former Ottoman territory, then inducing Germany, Austria, Great Britain, France, and Italy to organize a Berlin Congress that contained Russian advances. As a result, in 1878 Romania, Serbia, Montenegro, and part of Bulgaria acquired formal independence, while Bosnia and Herzegovina (still nominally subordinate to the Ottomans) be-came Austrian protectorates. In succeeding years, European powers also induced the Ottoman regime to strengthen the rights of non-Muslim mi-norities within its remaining lands. With the Balkan wars of 1908–13, the Ottoman Empire lost all its European territory save a small strip adjacent to Istanbul.

The struggles of 1815 to 1913 transformed the Balkan map. They did not, however, implant durable democracy anywhere in the region. Citizens of Croatia, Slovenia, Bosnia, and Herzegovina gained some protections as subjects of the Austro-Hungarian Empire, while Bulgaria, Serbia, and Greece fitfully installed and overturned formally democratic regimes. The region as a whole spent the century in undemocratic petty tyranny. Yet as a cockpit of war, the Balkans played a crucial part in precipitating the next major round of European democratization. War between Greece and Turkey (1896), Austria's annexation of Bosnia and Herzegovina (1908), war pitting Bulgaria, Serbia, and Greece against the Ottoman Empire (1912), and a second war of Serbia, Greece, Romania, and the Ottomans against Bulgaria (1913) all resulted from regional jockeying for power and land in the Balkans. The Ottoman Empire was literally losing ground, furthermore; the conflict of 1913, for example, carved an independent Albania from a flank of the empire.

By the time a Bosnian nationalist assassinated the Austrian archduke in Sarajevo, Bosnia (28 June 1914), battle lines were already drawn. The Austrians accused Serbia of backing the Black Hand assassin. Their German allies assured Austria-Hungary of military support in the event of war against Serbia. After a month of frenzied international negotiations, Austria-Hungary declared war on Serbia. Almost immediately, Austria's German ally declared war on Russia, France, and Belgium, launching an invasion of Belgium on its way into France. Great Britain replied by going to war with Germany. Almost as soon, Montenegro declared war on Austria and Germany, Austria on Russia, and Serbia on Germany. Within five days, all the major European powers, plus some minor states, had joined the war.

War's end brought the disintegration of the Russian, Austro-Hungarian, and Ottoman empires, extensive redrawing of the European political landscape, multiple revolutions, and an important cycle of democratization. Within the Balkans, the formation of a new Serbian-dominated Kingdom of the Serbs, Croats, and Slovenes marked the most important single mutation. Despite resolute Croatian resistance, the composite state managed a chaotic semblance of parliamentary rule until 1929, when King Alexander established a dictatorship and renamed his country Yugoslavia. Assassination of the king (1934) by a Croatian nationalist brought Yugoslavia close to war with Hungary, which had harbored the assassin. During the remainder of the 1930s, the country experimented unsuccessfully with democratic forms, but joined Axis forces in World War II. Partisans led by Marshal Tito and backed by the Soviet Union seized power as the war ended.

Although relatively free elections to a constituent assembly confirmed Tito's Communist-dominated National Front, Yugoslavia soon became a one-party state on the Soviet model. Governmental capacity increased dramatically, but protected consultation did not. Despite Tito's death in 1980, not until the federation started to splinter with external recognition of an independent Slovenia in 1990 did any part of Yugoslavia move decisively into democratic territory. After civil war and substantial loss of territory to Serbia, Croatia likewise moved away from petty tyranny toward higher capacity protected consultation.

As Caramani's compilation earlier indicated, Greece repeatedly adopted democratic forms during the century after independence in 1830, but never secured them for long. After World War I shattered the Ottoman Empire, Greek nationalists sought to realize a widely shared 19th-century dream by bringing all of the empire's major clusters of Greek-speaking people, including those of Istanbul, into a single state. Greek defeat in the fierce Greek-Turkish war of 1919–22 discredited that dream, and the regime that pursued it. After the military drove out King George II (1923), a 1924 plebiscite established a republic.

Parliaments nominally ruled the country thereafter, but only in the face of repeated military intervention and intermittent military rule. Conquest by Germany and Italy in 1941 preceded civil war that did not really end until 1949. By that time the United States was providing substantial aid to anticommunist forces in Greece. Meanwhile, Yugoslavia, increasingly at odds with the Soviet Union, was closing its frontiers against Greek communist rebels. From 1950, Greece staggered through unstable regimes including military coups in 1967 and 1973. To establish domestic and international credibility, the junta began cautious restoration of civil liberties in 1968, and suspended martial law through most of the country in 1971. Nevertheless, student risings in 1973 incited reestablishment of martial law.

During the 1960s, Greece's right-wing forces had begun to split between hard-line supporters of military rule and backers of the monarchy (Diamandouros 1986: 146–49). Turkey's invasion of Cyprus (1974) discredited the Greek military sufficiently to bring down the junta and initiate civilian rule. The conservative New Democracy Party of Konstantinos Karamanlis (who engineered the transition of 1974 and became president in 1980) then governed until 1981. At that point Greek voters brought the social democratic party PASOK to power. Greek public politics began to resemble that of other contentious European democracies. As of 2001, Freedom House awarded Greece a 1 for political rights, but only a 3 for civil liberties, the lower score largely because of discrimination against Muslim and Roma minorities as well as recent immigrants (see also Human Rights Watch 2000: 271–72).

In 2001, the only Balkan countries that had achieved high rankings for both rights and liberties in Freedom House assessments were Slovenia, Croatia, Romania, Bulgaria, and Greece. Slovenia exited quickly, and Croatia with much more trouble, from Yugoslavia. Both countries were operating quasidemocratic systems by 2001. Romanians threw over the Ceausescu regime in one of 1989's more violent departures from state socialism, passed through a period of extensive struggle, but after 1995 settled into something like democratic public politics despite substantial discrimination against Hungarian and Roma minorities. Bulgaria (which by 2001 had joined Greece in Freedom House's 2, 3 rating) continued to rival its neighbors in mistreatment of Roma and Turks as well as in seriously restricting freedoms of speech and association. Yet Bulgaria, too, had distinguished itself from such Balkan countries as Serbia and Albania by establishing relatively broad, equal, binding, and protected consultation as its system of rule. For the first time in history, significant sections of the Balkans were democratizing (Rakowska-Harmstone 2000).

Iberia

Chapter 3 left Iberia in 1850, amid repeated experiments with democratic forms, some of them backed by military force, and equally repeated reversals of democratization. For comparability with Russia and the Balkans, however, we may as well backtrack to the close of the Napoleonic Wars. In 1815, both Spain and Portugal had just emerged from French conquest, Spain with a restored monarchy and Portugal as part of an empire temporarily ruled from Brazil. King John returned to Portugal as constitutional monarch in 1820, leaving his son Pedro to rule Brazil. Brazil then severed its formal ties to Portugal in 1822, cutting off its European counterpart from a great source of revenue.

Despite restoration of the Spanish and Portuguese Inquisitions in 1814, both countries continued to dispossess the Catholic Church, crown lands, and great landlords in favor of bourgeois – but not peasant – property. In both countries, the armed forces continued to intervene in national politics for well over a century. Both countries fought multiple civil wars over disputed royal successions. Both countries, finally, alternated rapidly among ostensibly democratic, willfully oligarchic, would-be revolutionary, and temporarily authoritarian regimes – both the revolutionary and authoritarian versions typically led by military men.

Socialist, anarchist, and liberal political movements grew impressively in both Portugal and Spain during the 19th century. In response, ruling classes aligned themselves fearfully with authoritarian leaders. A government-backed propaganda war began on behalf of social and public order; between 1870 and 1876, for example, more than 300 pamphlets attacking the International, socialism, and the right to strike appeared in Spain (González Calleja 1998: 25). At the same time, regimes made frequent but ultimately unsuccessful attempts to repress working-class activism (González Calleja 1998: 219–302).

Despite popular militancy, nothing like a durable democratic regime emerged in either Spain or Portugal before World War I. During the war, Spain (formally neutral) and Portugal (intermittently engaged on France's side, but riven by pro-German factions) repeatedly approached civil war. Spanish postwar struggles culminated in the 1923 coup of Miguel Primo de Rivera, who ruled until just before he died in 1930. After a period of widespread struggle, King Alfonso XIII restored the nominally democratic constitution (1931) and called elections. Republicans and socialists won overwhelmingly. The king fled. Under a new republican constitution of December 1931, formal democracy prevailed despite sharp divisions between Catalan autonomists and Castilian centralists, on one side, and pro- and anticlerical forces, on the other.

With a weak, divided central government facing strikes by agricultural workers and miners and separatist movements in Catalonia and Asturias, the end of 1934 almost finished the republic. By 1935 significant elements of the army (impressively neutral up to that point) were aligning with conspiracies against the regime. "The post-1934 situation," remarks Juan Linz,

was unique in democratic regimes, for it involved a revolution and a confused attempt at secession (or at least, what was perceived as such) that led not to the establishment of an authoritarian regime but to continuation of democratic legal institutions using emergency powers of repression and allowing an election less than a year and a half later in which the disloyal oppositionists won. The psychological impact on the counter-revolutionaries who felt threatened by the electoral victory of their opponents and their desire to turn the tables, was a situation without parallel in countries with democratic regimes. (Linz 1978: 191)

The "disloyal oppositionists" brought together Republicans, Socialists, Syndicalists, and Communists in the Popular Front of 1936. A spreading military rebellion eventually turned into a direct assault on that leftist government and its successors. The bloody civil war of 1936–39 ended with General Francisco Franco's victory and the establishment of a new authoritarian regime (Smith 2000). To the very end of Franco's regime, the military retained responsibility for political policing. As demonstrations and strikes multiplied after 1969, indeed, the frequency of trials by military tribunal for "insults to the armed forces" actually increased (Ballbé 1983: 450).

Only with Franco's death in 1975 did durable democratization occur in Spain. But then it occurred with startling rapidity. In 1969, Franco had designated Prince Juan Carlos de Borbon as his eventual successor and heir to the Spanish throne. Within three years of Franco's death, King Juan Carlos and his prime minister Adolfo Suárez had pushed ratification of a secular constitutional monarchy through a reinvigorated Cortes, legalized the Communist Party, and reinstated electoral competition for power at the national level. In 1977, Suárez failed to hammer out agreements with the leaders of competing labor and business blocs. But he later negotiated a deal with the major leftist parties – the Moncloa Pact of October 1978 – that confirmed inclusion of all but the far right and extreme nationalists in public politics. The Moncloa agreement gained acceptance by labor's parliamentary representatives of widespread economic reforms in exchange for governmental guarantees of substantial aid for displaced workers.

The cross-class compact emerged against the background of vast popular mobilizations and violent direct action by Basque nationalists. Manuel Pérez Ledesma summarizes:

As in other political change processes our country has experienced, in this case popular mobilization played a decisive role. Not only through the numerous demonstrations in favor of freedom of association, amnesty for political prisoners, and recognition of regional autonomies during the early months of the transition but also the strike wave during the first quarter of 1976 blocked in mid-passage the mini-reform proposed by the Arias Navarro government. That mobilization forced the new prime minister, Adolfo Suárez, to accelerate the process of change. (Pérez Ledesma 1990: 242)

Nevertheless, the 1978 pact resolved a crisis that could easily have turned into yet another civil war.

Three years later, in fact, the Spanish regime survived an attempted military coup (1981) that held the Cortes captive for eighteen hours and brought rebel tanks into the streets of Valencia. Leopoldo Calvo Sotelo, who was being sworn in as the new prime minister when the coup attempt began, later described it as the "Waterloo of Francoism," because it demonstrated that authoritarians no longer enjoyed the public support they had long commanded (Alexander 2002: 4). Government civilized: whereas a third of Franco's ministers had been military men, during the period of transition the proportion dropped to 7 percent. Meanwhile, university professors rose from 13 to 26 percent of the ministers (Genieys 1997: 234–35). By 1982, with the election of a social democratic government, Spain had moved into a turbulent version of Western European democratic routines.

In Portugal, World War I initiated a period of violent struggles for control of the government. Coups, assassinations, and uprisings continued at the rate of about one per year from 1915 to 1928. Nevertheless, a republic of sorts staggered on between 1918 and 1926. At that point, a more stable military junta took charge. By 1932 the nonmilitary economist Antonio de Oliveira Salazar had taken dictatorial powers with military backing. Salazar installed a quasidemocratic constitution, but brooked no political opposition. His regime sided with Franco's insurgents during the Spanish civil war, adopted the trappings of fascist public politics, but allowed the antifascist Allies to station troops in the Azores during World War II.

Salazar's incapacitation (1968) and death (1970) did not shake the Portuguese regime as deeply as Franco's departure shook Spain's. Nevertheless, the successor regime under Marcello Caetano loosened some central controls, permitting an antifascist opposition to run candidates in 1973 and tolerating a strike wave that began late that year. The new regime also began withdrawal of Portugal from Guinea-Bissau, Cape Verde, Mozambique, São Tomé-Principé, and Angola. That withdrawal incited a military coup (1974), bringing in not conservatives but a left-leaning junta based on junior officers. Popular mobilization accelerated over much of the country (Downs 1989). At the same time, the new government nationalized a wide range of businesses.

Rapidly, the military-backed government called a constituent assembly, which enacted a social democratic constitution and held elections that (to the military rulers' chagrin) brought in centrists and moderate socialists. A second coup by higher-ranking army moderates (November 1975) evicted the radical junta, and thus led to formation of a new socialist government. A military-dominated Council of the Revolution continued to exercise veto power over parliamentary legislation. Under pressure from major European powers and the United States, however, Portugal's military rulers gradually ceded ground to civilian parties (Diamandouros 1997: 6–7). A 1982 revision of the constitution finally abolished the council and excluded the military from direct participation in public politics. By the late 1970s, Portugal was escaping from centuries of military intervention. It was actually preceding its neighbor, Spain, in the shift toward protected consultation.

Russia, the Balkans, and Iberia in Comparative Perspective

Relative to other European regimes, Russia, the Balkans, and Iberia came late and uncertainly to democracy. As of 2000, Russia had established competitive elections and universal suffrage but had not managed to create firm democratic protections or relatively equal participation of minorities. The Balkans then divided between a minority of decisively democratizing countries and a majority in which democratic institutions remained threatened or unknown. Iberia had recently emerged from centuries of military intervention in public politics and a long period of fluctuation between semi-democratic and authoritarian regimes. The three regions had amply demonstrated both the contingency of democratization and its close connection with contentious politics.

On the basis of these narratives for Russia, the Balkans, and Iberia, what causal efficacy can we reasonably assign to our crucial causal mechanisms – changes in trust networks, categorical inequality, public politics, and their interactions? Frankly, none. The narratives do not reach far enough into change processes to justify a verdict pro or con. They merely set an agenda for further inquiry. They hint, for example, that in Russia the widely noted collapse of government-backed social security coupled with the reshaping of patron-client chains and relations of mutual aid to promote widespread segregation of interpersonal trust networks from public politics as well as a dramatic decline in protection from arbitrary action by governmental agents (Humphrey 1999, 2001; Ledeneva 1998; Varese 2000, 2001; Volkov 2002; Woodruff 1999). Only further research of density at least equal with the earlier inquiries into France, Britain, and Switzerland, however, will clarify the connections among democratization, de-democratization, and the supposedly fundamental causal mechanisms elsewhere in Europe.

Russia, the Balkans, and Iberia do nevertheless underscore some important lessons from elsewhere in Europe. Contrary to the idea of independent national trajectories toward (or away from) democracy, external parties loom large in these regions, as they do in other parts of Europe. In the Balkans, for example, rapid German recognition of Slovenia's independence in 1990 not only hastened Yugoslavia's fragmentation but also provided patronage for Slovenian reformers. U.S. military presence on Spanish and Portuguese territory during the 1970s offered guarantees of stabilization for whatever regimes currently commanded support in Iberia (Powell 2001). German political foundations provided direct support for Iberian democratizers during the 1970s. In all these regions and across the rest of Europe, the European Union exerted pressure on member governments as well as prospective members to adopt at least the outward forms of democracy.

Outside Russia, the Balkans, and Iberia, furthermore, Allied occupations at the end of World War II guided restorations of democratic institutions in France, Germany, Italy, and Austria. External parties do their democratizing work, when they do, by activating mechanisms that insulate categorical inequality from public politics, integrate trust networks into public politics, and directly promote broad, equal, protected, and binding relations between citizens and governmental agents.

External parties also act on domestic politics through international war. Positively and negatively, major wars exerted remarkably strong influences on democratic prospects. Wars mattered in multiple ways:

- because they mobilized participation (especially but not exclusively by fighting men) that then or later established claims for political rights
- because, at least at first, they typically built up governmental capacity
- because ends of wars brought both demobilization and payoffs to participation
- because governmental debt (most often owed to the government's own subjects) usually rose significantly during wartime
- because losses of wars brought some combination of military defections, discredit of existing authorities, and occupation by foreigners

In the case of Russia, the Napoleonic Wars, the Crimean War, the Russo-Japanese War, World War I, and the Afghan War all seriously affected the regime's capacity and its moves toward or away from protected consultation. They wrought their effects by activating or reversing the standard mechanisms of trust networks, categorical inequality, and public politics. Across Europe as a whole, the Napoleonic Wars, World War I, and World War II all figured significantly in the advancement – temporary or long-lasting – of democracy.

War mattered in another regard as well: in its effects on the political autonomy of military forces. Although Russia had subordinated its military forces to civilian rule fairly effectively by the middle of the 19th century, only

Trotsky's gargantuan effort again contained the armies that overran Russia between 1917 and 1921. Subordination of the army, navy, and security forces to the Communist Party by no means guaranteed democracy, but it did at least promote civilian rule after 1989. (Nevertheless, disbanded security forces seriously threatened Russian political rights and liberties during the 1990s; Varese 2001; Volkov 2002). The Balkans and Iberia dramatize the barriers to democratization erected by politically autonomous military forces. Such forces not only seize power on their own behalf, but also regularly ally with powerful classes having an interest in subversion of democratic rule.

Despite the contrary example of Switzerland, the experiences of Russia, the Balkans, and Iberia likewise confirm the importance of relatively high governmental capacity to democratization. Rapid weakening of the central government, to be sure, sometimes opens the path to democratizing revolutions, as in the France of 1870–71. Finland and the Baltic states exited from the Russian Empire in 1917 and thereafter with at least temporarily and shakily democratic arrangements. But at varying intervals Russia, Hungary, and Germany followed revolutions that had been facilitated by wartime governmental collapse with restored versions of authoritarianism. Since 1991, the sapping of the Russian central government's powers has allowed petty tyranny and civil war to reverse what little democratization occurred between 1985 and 1991 in some segments of the Russian Federation.

Spain and Portugal of the 1970s, in contrast, document the possibility of rapid transitions to democratic civilian rule where central governments already possess the capacity to enforce democratic rights and obligations. In that regard, Iberian experience follows the examples of France and the British Isles, where the undemocratic building up of governmental capacity laid the foundation for effective democratization. For all their cruelty in other regards, relatively strong-state trajectories toward democracy seem to have promoted more durable democratic outcomes than did weak-state trajectories. Switzerland constitutes a brilliant exception rather than a prominent exemplar.

Examined over the entire period from 1650 to 2000, nevertheless, democratization looks contingent, fragile, incomplete, and readily reversible. Repeatedly, we have seen predatory aspirants to rule overturning partly democratic regimes. Threats to democratization come from both inside and outside regimes: reversals in the name of national defense during the French Revolution couple with conquests such as the Nazi overrunning of the Low Countries. Of countries we have encountered, not only Belgium and the Netherlands but also France, Great Britain, Ireland, Germany, Austria, the Baltic states, Yugoslavia, and most of those places that adopted state socialism after World War II have all followed periods of substantial democratization with phases of authoritarianism and/or petty tyranny. Despite the optimism of Freedom House rankings, even stalwarts of European democratization such as Great Britain and France remain vulnerable to substantial reversals through xenophobia and religious conflict.

In the long run and on the average, Europe's revolutions promoted democratization by activating the three characteristic bundles of mechanisms – insulating categorical inequality from public politics, integrating trust networks into public politics, and broadening, equalizing, protecting, and increasing the impact on governmental action of public politics. Yet with impressive frequencies the histories we have reviewed reveal the short-term emergence of authoritarian regimes from revolutionary transformations, especially where revolutionaries built up governmental capacity in the process of consolidating their gains. The variable histories of postsocialist regimes show us just such contingencies in action.

Another implication follows. Constitutions as such make less difference than a strictly legalist account of democratization suggests. These days almost every European state has enacted a formally democratic constitution, but sharp differences in breadth, equality, protection, and consultation still appear across the continent. One might try to explain those differences by means of variation in national culture or in market penetration. But the European experiences we have compared indicate that national culture, market penetration, and other such general factors wield their influence on democratization not directly but through their activation of mechanisms within the realms of trust networks, categorical inequality, and public politics.

Models of democratic organization likewise appear to have played peculiar roles in European democratization: not somehow attracting cumulative popular support until they became irresistible alternatives to more authoritarian regimes, but arriving typically instead as solutions to crises. We have seen the crisis adoption of democratic institutions in three different variants: as the compromise settlement of deep internal divisions (e.g., Switzerland in 1848), as an elite bid for domestic and international legitimacy (e.g., Spain in 1978), and as the price of external military occupation (e.g., Germany in 1945). Russia and the Balkans demonstrate amply, however, that even crisis adoption of democratic forms does not suffice to produce stable democracy in the absence of necessary changes in categorical inequality, trust networks, and public politics.

Similarly, the prevalence of democratic ideologies matters much less to European histories of democratization than democrats themselves commonly suppose. That in two surprising ways:

First, however grudgingly, oligarchs and authoritarians adapt with impressive rapidity to democratic arrangements when those arrangements begin to look durable and inevitable; Spanish and Portuguese democratization did not result from massive conversions among the elites that had so long worked hand in glove with autocracies. Even the Iberian military, so long the backbone of the region's authoritarian regimes, adapted quickly to civilian rule during the 1970s.

Second, peasants, workers, and other plebeians less often subscribe to thoroughgoing programs of democratization than to demands for particular forms of justice – protection from exploitation by employers, defense of their property, freedom to associate, and so on. Although such demands, when successful, did commonly promote democracy and sometimes crystallized into articulate calls for democracy as such, they often coupled with extensive gender discrimination, victimization of minorities, and denial of rights to the putatively unworthy poor.

At least as seen in European experience, widespread, self-conscious belief in democracy as such does not look like a necessary condition of democratization.

As promised, my accounts of Russia, the Balkans, and Iberia have stayed away from the detailed pinpointing of democracy-promoting mechanisms that studded the earlier treatments of France, the British Isles, and Switzerland. Nevertheless, the stories of democratization and de-democratization in the three regions generally confirm the importance of our main bundles of mechanisms – those that equalized wealth, income, power, and prestige across major categories of the population, buffered politics from categorical inequality, dissolved trust networks previously insulated from public politics, created politically connected trust networks, directly broadened political participation, equalized political participation, enhanced collective control over government by political participants, and/or inhibited the arbitrary exercise of power by governmental agents.

When the opposites of these mechanisms operated – as happened recurrently in the Balkans and Iberia during crisis periods between 1815 and 1970, and as happened in Russia and parts of Yugoslavia after 1989 – de-democratization resulted. Massive de-democratization in the recent past should suffice to remind us that democracy itself remains a contingent, contested product of contentious politics.

The Rest of Europe

My survey has neglected some European regimes: the Nordic countries, Germany, Austria, Italy, Poland, Czechoslovakia, Hungary, and a number of microstates. Each regime followed a somewhat different path toward and away from protected consultation over the 350 years between 1650 and 2000. Would including them in the analysis change the conclusions substantially? I think not. Consider Italy as a case in point. Italy would certainly add to our histories a fascinating sequence of consolidation from smaller autonomous regimes through conquest, confrontation, and revolution. A survey of Italy from 1650 onward would display:

- a dazzling array of tyrannies and oligarchies during the 17th and 18th centuries
- French conquest, temporary unification, and partial democratization under Napoleon
- post-Napoleonic segmentation and de-democratization
- shaky democratization of some segments during state consolidation from 1848 to World War I
- near-revolutionary conflict during and after the war
- formation of a fascist postwar regime
- destruction of that regime in World War II
- more durable democratization initiated by Allied occupation as the war ended
- establishment of a vulnerable, distinctive, but recognizable version of protected consultation during the postwar years
- persistent (if changing) regional differences in relationships to the central government

Piedmont enacted modest concessions to representative government in 1848, and retained relatively democratic institutions as it became the core of a uniting Italy from 1859 onward. Sicily had a very different experience. With widespread support from bourgeois and landless peasants, Garibaldi made Sicily his base for his version of democratic nationalism. The defeat of his movement at the hands of Piedmontese forces backed by France in the civil war of 1860–62 checked Garibaldi's initiative and integrated the south into the new regime on the north's terms. "What made Sicily different from Piedmont," reflects Lucy Riall,

was a profoundly different relationship between state and society, which had developed largely as a result of Bourbon reforms in the late eighteenth and early nineteenth centuries. It is therefore ironic that while both the Bourbons and the Right realized that effective reform was the key to governing Sicily, their attempts to implement reform actually made the problem worse. By increasing the power of the state in rural areas they simultaneously introduced new elements of conflict into the communities and reinforced the positions of those groups who had most at stake in maintaining the status quo. Administrative centralization added another layer of corruption to local government and made Sicily more, not less ungovernable than before. (Riall 1998: 228)

Yet, as Antonio Gramsci later made memorable, it was a failed democratic revolution – *la rivoluzione mancata* – that produced such an undemocratic outcome (Gramsci 1952). In this and many other respects, Italy's rocky history of democratization and de-democratization brings together mechanisms and processes we have seen operating widely elsewhere in Europe, but brings them together in distinctive combinations and sequences.

Italian fascism itself came into being as a virulently antidemocratic movement and established an emphatically authoritarian regime. Yet with its partial insulation of existing categorical inequalities from public politics, its partial suppression and integration of previously segregated trust networks, and its forcible installment of authoritarian citizenship, fascism altered relations between Italians and their state in directions that promoted democratization under military defeat and foreign conquest. After the fascist collapse of July 1943, German forces overran almost all of the peninsula, meeting concerted popular resistance only in Naples. The nearly two years it took the Allies, with increasing help from Italians themselves, to drive out the Germans built bridges between Italy's civilian population and the occupying forces, thus providing some basis for mutual trust. On those bridges rose the fragile foundations of a newly democratic regime. In Italy, as elsewhere in Europe, contention drove democratization.

8

Europe and Elsewhere

Colonization, conquest, confrontation, and revolution all played their parts in European democratization outside Europe. In a vivid contradiction, 19th-century Europeans simultaneously promoted the spread of both democracy and tyranny outside their home continent. They promoted democracy among European colonists and their descendants, but they promoted tyranny over and among the peoples they colonized. We can distinguish four modes of colonial penetration: settler colonies, seizure of complex economies, coerced-labor systems, and exploitative but thin control (for a more complicated – but also more accurate – classification, see Abernethy 2000: 55–63).

In territories that were becoming settler colonies, European powers generally exterminated, enslaved, or ghettoized indigenous populations. Regions of extensive European settlement in the Americas, Africa, and Oceania all started with relatively authoritarian regimes; they typically began as plantations, properties of chartered companies, penal colonies, or regions under military administration. European settlers then established partly democratic regimes among themselves, but only slowly and reluctantly opened public politics to whatever remained of indigenous populations.

Seizure of complex economies went differently, and with much lower densities of European settlement. In Africa and (especially) Asia, Europeans sometimes sought to wring revenues and trade from differentiated agricultural and industrial establishments that remained largely under non-European control; British India provides the extreme case. In such circumstances, new composite political regimes generally emerged, borrowing some of their organization from the colonial power and remaining under the colonial power's influence, but bargaining out considerable autonomy

243

even before independence. Long before Indian independence from Britain (1950), Indian activists connected by the Indian National Congress (formed in 1885) had been associating, petitioning, and agitating in India and Great Britain alike.

Where settlers built their economies on coerced, legally stigmatized labor – indigenous, immigrant, or imported – they approached democracy only through massive struggle over terms of political incorporation for those subordinated workers and their descendants. Haiti and Jamaica offer extreme contrasting examples. Haiti threw off European rule in the 1790s but never securely established protected consultation because the leading liberators then diverted what remained of the governmental apparatus to their own advantage. British-backed emancipation of Jamaican slaves (1834) started a struggle-ridden movement toward flawed but genuine democratic practice (Sheller 2000). In contrast to both Haiti and Jamaica, European colonizers of what became the United States began by exterminating, uprooting, and segregating their territories' native populations, based the economies of major regions on the labor of enslaved Africans, and fought a terrible civil war over regional differences in that regard. Although massive migration of freed slaves and their descendants northward eventually eliminated the sharp contrast between free white labor in the north and unfree black labor in the south, even today the United States falls farthest short of genuine democracy with respect to the rights of African Americans.

Neighboring Canada produced a parallel north-south split, but of a different kind. The band just north of what eventually became the U.S. border greatly resembled the northern United States in its extermination of indigenous populations. It also drew large numbers of settlers from south of the border both in the revolutionary era and during the early 19th century. But Europeans settled only thinly as traders, miners, soldiers, and service providers in the vast northern reaches of Canada. There they relied heavily on the indigenous population for custom, labor, and subsistence. In Canada and elsewhere, European settlement remained thin where the colonists' activity consisted essentially of trading and exporting raw material. In general, little or no democratization occurred under such thin colonial regimes. In some such colonies, Europeans installed or maintained local systems of tyranny. In others, they essentially established European enclaves with no more than economic and political tentacles reaching into the hinterland. For such European colonies, whatever democratization occurred grew out of anticolonial or postcolonial struggles. In different periods, Latin America, Africa, Asia, and Oceania all resounded with anticolonial and postcolonial rebellions. As of 2000, the vast majority of such post-colonial regimes had installed the formal structures of democratic rule, but despite contested elections and civilian rule fell far short of genuinely protected consultation.

With ample assistance from its settler colonies, Europe set the world's prevailing models for democratization after 1800. Democratizing regimes typically established legislatures, judiciaries, executives, contested elections, political parties, enumerations of political rights, and public guarantees of civil liberties. They did so, furthermore, in an individualistic mode. Despite long restrictions on who actually counted as a public political individual, they mainly enforced political rights and obligations one person at a time. To be sure, they also recognized the rights of firms, households, churches, associations, and other collective entities to exist and do business. By and large, however, such organizations did not acquire formal representation, voting privileges, and the other appurtenances of democratic participation. Indeed, most democratic regimes invested considerable energy in restricting the influence of collective entities on individual political rights.

The European constitutional model did not prevail because it embodied the only logically possible version of protected consultation. Even within the European experience, two other clumps of programs and practices sometimes competed with high-capacity, individualistic democratic forms. The first called for segmentation of centralized states into largely self-governing and internally democratic units – villages, regions, cooperatives, and congregations. Europe's religious communities, anarchists, communists, and radical democrats repeatedly dreamed of local democracy un-encumbered by constitutions and central power. Now and then they even put those dreams into practice for a while. France's multiple Communes of 1871 organized around decentralizing visions of this sort. As recently as 1975, Portuguese revolutionaries actually experimented with small-scale producers' democracy after a left-leaning military junta seized control of the central state (Downs 1989).

European socialists, in contrast, sometimes theorized and even began to implement democratization in a collectivist mode. Europe had a long tradition of representing corporate entities – Estates, communities, guilds, congregations, and more – formally in public politics. Socialists turned that tradition to their own uses. In many models of state-based socialism, not individuals but collectivities acquire relatively broad, equal, binding, and protected consultation. In socialist visions, such collectivities most frequently took the form of economic units: factories, farms, producers of a given commodity, and so forth. They also sometimes included nationalities and/or localities.

In their initial phases, 20th-century state socialist regimes did often effect partial democratization in comparison with the authoritarian or oligarchic regimes they displaced. That they all subsequently moved back toward authoritarianism does not gainsay the logical possibility of democratization based on collective representation. Indeed, the upper houses of bicameral constitutional regimes that unquestionably operate democratically in other regards commonly balance the popular representation of lower houses with concessions to established elites and regional powers. Social movement and interest-group politics, furthermore, often create semi-formal links between collectivities and governments; organized farmers, for instance, negotiate with ministries of agriculture, as organized workers negotiate with ministries of labor. Clearly, some collective representation occurs despite the bias toward individual citizenship.

Europe and its settler colonies established the model of individualist constitutional democracy based on a high-capacity government. (For convenience, let us follow Guillermo O'Donnell (1999) in calling both European democratic regimes and their overseas counterparts in the Americas and Oceania "the Northwest.") Once they did so, that model prevailed throughout the world. Many people suppose that the model prevailed because, even in principle, all other versions of democracy harbored fatal flaws. Since the world ran the experiment only once, it is hard to disentangle superior efficacy from the effects of western political and economic domination during the major periods of democratization. As history actually unfolded, northwestern recognition of any particular regime as democratic offered visible advantages to that regime's rulers. Recognition came more easily if the regime adopted the familiar organizational forms and practices of northwestern democracy.

Indeed, Northwest powers did not simply provide prestigious models of democratization; they often imposed those models. Laurence Whitehead points out that as Britain granted independence to its Caribbean colonies, it made decolonization more palatable to its own domestic constituency by insisting on installation of the Westminster political model for the new regimes; thus after 1945 in rapid sequence Trinidad, Barbados, St. Lucia, Dominica, and Antigua all adopted constitutions on British models (Whitehead 2001: 10). Similarly, the United States pushed its Latin American clients – the Dominican Republic, Grenada, Panama, Nicaragua, El Salvador, and Guatemala – to organize public politics in something like the North American manner, thus distinguishing themselves from dangerously socialistic Cuba (Whitehead 2001: 8). Regimes did not simply choose the most attractive forms of democratic government, but responded to strong international pressure.

The enormous influence of northwestern democratic models raises two significant questions for our inquiry. First, to what extent and how could latecomers to democratization simply borrow organizational forms and lock them into place without undergoing the sorts of painful struggle we have seen occurring so widely in the course of European democratization? If painless borrowing happened, it would raise doubts about the causal connection between contention and democratization argued in previous chapters. It would at least force us to ask why Europeans had so much trouble accomplishing what their successors achieved so easily. Second, did alterations in categorical inequality, trust networks, and public politics originate and interact elsewhere as they did in Europe? If not, maybe the necessary conditions I have stipulated were not so necessary after all. Perhaps Europe as a whole is a special case, the struggling inventor fated to see others profit from the invention without enduring the travail that brought the innovation into being.

Contentious Transitions Elsewhere

We have reasons to doubt it, however. Painless borrowing? No nonnorthwestern examples come to mind. Such democratization as has actually happened in Latin America, Africa, and Asia has occurred in fits and starts through conquest, confrontation, and/or revolution. Surely, the histories of Japan, Korea, and Taiwan after World War II couple democratization with intense struggle and powerful external intervention. Elsewhere in Asia, Indonesia, Israel, Mongolia, and Samoa offer examples of embattled and incomplete democratization. In Africa, Benin, Botswana, Cape Verde, Ghana, Madagascar, Malawi, Mali, Namibia, São Tomé-Príncipé, Seychelles, and South Africa all illustrate contention-filled, and often reversed, paths toward democracy (Bratton and van de Walle 1997: 286). In Latin America, even the fabled democratization of Costa Rica resulted from the settlement of a civil war (Yashar 1997).

Consider the record of the later 20th century. Figure 8.1 displays trends in Freedom House ratings for all the world's independent countries from 1981 to 2002, showing the share of world population in each of three categories. "Free," according to Freedom House's generous standard, means

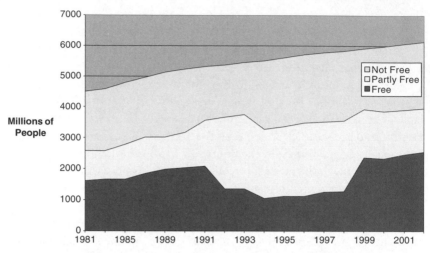

Figure 8.1: Freedom House ratings of all countries by total population, 1981–2002. *Source*: Freedom House 2002.

that a country's ratings for political rights and civil liberties averaged 3 or less (e.g., 5, 1; 4, 2; 3, 3; and so on). "Partly free" means an average of 3.5 to 5.5, "not free" an average higher than 5.5. Free, as we saw in Chapter 7, equates roughly with democratic. By these standards, 36 percent of the world's people lived in democratic countries at the series' starting point, in 1981. The low point arrived in 1994, a fierce year of civil war, genocide, and terror across the world. At the start of 1994, by Freedom House estimates, only 19 percent of the world's population lived under free regimes. Reclassification of India from partly free to free in 1999 produced the large apparent increase in freedom after 1998. With that boost and some minor border crossings elsewhere, Freedom House estimated that 41 percent of the world's people lived in free countries at the terminus of 2002. Meanwhile, the proportion living in the wretched not free countries declined modestly from 42 to 35 percent between 1981 and 2002. These shifts invariably occurred in the midst of intense contention. Nowhere did democracy come cheap.

Of the 192 regimes catalogued in 2002, 86 (45 percent) qualified as free, 58 (30 percent) as partly free, and 48 (25 percent) as not free. At that point, about half of the world's not free people, by Freedom House's evaluation, lived in China. Obviously some very large states remained undemocratic. Among the big countries that Freedom House relegated to its bottom category in 2002 fell not only China (7 on rights, 6 on liberties) but also Iran

(6, 6) and Pakistan (6, 5). In Europe, only little Belarus (6, 6) qualified for the not free rating (Freedom House 2002). It looks very unlikely that any of these countries, large or small, will democratize substantially without deep internal struggles and/or external conquest.

What about categorical inequality, trust networks, and public politics? Without the sorts of detailed historical investigations earlier chapters have reported for European countries, it remains hard to say whether the mechanisms and processes I claim to have detected at work in European democratization operate similarly elsewhere. We are looking for bundles of mechanisms that

1. equalized wealth, income, power, and prestige across major categories of national populations (e.g., dissolution of governmental controls supporting currently unequal relations among social categories)
2. buffered national public politics from categorical inequality (e.g., reduction or governmental containment of privately controlled armed force)
3. dissolved trust networks that had worked in insulation from public politics (e.g., governmental absorption or destruction of previously autonomous patron-client networks)
4. created trust networks connecting to public politics either through direct governmental ties or through attachment to established political actors (e.g., increase of governmental resources and arrangements for risk reduction and/or compensation of loss)
5. directly broadened political participation (e.g., coalition formation between segments of ruling classes and constituted political actors that are currently excluded from power)
6. equalized political participation (e.g., brokerage of coalitions across unequal categories and/or distinct trust networks)
7. enhanced collective control over government by political participants (e.g., central co-optation or elimination of previously autonomous political intermediaries), and/or
8. inhibited the arbitrary exercise of power by governmental agents (e.g., bureaucratic containment of previously autonomous military forces)

Some faint encouragement comes from research by Adam Przeworski and his collaborators. The group analyzed year-to-year survival and reversal of democracy in 135 countries throughout the world over the period from 1950 to 1990. Democracy, for them, takes an electoral form: "all regimes that hold elections in which the opposition has some chance of winning and taking office" (Przeworski et al. 1997: 295). Over the forty-one years under investigation, fifty transitions from nondemocracy to democracy occurred (in some countries more than once), but so did forty transitions from democracy to nondemocracy. The volatility of movements across the boundary we have witnessed in Europe since 1650 reappears in the world at large between 1950 and 1990.

What features of a regime, Przeworski and collaborators ask, predict the survival of democracy from one year to the next? Their analysis identifies as strong positive predictors of survival the following conditions: high per capita income, relatively rapid economic growth, moderate (but not extremely low or high) inflation, declining income inequality, presence of a parliamentary (rather than presidential) regime, and current proportions of democracies elsewhere in the region and the world. These features interacted: although plenty of authoritarian regimes remained authoritarian despite substantial economic growth, for example, whether established democracies survived varied dramatically with their current income levels:

What is most striking is how fragile poor democracies are in the face of economic crises. In poor countries, those with per capita income under $2,000, of the 107 years during which a decline of incomes occurred, twelve democracies fell the following year: the expected life of democracy under such conditions is about nine years. Even among countries with incomes between $2,001 and $6,000, a decline of incomes resulted in the fall of six democracies in 120 years during which this happened: these democracies could expect to last 20 years. And then, above $6,055 a miracle occurs: in the 252 years during which wealthy democracies experienced economic crises, none ever fell. (Przeworski and Limongi 1997: 165; the odd figure of $6,055 marks high-income Argentina's 1975 slide into military rule)

European historical knowledge might lead us to cavil that not only internal disintegration, but also external conquest sometimes produce abrupt transitions from democracy to tyranny, as in the cases of relatively rich and relatively democratic France, Belgium, and the Netherlands during 1940. Under German occupation or influence, they all experienced shifts from democratic to authoritarian regimes. But the reversals we have examined in Iberia, Greece, Germany, Italy, and elsewhere generally confirm the threat to democracy posed by the arrival of economic crisis in low-income countries.

I do not claim the findings of Przeworski and collaborators as evidence for my account of European democratization. I claim only that my account offers an interesting possible interpretation of the Przeworski findings. If this book's arguments are both correct and generally applicable, close inspection of such retrogressive episodes should uncover reversals of the basic mechanisms and processes. We should find that in relatively poor but still democratic countries economic crises promote sharpening inequality, ruptures of cross-class coalitions, failures of governmental programs for risk-reduction, severing of connections between trust networks and governmental agents, emergence of autonomous political intermediaries, weakening of bureaucratic controls over armed forces, and so on through the inventory of relevant mechanisms.

More generally, in times of crisis we should detect increasing intrusion of existing categorical inequalities into public politics, growing insulation of trust networks from public politics, and direct attacks on protected consultation by actors that had previously participated, however grudgingly, in democratic politics (for some encouragement from a study of governmental change between 1948 and 1982, see Arat 1991: chapters 4 and 5). We have seen those processes repeatedly in Europe's many movements away from democracy. If European history serves as a guide, actors who are powerful, small in number, internally connected, and well placed to benefit from government action on their behalf – large property holders and military officers provide obvious examples – have a greater propensity to defect from the democratic compact. Higher-income democracies, runs the argument, weather economic crises without serious activation of these democracy-destroying mechanisms and processes. They survive as democracies, we might speculate, because in their polities crisis actually generates solidarity and remedial action.

Extrapolations

If European history serves as a guide! On the fantastic hypothesis that the explanations of European democratization and de-democratization in previous chapters will hold up to fuller evidence, let us think through what they imply for the rest of the world. Outside Europe, what should we find? Returning to an earlier summary, here are the main points:

1. *Differing combinations of coercion, capital, and commitment in various regions promote the formation of significantly different kinds of regimes, and different directions of regime change, within those regions.*

   As in Europe, we should find that (a) governmental capacity increased earlier and further where coercion, capital, and commitment accumulated and concentrated in relatively equal degrees; (b) within

251

those limits, regimes in regions of greater coercive concentration ended up more authoritarian; whereas (c) greater concentrations of capital and/or commitment promoted the formation of regimes featuring somewhat less governmental capacity and somewhat more extensive protected consultation. The histories of high-capacity France and low-capacity Switzerland will not repeat themselves outside Europe, but the processes that produced them apply more generally.

2. *Trajectories of regimes within a two-dimensional space defined by (a) degree of governmental capacity and (b) extent of protected consultation significantly affect both their prospects for democracy and the character of their democracy if it arrives.*

Outside Europe, we should also expect to find variation from strong-state to weak-state trajectories toward democracy, with weak-state paths less likely ever to produce democracy because of their vulnerability to fragmentation, exploitative monopoly, and conquest. To that extent, we discover broad equivalents of the British Isles' strong-state path outside Europe.

3. *In the long run, increases in governmental capacity and protected consultation reinforce each other, as government expansion generates resistance, bargaining, and provisional settlements, on one side, while on the other side protected consultation encourages demands for expansion of government intervention, which promote increases in capacity.*

Trajectories that actually reach some form of democracy should therefore concentrate along the diagonal of the capacity-protection space, but fall disproportionately on its strong-state side. Although patronage by major powers, international exploitation of local economic resources, and protection by international organizations may have tipped the balance somewhat toward weaker states after World War II, we should still discover a strong-state advantage in moves toward democracy.

4. *At the extremes, where capacity develops further and faster than consultation, the path to democracy (if any) passes through authoritarianism; if protected consultation develops further and faster than capacity and the regime survives, the path then passes through a risky zone of capacity building.*

This claim follows obviously from the previous points. It does not mean, however, that authoritarianism is a necessary prelude to democratization or that (as was once widely believed) authoritarian regimes generate greater economic growth, and thereby favor democratization in the long run (Przeworski et al. 2000).

5. *Although the organizational forms – elections, terms of office, areal representation, deliberative assemblies, and so on – adopted by democratizing regimes often emulate or adapt institutions that have strong precedents in villages, cities, regional jurisdictions, or adjacent national regimes, they almost never evolve directly from those institutions.*

Despite the frequent claims of new states' leaders to be creating democracy by means of indigenous institutions, we should rarely find local and regional versions of those institutions becoming means of government at the national scale. Even in tradition-rich Mexico, for example, national political forms on northwestern models articulate with a wide variety of local political structures without incorporating those local structures directly into protected consultation at the national scale (Fox 1994; Ortega Ortiz 2001; Rubin 1997).

6. *Creation of citizenship – rights and obligations linking whole categories of a regime's subject population to governmental agents – is a necessary but not sufficient condition of democratization.*

Everywhere we should find regimes shifting from embedded to detached identities as bases of political rights and obligations, with broad categories of citizenship at least partially displacing other identities as protected consultation expands. Exactly as European experience of religious qualifications for citizenship would lead us to expect, direct representation of existing religious divisions in public politics proves to set up significant barriers against democratization and to foment intense struggle over the boundary between inclusion and exclusion.

7. *In high-capacity regimes, nondemocratic citizenship sometimes forms and with extensive integration of citizens into regimes even reduces or inhibits democracy.*

Where rulers have managed to gain control of major national concentrations of coercion, capital, and/or commitment – for example, military forces, major export commodities, and/or dominant religious organizations – we should find them building authoritarian regimes with top-down definitions of citizenship. As in Europe, few non-European rulers who already control effective means of drawing power and resources from the existing regime concede protected consultation except in the face of unmanageable popular opposition and/or strong external pressure.

8. *Nevertheless, the prior presence of citizenship, other things equal, generally facilitates democratization.*

The prior equalization of political rights and obligations over large categories of the population should increase the likelihood that crises and struggles will move regimes toward protected consultation. China, for example, looks like an impossibly recalcitrant case of lingering authoritarianism, yet the Communist leveling of rights and obligations for all but the party elite has encouraged a surprising range of mass action and will eventually facilitate a rapid shift toward protected consultation (Bernstein and Lü 2002; Lee 2002; O'Brien 1996; Perry 2002).

9. *Both creation of citizenship and democratization depend on changes in three arenas – categorical inequality, trust networks, and public politics – as well as on interactions among those changes.*

Outside Europe, as in Europe since 1650, we expect to find that the combination (and only the combination) of (a) segregation of public politics from categorical inequalities, (b) integration of trust networks into public politics, and (c) broadening, equalization, protection, and enforcement of ties among major political actors promotes democratization. Verification, falsification, or modification of this claim will require massive new research on non-European democratization, as well as reinterpretation of existing national studies.

10. *Regularities in democratization consist not of standard general sequences or sufficient conditions but of recurrent causal mechanisms that in varying combinations and sequences produce changes in categorical inequality, networks of trust, and public politics.*

We have reason to think that the causal mechanisms in European bundles (a), (b), and (c) above operated in similar fashions outside Europe, for example, that everywhere reduction or governmental containment of privately controlled armed force hindered the translation of categorical inequality into public politics and that everywhere creation of external guarantees for governmental commitments promoted integration of trust networks into public politics. In fact, expressed in other terms, both of these specific points have become commonplaces of contemporary analyses (see, e.g., Linz and Stepan 1996: 219–21; Sørensen 1998: chapter 2).

11. *Under specifiable circumstances, revolution, conquest, confrontation, and colonization accelerate and concentrate some of those crucial causal mechanisms.*

    We should find that each sort of crisis accelerates democratization or de-democratization precisely to the degree that it activates or reverses mechanisms in our basic inventories. Confrontation, for example, should promote democratization to the extent that it activates cross-class coalitions, especially coalitions including dissident members of ruling classes. Again, checking of this claim will require either substantial new research or astute reviews of existing national studies.

12. *Almost all crucial democracy-promoting causal mechanisms involve popular contention – politically constituted actors' making of public, collective claims on other actors, including agents of government – as correlates, causes, and effects.*

    Struggle should invariably accompany democratization elsewhere, as it did in Europe. Certainly, we have no reason to believe that the non-European world has settled into an orderly, peaceful progression toward democracy (see, e.g., Auyero 2001; Bratton and van de Walle 1997; Gurr 2000; Horowitz 2001; Tilly 2003c: chapter 3; Tishkov 1997).

13. *In the course of democratization, repertoires of contention (arrays of widely available claim-making performances) shift from predominantly parochial, particular, and bifurcated interactions based largely on embedded identities to predominantly cosmopolitan, modular, and autonomous interactions based largely on detached identities.*

    Except for Mark Beissinger's massive study of the collapsing Soviet Union (Beissinger 1993, 2001), no one has constructed the sorts of detailed event catalogs for democratizing non-European countries that this book has drawn on for the Low Countries, France, and Great Britain. It does appear, however, that the social movement's claim-making forms have proliferated in democratizing polities across the world (Edelman 1999, 2001; Foweraker and Landman 1997; Markoff 1996b).

14. *So long as military forces retain extensive political autonomy, democratization does not advance.*

    The rule should apply just as forcefully outside Europe as it did inside Europe. For guides to the (vast) literature, see Feaver 1999 and Geddes 1999.

15. *Inscription of religious identities into public politics – especially exclusion of whole categories from full citizenship on religious grounds – likewise constitutes an almost impenetrable barrier to democratization.*

Although the partly democratic instances of Greek Cyprus, India, and Israel might shake our confidence in this item as a universal principle, it looks like a promising generalization outside Europe. For European postsocialist countries and the world at large outside Europe, we should no doubt add race and ethnicity to the disabling inscriptions; in such countries as Kazakhstan and Malaysia, the legal priority given to a titular nationality (Kazakh and Malay, respectively) will surely erect a formidable barrier to democratization. On the whole, European histories of democratization and de-democratization should make us dubious about common proposals to reduce strife and promote political accommodation by assigning religious, ethnic, racial, and other well-organized social categories their own distinctive niches, including territorial niches, within national regimes. In contrast, European experience suggests that partial democratization can occur despite inscription of gender into citizenship, probably because politically excluded women exercise some influence through closely related males.

16. *Relations with other countries and with the international system as a whole repeatedly affect the path and timing of democratization or de-democratization.*

Although this statement leaves indeterminate *how* external relations affect democratization, if anything the principle appears to apply even more strongly outside Europe than it did inside Europe; war, colonization, decolonization, external certification, and externally sponsored internal mobilizations have all deeply marked democratization and de-democratization in the non-European world. The American occupation, for example, profoundly shaped Japan's democratization after World War II, while in nearby Korea and Taiwan, the United States first supported authoritarian regimes before reorienting its influence toward democratization. In times of crisis, regimes often adopt models of political organization from elsewhere as least bad compromises among national contenders, as means of internal and external legitimation, and/or as concessions to external powers. How well those models work, however, depends on the same sorts of transformations we have followed closely across

Europe: alterations in categorical inequality, trust networks, public politics, and their interplay.

To Promote Democratization

Governments in the non-European world's emphatically undemocratic regimes range from high-capacity (e.g., China) to low-capacity (e.g., Sierra Leone). Suppose that you want to promote democratization in a high-capacity undemocratic regime. What practical instructions can you draw from this book's tentative conclusions? First, you should resist the temptation to start by drafting constitutions, staging elections, and imposing the formal structures of western democracies. You should also resist the fashionable program of recruiting people into voluntary associations with the hope of building "civil society." In the absence of other changes, those tempting interventions will cause more harm than good. They will make it possible for those who already hold power to bend the new governmental apparatus toward their own interests. As European experience has shown us abundantly, de-democratization often occurs in the company of constitution making and expanding political participation. Europe's authoritarian regimes often insisted on both. Do not emulate them.

Instead, you should begin by analyzing current governmental operations: who staffs the government, how do they get to power, to whom (if anyone) are they accountable, how do they control resources, activities, and people within the government's jurisdiction? You should look especially hard at relations between the government's civilian staff and groups that control major concentrations of coercion, capital, and commitment – generals, tycoons, and priests, for short. You should continue by inspecting the intersections of categorical inequality, trust networks, and public politics. Only then can you sensibly start thinking about intervention.

You may discover, for example, that the principal obstacles to democratization lie in the insulation of major trust networks – of kinship, religion, credit, trade, and ritual solidarity – from public politics. In that case, devise programs that create external guarantees for governmental commitments to citizens, help the government extend its meeting of commitments to previously excluded populations, increase governmental resources for risk reduction and compensation for loss, and work to integrate existing patron-client networks into public politics while undermining the autonomous power of the patrons involved. In short, treat the relevant causal mechanisms as potential sites for intervention.

What if the undemocratic regime in question centers on a low-capacity government, as in contemporary Sierra Leone or Haiti? Your task will be both more urgent and more difficult. It will be more urgent because citizens of low-capacity undemocratic regimes, on the average, suffer from the worst ills of bad government: extreme poverty, corrupt rulers, marauding militaries, petty tyrants of all sorts, execrable public services, and weak governmental protection of citizens from thugs, exploiters, and officials alike. You should even more assiduously avoid rushing toward constitutional reform and creation of voluntary associations. Instead, your difficult work will consist of helping the regime edge its way up the capacity-protection diagonal without veering into authoritarianism.

Yet in low-capacity undemocratic regimes some parts of the job will be obvious, if arduous and risky:

- reinforcing protections of ordinary citizens from predators both inside and outside the government
- guaranteeing and dramatizing the availability and advantage of even-handed treatment by governmental agents
- dissolution or bureaucratic containment of autonomous military forces
- securing responsible government control over valuable and easily transferable resources such as minerals and drugs
- organizing the supply of reliable, low-cost public services such as education, clean water, electricity, and telephones
- providing small entrepreneurs with reliable access to credit and protection of their commerce
- forming coalitions across unequal categories and distinct trust networks as you pursue these activities
- generally building bottom-up connections with government as from the top down you work toward reliable, equitable systems of taxation, investment, accountability, and delivery of services.

In the course of such an effort, of course, you may discover reasons to ignore my initial warnings. Both elections and voluntary associations may become valuable instruments for achieving one or more of these difficult objectives.

So doing, you will actually be following this book's more fundamental teaching: elections, voluntary associations, and institutional forms do not constitute democracy in themselves. In some circumstances, nevertheless, they serve as tools to move a regime toward broad, equal, protected, and binding consultation of the population at large – toward democracy. They serve as organized equivalents of the revolution, confrontation, colonization, and conquest that repeatedly accelerated and activated democracy-promoting processes in Europe between 1650 and 2000. They promote the insulation of categorical inequalities from public politics, the integration of trust networks into public politics, and the alteration of relations between citizens and governmental agents in the directions of breadth, equality, protection, and mutual binding. They will surely continue to generate struggle and resistance. But they point toward the possibility of democratic reconstruction across the world.

References

Abernethy, David B. 2000. *The Dynamics of Global Dominance: European Overseas Empires 1415–1908.* New Haven: Yale University Press.

Adams, Julia. 1994. "Trading States, Trading Places: The Role of Patrimonialism in Early Modern Dutch Development." *Comparative Studies in Society and History* 36: 319–355.

Agirreazkuenaga, Joseba, and Mikel Urquijo, eds. 1994. *Historias Regionales - Historia Nacional: La Confederación Helvetica.* Bilbao: Servicio Editorial, Universidad del País Vasco.

Agulhon, Maurice. 1966. *La Sociabilité méridionale (Confréries et associations dans la vie collective en Provence orientale à la fin du 18e siècle)*, 2 vols. Aix-en-Provence: Publications des Annales de la Faculté des Lettres.

_____. 1970a. *La République au village (Les populations du Var de la révolution à la seconde république).* Paris: Plon.

_____. 1970b. *La Vie sociale en Provence intérieure au lendemain de la révolution.* Paris: Société des Etudes Robespierristes.

_____. 1977. *Le Cercle dans la France bourgeoise 1810–1848: Étude d'une mutation de sociabilité.* Paris: Armand Colin.

_____. 1993. *The French Republic 1879–1992.* Oxford: Blackwell.

Alapuro, Risto. 1988. *State and Revolution in Finland.* Berkeley: University of California Press.

Alexander, Gerard. 2002. *The Sources of Democratic Consolidation.* Ithaca, N.Y.: Cornell University Press.

Aminzade, Ronald. 1993. *Ballots and Barricades: Class Formation and Republican Politics in France, 1830–1871.* Princeton: Princeton University Press.

Anderson, Eugene N., and Pauline R. Anderson. 1967. *Political Institutions and Social Change in Continental Europe in the Nineteenth Century.* Berkeley: University of California Press.

Andrey, Georges. 1986. "La Quête d'un État national." In Jean-Claude Fayez, ed., *Nouvelle Histoire de la Suisse et des Suisses.* Lausanne: Payot.

Arat, Zehra F. 1991. *Democracy and Human Rights in Developing Countries.* Boulder, Colo.: Lynne Rienner.

Armitage, David. 1994. "'The Projecting Age': William Paterson and the Bank of England." *History Today* 44: 5–10.

Armstrong, John A. 1982. *Nations before Nationalism*. Chapel Hill: University of North Carolina Press.

Aron, Jean-Paul, Paul Dumont, and Emmanuel Le Roy Ladurie. 1972. *Anthropologie du conscrit français d'après les comptes numériques et sommaires du recrutement de l'armée 1819–1826*. Paris: Mouton.

Ashforth, Adam. 1990. *The Politics of Official Discourse in 20th-Century South Africa*. Oxford: Clarendon.

Aubrey, John. 2000. *Brief Lives, Together with an Apparatus for the Lives of our English Mathematical Writers and The Life of Thomas Hobbes of Malmesbury*, John Buchanan-Brown, ed. London: Penguin.

Auyero, Javier. 2001. "Global Riots." *International Sociology* 16: 33–53.

Bairoch, Paul. 1976. "Europe's Gross National Product, 1800–1975." *Journal of European Economic History* 5: 273–340.

_____. 1988. *Cities and Economic Development*. Chicago: University of Chicago Press.

Bairoch, Paul, and Maurice Lévy-Leboyer. 1981. *Disparities in Economic Development since the Industrial Revolution*. London: Macmillan.

Ballbé, Manuel. 1983. *Orden público y militarismo en la España constitucional (1812–1983)*. Madrid: Alianza.

Barber, Benjamin. 1974. *The Death of Communal Liberty: The History of Freedom in a Swiss Mountain Canton*. Princeton: Princeton University Press.

Bartlett, Robert. 1993. *The Making of Europe: Conquest, Colonization and Cultural Change 950–1350*. Princeton: Princeton University Press.

Bax, Mart. 1976. *Harpstrings and Confessions: Machine Style Politics in the Irish Republic*. Assen and Amsterdam: Van Gorcum.

Bearman, Peter S. 1991. "Desertion as Localism: Army Unit Solidarity and Group Norms in the U.S. Civil War." *Social Forces* 70: 321–42.

_____. 1993. *Relations into Rhetorics. Local Elite Social Structure in Norfolk, England, 1540–1640*. New Brunswick, N.J.: Rutgers University Press.

Beddard, Robert. 1991. "The Unexpected Whig Revolution of 1688." In Robert Beddard, ed., *The Revolutions of 1688*. Oxford: Clarendon.

Beissinger, Mark. 1993. "Demise of an Empire-State: Identity, Legitimacy, and the Deconstruction of Soviet Politics." In Crawford Young, ed., *The Rising Tide of Cultural Pluralism*. Madison: University of Wisconsin Press.

_____. 2001. *Nationalist Mobilization and the Collapse of the Soviet State*. Cambridge: Cambridge University Press.

Bermeo, Nancy, and Philip Nord, eds. 2000. *Civil Society before Democracy: Lessons from Nineteenth-Century Europe*. Lanham, Md.: Rowman & Littlefield.

Bernstein, Thomas P., and Xiaobo Lü. 2002. *Taxation without Representation in Contemporary Rural China*. Cambridge: Cambridge University Press.

Birmingham, David. 1993. *A Concise History of Portugal*. Cambridge: Cambridge University Press.

Birnbaum, Pierre. 1992. *Les Fous de la république: Histoire politique des Juifs d'Etat de Gambetta à Vichy*. Paris: Fayard.

References

_____. 1994. *L'Affaire Dreyfus: La République en peril.* Paris: Découvertes Gallimard.

_____. 1995. *Destins Juifs: De la révolution française à Carpentras.* Paris: Calmann-Lévy.

_____. 1998. *Le Moment antisémite: Un tour de la France en 1898.* Paris: Fayard.

_____. 2002. *Sur la corde raide: Parcours juifs entre exil et citoyenneté.* Paris: Flammarion.

Blickle, Peter. 1988. *Unruhen in der ständischen Gesellschaft, 1300–1800.* Enzyklopädie Deutscher Geschichte, vol. 1. Munich: Oldenbourg.

Blickle, Peter, ed. 1997. *Resistance, Representation, and Community.* Oxford: Clarendon.

Blockmans, Wim. 1988. "Alternatives to Monarchical Centralisation: The Great Tradition of Revolt in Flanders and Brabant." In Helmut Koenigsberger, ed., *Republiken und Republikanismus im Europa der Frühen Neuzeit.* Munich: Oldenbourg.

_____. 1996. "The Growth of Nations and States in Europe before 1800." *European Review* 4: 241–51.

Bois, Paul. 1981. "Aperçu sur les causes des insurrections de l'Ouest à l'époque révolutionnnaire." In J.-C. Martin, ed., *Vendée-Chouannerie.* Nantes: Reflets du Passé.

Böning, Holger. 1998. *Der Traum von Freiheit und Gleichheit: Helvetische Revolution und Republik (1798–1803) – Die Schweiz auf dem Weg zur bürgerlichen Demokratie.* Zurich: Orell Füssli.

Bonjour, Edgar, H. S. Offler, and G. R. Potter. 1952. *A Short History of Switzerland.* Oxford: Clarendon.

Braddick, Michael J. 2000. *State Formation in Early Modern England c. 1550–1700.* Cambridge: Cambridge University Press.

te Brake, Wayne. 1989. *Regents and Rebels: The Revolutionary World of the 18th Century Dutch City.* Oxford: Blackwell.

_____. 1990. "How Much in How Little? Dutch Revolution in Comparative Perspective," *Tijdschrift voor Sociale Geschiedenis* 16: 349–63.

_____. 1998. *Shaping History: Ordinary People in European Politics 1500–1700.* Berkeley: University of California Press.

Bratton, Michael, and Nicolas van de Walle. 1997. *Democratic Experiments in Africa: Regime Transitions in Comparative Perspective.* Cambridge: Cambridge University Press.

Braun, Rudolf. 1960. *Industrialisierung und Volksleben.* Zurich: Rentsch.

_____. 1965. *Sozialer und kultureller Wandel in einem ländlichen Industriegebiet.* Zurich: Rentsch.

_____. 1975. "Taxation, Sociopolitical Structure, and State-Building: Great Britain and Brandenburg-Prussia." In Charles Tilly, ed., *The Formation of National States in Western Europe.* Princeton: Princeton University Press.

Brewer, John. 1989. *The Sinews of Power: War, Money and the English State, 1688–1783.* New York: Knopf.

Brock, Michael. 1974. *The Great Reform Act.* New York: Humanities Press.

Bucher, Erwin. 1966. *Die Geschichte des Sonderbundskrieges.* Zurich: Berichthaus.

Campos, Nauro F., and Fabrizio Coricelli. 2002. "Growth in Transition: What We Know, What We Don't, and What We Should." *Journal of Economic Literature* 40: 793–836.

Cannon, John. 1973. *Parliamentary Reform, 1640–1832*. Cambridge: Cambridge University Press.

de Capitani, François. 1986. "Vie et mort de l'Ancien Régime." In Jean-Claude Fayez, ed., *Nouvelle Histoire de la Suisse et des Suisses*. Lausanne: Payot.

Caramani, Daniele. 1997. "The Nationalization of Electoral Politics: A Comparative and Historical Analysis of Territories, Elections, and Parties in Western Europe." Ph.D. dissertation, European University Institute, Florence.

————. 2000. *The Societies of Europe: Elections in Western Europe since 1815: Electoral Results by Constituencies*. London: Macmillan.

————. 2003. *The Formation of National Electorates and Party Systems in Europe*. Cambridge: Cambridge University Press.

Carothers, Thomas. 2002. "The End of the Transition Paradigm." *Journal of Democracy* 13, no. 1: 5–21.

Casparis, John. 1982. "The Swiss Mercenary System: Labor Emigration from the Semi-Periphery." *Review* 5: 593–642.

Cerutti, Simona, Robert Descimon, and Maarten Prak, eds. 1995. "Cittadinanze." *Quaderni Storici* 30, no. 89: 281–514.

Chassin, Charles-Louis. 1892. *La Préparation de la guerre de Vendée*, 3 vols. Paris: Dupont.

Cholvy, Gérard. 1974. "Recrutement militaire et mentalités languedociennes au XIXème siècle. Essai d'interprétation." In Centre d'Histoire Militaire et d'Études de Défense Nationale, *Recrutement, Mentalités, Sociétés*. Montpellier: Université Paul Valéry.

Clark, J. C. D. 1985. *English Society 1688–1832*. Cambridge: Cambridge University Press.

Clarke, Aidan. 2001. "The Colonisation of Ulster and the Rebellion of 1641, 1603–1660." In T. W. Moody and F. X. Martin, eds., *The Course of Irish History*, 4th ed. Lanham, Md.: Roberts Rinehart.

Colley, Linda. 1992. *Britons: Forging the Nation 1707–1837*. New Haven: Yale University Press.

Collier, David, and Steven Levitsky. 1997. "Democracy with Adjectives: Conceptual Innovation in Comparative Research." *World Politics* 49: 430–51.

Collier, Ruth Berins. 1999. *Paths Toward Democracy: The Working Class and Elites in Western Europe and South America*. Cambridge: Cambridge University Press.

Comninel, George C. 1987. *Rethinking the French Revolution: Marxism and the Revisionist Challenge*. London: Verso.

Craig, Gordon A. 1988. *The Triumph of Liberalism: Zürich in the Golden Age, 1830–1869*. New York: Scribner's.

Cronin, Maura. 2000. "'Of One Mind'? O'Connellite Crowds in the 1830s and 1840s." In Peter Jupp and Eoin Magennis, eds., *Crowds in Ireland c. 1720–1920*. London: Macmillan.

References

Crotty, Raymond D. 2001. *When Histories Collide: The Development and Impact of Individualistic Capitalism*. Lanham, Md.: AltaMira.

Dahl, Robert A. 1998. *On Democracy*. New Haven: Yale University Press.

Daunton, Martin. 2001. *Trusting Leviathan: The Politics of Taxation in Britain, 1799–1914*. Cambridge: Cambridge University Press.

Davids, Karel. 1995. "Shifts of Technological Leadership in Early Modern Europe." In Karel Davids and Jan Lucassen, eds., *A Miracle Mirrored: The Dutch Republic in European Perspective*. Cambridge: Cambridge University Press.

Dawson, Philip. 1972. *Provincial Magistrates and Revolutionary Politics in France, 1789–1795*. Cambridge, Mass.: Harvard University Press.

Dekker, Rudolf. 1982. *Holland in beroering: Oproeren in de 17de en 18de eeuw*. Baarn: Amboeken.

———. 1987. "Women in Revolt: Popular Protest and Its Social Basis in Holland in the 17th and 18th Centuries." *Theory and Society* 16: 337–62.

Deneckere, Gita. 1997. *Sire, het volk mort: Sociaal protest in België (1831–1918)*. Antwerp: Baarn; Ghent: Amsab.

Deutsch, Karl. 1976. *Die Schweiz als ein paradigmatischer Fall politischer Integration*. Bern: Haupt.

Diamandouros, P. Nikiforos. 1986. "Regime Change and the Prospects for Democracy in Greece: 1974–1983." In Guillermo O'Donnell, Philippe C. Schmitter, and Laurence Whitehead, eds., *Transitions from Authoritarian Rule: Southern Europe*. Baltimore: Johns Hopkins University Press.

———. 1997. "Southern Europe: A Third Wave Success Story." In Larry Diamond, Marc F. Plattner, Yun-han Chu, and Hung-mao Tien, eds., *Consolidating the Third Wave Democracies: Regional Challenges*. Baltimore: Johns Hopkins University Press.

Diamond, Larry. 1999. *Developing Democracy: Toward Consolidation*. Baltimore: Johns Hopkins University Press.

Diaz del Moral, Juan. 1984. *Historia de las agitaciones campesinas andaluzas – Córdoba*, 4th ed. Madrid: Alianza.

Dodgshon, Robert A. 1987. *The European Past: Social Evolution and Spatial Order*. London: Macmillan.

Downing, Brian M. 1992. *The Military Revolution and Political Change: Origins of Democracy and Autocracy in Early Modern Europe*. Princeton: Princeton University Press.

Downs, Charles. 1989. *Revolution at the Grassroots: Community Organizations in the Portuguese Revolution*. Albany: State University of New York Press.

Doyle, William. 1986. *The Ancien Régime*. Atlantic Highlands, N.J.: Humanities Press.

Ebbinghaus, Bernhard. 1995. "The Siamese Twins: Citizenship Rights, Cleavage Formation, and Party-Union Relations in Western Europe." In Charles Tilly, ed., *Citizenship, Identity and Social History*. Cambridge: Cambridge University Press.

Edelman, Marc. 1999. *Peasants against Globalization: Rural Social Movements in Costa Rica*. Stanford: Stanford University Press.

———. 2001. "Social Movements: Changing Paradigms and Forms of Politics." *Annual Review of Anthropology* 30: 285–317.

Egret, Jean. 1962. *La Pré-révolution française*. Paris: Presses Universitaires de France.

Evans, Eric J. 1983. *The Forging of the Modern State: Early Industrial Britain 1783–1870*. London: Longman.

Feaver, Peter D. 1999. "Civil-Military Relations." *Annual Review of Political Science* 2: 211–41.

Fish, M. Steven. 2001. "The Dynamics of Democratic Erosion." In Richard D. Anderson, Jr., et al., *Postcommunism and the Theory of Democracy*. Princeton: Princeton University Press.

Forrest, Alan. 1975. *Society and Politics in Revolutionary Bordeaux*. Oxford: Oxford University Press.

———. 1989. *Conscripts and Deserters: The Army and French Society during the Revolution and the Empire*. Oxford: Oxford University Press.

Foster, R. F. 1989. *Modern Ireland 1600–1972*. London: Penguin.

Foweraker, Joe, and Todd Landman. 1997. *Citizenship Rights and Social Movements: A Comparative and Statistical Analysis*. Oxford: Oxford University Press.

Fox, Jonathan. 1994. "The Difficult Transition from Clientelism to Citizenship: Lessons from Mexico." *World Politics* 46: 151–84.

Franzosi, Roberto. 1998. "Narrative as Data: Linguistic and Statistical Tools for the Quantitative Study of Historical Events." *International Review of Social History* 43, Supplement 6: New Methods for Social History, 81–104.

Frêche, Georges. 1974. *Toulouse et la region Midi-Pyrénées au siècle des Lumières (vers 1670–1789)*. Paris: Cujas.

Freedom House. 2002. "Freedom in the World 2002: The Democracy Gap." www.freedomhouse.org/research/survey2002.htm, 29 March.

Frey, Bruno S., and Alois Stutzer. 2002. "What Can Economists Learn from Happiness Research?" *Journal of Economic Literature* 40: 402–35.

Gaillard, Jeanne. 1971. *Communes de Province, Commune de Paris 1870–1871*. Paris: Flammarion.

Garrard, John. 2002. *Democratization in Britain: Elites, Civil Society and Reform since 1800*. New York: Palgrave.

Geddes, Barbara. 1999. "What Do We Know about Democratization after Twenty Years?" *Annual Review of Political Science* 2: 115–44.

Genieys, William. 1997. *Les Élites espagnoles face à l'état: Changements de régimes politiques et dynamiques centre-péripheries*. Paris: L'Harmattan.

Gentles, Ian. 1992. *The New Model Army in England, Ireland and Scotland, 1645–1653*. Oxford: Blackwell.

———. 2001. "The Agreements of the People and Their Political Contexts, 1647–1649." In Michael Mendle, ed., *The Putney Debates of 1647: The Army, the Levellers, and the English State*. Cambridge: Cambridge University Press.

Gérard, Alain. 1999. *"Par principe d'humanité…": La Terreur et la Vendée*. Paris: Fayard.

Gildea, Robert. 2002. *Marianne in Chains: In Search of the German Occupation 1940–45*. London: Macmillan.

Gilliard, Charles. 1955. *A History of Switzerland*. London: George Allen & Unwin.

References

Giugni, Marco, and Florence Passy. 1997. *Histoires de mobilisation politique en Suisse: De la contestation à l'intégration*. Paris: L'Harmattan.

González Calleja, Eduardo. 1998. *La Razón de la fuerza: Orden público, subversion y violencia política en la España de la Restauración (1875–1917)*. Madrid: Consejo Superior de Investigaciones Científicas.

———. 1999. *El Máuser y el sufragio: Ordén público, subversión y violencia política en la crisis de la Restauración*. Madrid: Consejo Superior de Investigaciones Científicas.

Gossman, Lionel. 2000. *Basel in the Age of Burkhardt: A Study in Unseasonable Ideas*. Chicago: University of Chicago Press.

Gould, Roger V. 1995. *Insurgent Identities: Class, Community, and Protest in Paris from 1848 to the Commune*. Chicago: University of Chicago Press.

Gowa, Joanne. 1999. *Ballots and Bullets: The Elusive Democratic Peace*. Princeton: Princeton University Press.

Gramsci, Antonio. 1952. *La Questione meridionale*. Rome: Rinascità.

Greenberg, Louis. 1971. *Sisters of Liberty: Paris, Marseille, Lyon and the Reaction to the Centralized State*. Cambridge, Mass.: Harvard University Press.

Greer, Donald. 1935. *The Incidence of the Terror during the French Revolution*. Cambridge, Mass.: Harvard University Press.

Gruner, Erich. 1968. *Die Arbeiter in der Schweiz im 19. Jahrhundert*. Bern: Francke.

Gschwind, Franz. 1977. *Bevölkerungsentwicklung und Wirtschaftsstruktur der Landschaft Basel im 18. Jahrhundert*. Liestal: Kantonale Drucksachen- und Materialzentrale.

Gullickson, Gay L. 1996. *Unruly Women of Paris: Images of the Commune*. Ithaca, N.Y.: Cornell University Press.

Gurr, Ted Robert. 2000. *Peoples versus States: Minorities at Risk in the New Century*. Washington, D.C.: United States Institute of Peace Press.

Hanagan, Michael. 1998. "Irish Transnational Social Movements, Deterritorialized Migrants, and the State System: The Last One Hundred and Forty Years." *Mobilization* 13: 107–26.

Hanson, Philip. 2000. "Insiders, Mafiosi and Stationary Bandits: Some Stories about Russian Capitalism." In John Garrard, Vera Tolz, and Ralph White, eds., *European Democratization since 1800*. New York: St. Martin's.

Harris, Tim. 1987. *London Crowds in the Reign of Charles II: Propaganda and Politics from the Restoration until the Exclusion Crisis*. Cambridge: Cambridge University Press.

't Hart, Marjolein. 1991. "'The Devil or the Dutch': Holland's Impact on the Financial Revolution in England, 1643–1694." *Parliaments, Estates and Representation* 11: 39–52.

———. 1993. *The Making of a Bourgeois State: War, Politics and Finance during the Dutch Revolt*. Manchester: Manchester University Press.

Hart, Peter. 1997. "The Geography of Revolution in Ireland 1917–1923." *Past & Present* 155: 142–76.

Head, Randolph C. 1995. *Early Modern Democracy in the Grisons: Social Order and Political Language in a Swiss Mountain Canton, 1470–1620*. Cambridge: Cambridge University Press.

Heerma van Voss, Lex, ed. 2001. "Petitions in Social History." *International Review of Social History*, Supplement 9, entire issue.

Herr, Richard. 1989. *Rural Change and Royal Finances in Spain at the End of the Old Regime*. Berkeley: University of California Press.

Hinde, Wendy. 1992. *Catholic Emancipation: A Shake to Men's Minds*. Oxford: Blackwell.

Hobbes, Thomas. 1990. *Behemoth or the Long Parliament*, Ferdinand Tönnies, ed. Chicago: University of Chicago Press (written about 1668, first authorized publication 1682).

Hoffman, Philip T., Gilles Postel-Vinay, and Jean-Laurent Rosenthal. 2000. *Priceless Markets: The Political Economy of Credit in Paris*. Chicago: University of Chicago Press.

Hohenberg, Paul M., and Lynn Hollen Lees. 1985. *The Making of Urban Europe, 1000–1950*. Cambridge, Mass.: Harvard University Press.

van Honacker, Karin. 1994. *Lokaal Verzet en Oproer in de 17de en 18de Eeuw: Collectieve Acties tegen het centraal gezag in Brussel, Antwerpen en Leuven*. Heule: UGA.

————. 2000. "Résistance locale et émeutes dans les chef-villes brabançonnes aux XVIIe et XVIIIe siècles." *Revue d'Histoire Moderne et Contemporaine* 47: 37–68.

Hood, James N. 1971. "Protestant-Catholic Relations and the Roots of the First Popular Counter-Revolutionary Movement in France." *Journal of Modern History* 43: 245–75.

————. 1979. "Revival and Mutation of Old Rivalries in Revolutionary France." *Past & Present* 82: 82–115.

Horowitz, Donald L. 2001. *The Deadly Ethnic Riot*. Berkeley: University of California Press.

Human Rights Watch. 2000. *World Report 2000*. New York: Human Rights Watch.

Humphrey, Caroline. 1999. "Traders, 'Disorder' and Citizenship Regimes in Provincial Russia." In Michael Burawoy and Katherine Verdery, eds., *Uncertain Tradition: Ethnographies of Change in the Postsocialist World*. Lanham, Md.: Rowman & Littlefield.

————. 2001. "Inequality and Exclusion: A Russian Case Study of Emotion in Politics." *Anthropological Theory* 1: 331–53.

Hunt, Lynn. 1978. *Revolution and Urban Politics in Provincial France: Troyes and Reims, 1786–1790*. Stanford, Calif.: Stanford University Press.

————. 1984. *Politics, Culture, and Class in the French Revolution*. Berkeley: University of California Press.

Huntington, Samuel P. 1991. *The Third Wave: Democratization in the Late Twentieth Century*. Norman: University of Oklahoma Press.

Imig, Doug, and Sidney Tarrow, eds. 2001. *Contentious Europeans: Protest and Politics in an Emerging Polity*. Lanham, Md.: Rowman & Littlefield.

Inkeles, Alex, ed. 1991. *On Measuring Democracy: Its Consequences and Concomitants*. New Brunswick, N.J.: Transaction.

Jackson, Julian. 2001. *France: The Dark Years, 1940–1944*. Oxford: Oxford University Press.

Jessenne, Jean-Pierre. 1987. *Pouvoir au village et révolution: Artois, 1760–1848*. Lille: Presses Universitaires de Lille.

References

Johnson, Martin Phillip. 1996. *The Paradise of Association: Political Culture and Popular Organizations in the Paris Commune of 1871.* Ann Arbor: University of Michigan Press.

Johnson, Simon, Daniel Kaufman, and Oleg Ustenko. 1998. "Formal Employment and Survival Strategies after Communism." In Joan M. Nelson, Charles Tilly, and Lee Walker, eds., *Transforming Post-Communist Political Economies.* Washington, D.C.: National Academy Press.

Joris, Elisabeth. 1994. "Auswirkungen der Industrialisierung auf Alltag und Leben-szusammenhänge von Frauen im Zürcher Oberland (1820–1940)." In Joseba Agirreazkuenaga and Mikel Urquijo, eds., *Historias Regionales – Historia Nacional: La Confederación Helvetica.* Bilbao: Servicio Editorial, Universidad del País Vasco.

Joris, Elisabeth, and Heidi Witzig. 1992. *Brave Frauen, Aufmüpfige Weiber: Wie sich die Industrialisierung auf Alltag und Lebenszusammenhänge von Frauen auswirkte (1820–1940).* Zurich: Chronos.

Jupp, Peter. 1998. *British Politics on the Eve of Reform: The Duke of Wellington's Administration, 1828–30.* London: Macmillan.

Kaiser, Robert J. 1994. *The Geography of Nationalism in Russia and the USSR.* Princeton: Princeton University Press.

Kalb, Don. 1993. "Frameworks of Culture and Class in Historical Research." *Theory and Society* 22: 513–37.

———. 1997. *Expanding Class: Power and Everyday Politics in Industrial Communities, the Netherlands, 1850–1950.* Durham, N.C.: Duke University Press.

Karatnycky, Adrian, ed. 2000. *Freedom in the World: The Annual Survey of Political Rights and Civil Liberties.* Piscataway, N.J.: Transaction.

Kearney, Hugh. 1989. *The British Isles: A History of Four Nations.* Cambridge: Cambridge University Press.

Kellenbenz, Hermann. 1976. *The Rise of the European Economy: An Economic History of Continental Europe from the Fifteenth Century.* London: Weidenfeld and Nicolson.

Kelly, Patrick. 1991. "Ireland and the Glorious Revolution: From Kingdom to Colony." In Robert Beddard, ed., *The Revolutions of 1688.* Oxford: Clarendon.

Keogh, Dermot. 2001. "Ireland at the Turn of the Century: 1994–2001." In T. W. Moody and F. X. Martin, eds., *The Course of Irish History*, 4th ed. Lanham, Md.: Roberts Rhinehart.

Khazanov, Anatoly M. 1995. *After the USSR: Ethnicity, Nationalism, and Politics in the Commonwealth of Independent States.* Madison: University of Wisconsin Press.

Kindleberger, Charles P. 1996. *World Economic Primacy: 1500 to 1990.* New York: Oxford University Press.

Kishlansky, Mark. 1996. *A Monarchy Transformed: Britain 1603–1714.* London: Allen Lane/Penguin Press.

Kivelson, Valerie. 2002. "Muscovite 'Citizenship': Rights without Freedom." *Journal of Modern History* 74: 465–89.

Kohn, Hans. 1956. *Nationalism and Liberty: The Swiss Example.* London: George Allen & Unwin.

Kriesi, Hanspeter. 1993. *Political Mobilization and Social Change: The Dutch Case in Comparative Perspective.* Aldershot: Avebury.

Kriesi, Hanspeter. 1980. *Entscheidungsstrukturen und Entscheidungsprozesse in der Schweizer Politik*. Frankfurt: Campus.

———. 1981. *AKW-Gegner in der Schweiz. Eine Fallstudie zum Aufbau des Widerstands gegen das geplante AKW in Graben*. Diessenhofen: Verlag Rüegger.

Kriesi, Hanspeter, Ruud Koopmans, Jan Willem Duyvendak, and Marco Giugni. 1995. *New Social Movements in Western Europe: A Comparative Analysis*. Minneapolis: University of Minnesota Press.

Kriesi, Hanspeter, René Levy, Gilbert Ganguillet, and Heinz Zwicky. 1981. *Politische Aktivierung in der Schweiz, 1945–1978*. Diessenhofen: Verlag Rüegger.

van der Laarse, Robert. 2000. "Bearing the Stamp of History: The Elitist Route to Democracy in the Netherlands." In John Garrard, Vera Tolz, and Ralph White, eds., *European Democratization since 1800*. New York: St. Martin's.

Lafargue, Jérôme. 1997. "La Commune de 1871 ou l'ordre improbable." In *Désordre(s)*. Paris: Presses Universitaires de France.

———. 1998. *La Protestation collective*. Paris: Nathan.

Landes, David S. 1998. *The Wealth and Poverty of Nations: Why Some Are So Rich and Some So Poor*. New York: Norton.

Langford, Paul. 1991. *Public Life and the Propertied Englishman, 1689–1798*. Oxford: Clarendon.

Lebrun, François, and Roger Dupuy, eds. 1985. *Les Résistances à la Révolution*. Paris: Imago.

Ledeneva, Alena V. 1998. *Russia's Economy of Favours: Blat, Networking, and Informal Exchange*. Cambridge: Cambridge University Press.

Lee, Ching Kwan. 2002. "From the Specter of Mao to the Spirit of the Law: Labor Insurgency in China." *Theory and Society* 31: 189–228.

Lees, Lynn, and Charles Tilly. 1974. "Le Peuple de juin 1848." *Annales; Economies, Sociétés, Civilisations* 29: 1061–91.

Leff, Lisa Moses. 2002. "Jewish Solidarity in Nineteenth-Century France: The Evolution of a Concept." *Journal of Modern History* 74: 33–62.

Le Goff, T. J. A., and D. M. G. Sutherland. 1974. "The Revolution and the Rural Community in Eighteenth-Century Brittany." *Past & Present* 62: 96–119.

———. 1983. "The Social Origins of Counter-Revolution in Western France." *Past & Present* 99: 65–87.

———. 1984. "Religion and Rural Revolt in the French Revolution: An Overview." In János M. Bak and Gerhard Benecke, eds., *Religion and Rural Revolt*. Manchester: Manchester University Press.

Lenin, V. I. 1967. *Selected Works*, 3 vols. New York: International.

Lepetit, Bernard. 1982. "Fonction administrative et armature urbaine: Remarques sur la distribution des chefs-lieux de subdélégation en France à l'Ancien Régime." In Institut d'Histoire Économique et Sociale de l'Université de Paris I, *Recherches et Travaux* 2: 19–34.

———. 1988. *Les Villes dans la France moderne (1740–1840)*. Paris: Albin Michel.

Lerner, Marc H. 2003. "Privileged Communities or Equal Individuals: The Political Culture of *Freiheit* and *Liberté* in the Swiss Public Arena, 1798–1847." Ph.D. dissertation, Columbia University.

References

Levi, Margaret. 1997. *Consent, Dissent, and Patriotism*. Cambridge: Cambridge University Press.

Levi, Margaret, and Laura Stoker. 2000. "Political Trust and Trustworthiness." *Annual Review of Political Science* 3: 475–508.

Lewis, Gwynne. 1978. *The Second Vendée: The Continuity of Counter-Revolution in the Department of the Gard, 1789–1815*. Oxford: Clarendon.

Lewis, Gwynne, and Colin Lucas, eds. 1983. *Beyond the Terror: Essays in French Regional and Social History, 1794–1811*. Cambridge: Cambridge University Press.

Lijphart, Arend. 1999. *Patterns of Democracy: Government Forms and Performance in Thirty-Six Countries*. New Haven: Yale University Press.

Linz, Juan. 1978. "From Great Hopes to Civil War: The Breakdown of Democracy in Spain." In Juan J. Linz and Alfred Stepan, eds., *The Breakdown of Democratic Regimes. Europe*. Baltimore: Johns Hopkins University Press.

Linz, Juan J., and Alfred Stepan. 1996. *Problems of Democratic Transition and Consolidation: Southern Europe, South America, and Post-Communist Europe*. Baltimore: Johns Hopkins University Press.

Lissagaray, Prosper-Olivier. 1969. *Histoire de la Commune de 1871*. Paris: Maspéro.

Locke, John. 1937. *Treatise of Civil Government and a Letter Concerning Toleration*. New York: Appleton-Century-Crofts. First published in 1689.

Lonkila, Markku. 1999. *Social Networks in Post-Soviet Russia: Continuity and Change in the Everyday Life of St. Petersburg Teachers*. Helsinki: Kikimora.

Loret, Jean. 1857. *La Muze historique ou recueil des lettres en vers contenant les nouvelles du temps écrites á son Altesse Mademoizelle de Longueville, depuis duchesse de Nemour (1650–1665)*, 4 vols. Paris: Jannet.

Lucas, Colin. 1973. *The Structure of the Terror: The Example of Claude Javogues and the Loire*. Oxford: Oxford University Press.

Luebke, David Martin. 1997. *His Majesty's Rebels: Communities, Factions, and Rural Revolt in the Black Forest, 1725–1745*. Ithaca, N.Y.: Cornell University Press.

Lynch, John. 1992. *The Hispanic World in Crisis and Change, 1598–1700*. Oxford: Blackwell.

Lynn, John. 1984. *The Bayonets of the Republic: Motivation and Tactics in the Army of Revolutionary France, 1791–94*. Urbana: University of Illinois Press.

———. 1997. *Giant of the Grand Siècle: The French Army 1610–1715*. Cambridge: Cambridge University Press.

Lyons, Martyn. 1978. *Revolution in Toulouse: An Essay on Provincial Terrorism*. Bern: Lang.

———. 1980. *Révolution et terreur à Toulouse*. Toulouse: Privat.

Maclean, Fitzroy. 2000. *Scotland: A Concise History*, 2nd revised ed. London: Thames & Hudson.

Mamdani, Mahmood. 1996. *Citizen and Subject: Contemporary Africa and the Legacy of Late Colonialism*. Princeton: Princeton University Press.

———. 2001. "Beyond Settler and Native as Political Identities: Overcoming the Political Legacy of Colonialism." *Comparative Studies in Society and History* 43: 651–64.

Mann, Michael. 1986, 1993. *The Sources of Social Power,* vol. 1: *A History of Power from the Beginning to A.D. 1760,* vol. 2: *The Rise of Classes and Nation-States, 1760–1914.* Cambridge: Cambridge University Press.

Margadant, Ted. 1979. *French Peasants in Revolt: The Insurrection of 1851.* Princeton: Princeton University Press.

————. 1992. *Urban Rivalries in the French Revolution.* Princeton: Princeton University Press.

Markoff, John. 1996a. *The Abolition of Feudalism: Peasants, Lords, and Legislators in the French Revolution.* University Park: Pennsylvania State University Press.

————. 1996b. *Waves of Democracy: Social Movements and Political Change.* Thousand Oaks, Calif.: Pine Grove Press.

Marks, Shula, and Stanley Trapido, eds. 1987. *The Politics of Race, Class and Nationalism in 20th-Century South Africa.* London: Longman.

Marrus, Michael R., and Robert O. Paxton. 1995. *Vichy France and the Jews.* Stanford, Calif.: Stanford University Press.

Martin, Jean-Clément. 1987. *La Vendée et la France.* Paris: Seuil.

Martínez Dorado, Gloria. 1993. "La Formación del estado y la acción colectiva en España: 1808–1845." *Historia Social* 15: 101–18.

Marx, Anthony W. 1998. *Making Race and Nation: A Comparison of the United States, South Africa, and Brazil.* Cambridge: Cambridge University Press.

McAdam, Doug, Sidney Tarrow, and Charles Tilly. 2001. *Dynamics of Contention.* Cambridge: Cambridge University Press.

McCarthy, John D., Clark McPhail, and Jackie Smith. 1996. "Images of Protest: Estimating Selection Bias in Media Coverage of Washington Demonstrations 1982 and 1991." *American Sociological Review* 61: 478–99.

McPhee, Peter. 1988. "Les Formes d'intervention populaire en Roussillon: L'Exemple de Collioure, 1789–1815." In *Centre d'Histoire Contemporaine du Languedoc Méditerranéen et du Roussillon: Les pratiques politiques en province à l'époque de la révolution française.* Montpellier: Publications de la Recherche, Université de Montpellier.

Merriman, John M. 1978. *The Agony of the Republic: The Repression of the Left in Revolutionary France, 1848–1851.* New Haven: Yale University Press.

Mihalisko, Kathleen J. 1997. "Belarus: Retreat to Authoritarianism." In Karen Dawisha and Bruce Parrott, eds., *Democratic Changes and Authoritarian Reactions in Russia, Ukraine, Belarus, and Moldova.* Cambridge: Cambridge University Press.

Mill, John Stuart. 1887. *A System of Logic, Ratiocinative and Inductive: Being a Connected View of the Principles of Evidence and the Method of Scientific Investigation,* 8th ed. New York: Harper & Brothers.

Mjøset, Lars. 1992. *The Irish Economy in a Comparative Institutional Perspective.* Dublin: National Economic and Social Council.

Le Monde. 2002. "La Banalisation des actes antijuifs, nouvelle cause de tensions urbaines." *Le Monde Interactif,* 18 February.

Morgan, Edmund S. 1988. *Inventing the People: The Rise of Popular Sovereignty in England and America.* New York: Norton.

References

Muir, Edward. 1997. *Ritual in Early Modern Europe*. Cambridge: Cambridge University Press.

Muldrew, Craig. 1998. *The Economy of Obligation*. London: Macmillan.

Nabholz, Hans, Leonhard von Muralt, Richard Feller, and Edgar Bonjour. 1938. *Geschichte der Schweiz*, 2 vols. Zurich: Schultheiss.

Nicolas, Jean, ed. 1985. *Mouvements populaires et conscience sociale, XVIe-XIXe siècles*. Paris: Maloine.

O'Brien, Kevin. 1996. "Rightful Resistance." *World Politics* 49: 31–55.

O'Donnell, Guillermo. 1999. *Counterpoints: Selected Essays on Authoritarianism and Democratization*. Notre Dame, Ind.: University of Notre Dame Press.

O'Ferrall, Fergus. 1985. *Catholic Emancipation: Daniel O'Connell and the Birth of Irish Democracy 1820–30*. Dublin: Gill & Macmillan.

O'Gorman, Frank. 1989. *Voters, Patrons, and Parties: The Unreformed Electoral System of Hanoverian England 1734–1832*. Oxford: Clarendon.

Olzak, Susan. 1989. "Analysis of Events in the Study of Collective Action." *Annual Review of Sociology* 15: 119–41.

O'Neill, Joseph. 2001. *Blood-Dark Track: A Family History*. London: Granta.

Ortega Ortiz, Reynaldo Yunuen, ed. 2001. *Caminos a la Democracia*. Mexico City: El Colegio de México.

Outram, Quentin. 2002. "The Demographic Impact of Early Modern Warfare." *Social Science History* 26: 245–72.

Ozouf-Marignier, Marie-Vic. 1986. "De l'universalisme constituant aux intérêts locaux: Le Débat sur la formation des départements en France (1789–1790)." *Annales: Economies, Sociétés, Civilisations* 41: 1193–214.

Palmer, R. R. 1959, 1964. *The Age of the Democratic Revolution*, 2 vols. Princeton: Princeton University Press.

———. 1977. "The Fading Dream: How European Revolutionaries Have Seen the American Revolution." In Bede K. Lackner and Kenneth Roy Philp, eds., *The Walter Prescott Webb Memorial Lectures: Essays on Modern European Revolutionary History*. Austin: University of Texas Press.

Pepys, Samuel. 1985. *The Shorter Pepys*, Robert Latham, ed. Berkeley: University of California Press.

Pérez Ledesma, Manuel. 1990. *Estabilidad y conflicto social. España, de los iberos al 14-D*. Madrid: Editorial NEREA.

Perry, Elizabeth J. 2002. *Challenging the Mandate of Heaven: Social Protest and State Power in China*. Armonk, N.Y.: M. E. Sharpe.

Petitfrère, Claude. 1979. *Blancs et bleus d'Anjou (1789–1793)*. Paris: Maloine.

Phillips, John A. 1992. *The Great Reform Bill in the Boroughs: English Electoral Behaviour, 1818–1841*. Oxford: Clarendon.

Phillips, John A., and Charles Wetherell. 1991. "The Great Reform Bill of 1832 and the Rise of Partisanship," *Journal of Modern History* 63: 621–46.

Pomeranz, Kenneth. 2000. *The Great Divergence: China, Europe, and the Making of the Modern World Economy*. Princeton: Princeton University Press.

Powell, Charles. 2001. "International Aspects of Democratization: The Case of Spain." In Laurence Whitehead, ed., *The International Dimensions of Democratization: Europe and the Americas*. Oxford: Oxford University Press.

Prak, Maarten. 1991. "Citizen Radicalism and Democracy in the Dutch Republic: The Patriot Movement of the 1780s." *Theory and Society* 20: 73–102.

———. 1999. "Burghers into Citizens: Urban and National Citizenship in the Netherlands during the Revolutionary Era (c. 1800)." In Michael P. Hanagan and Charles Tilly, eds., *Expanding Citizenship, Reconfiguring States*. Lanham, Md.: Rowman & Littlefield.

Price, Richard. 1999. *British Society, 1680–1880: Dynamism, Containment and Change*. Cambridge: Cambridge University Press.

Przeworski, Adam, and Fernando Limongi. 1997. "Modernization: Theories and Facts." *World Politics* 49: 155–83.

Przeworski, Adam, Michael Alvarez, José Antonio Cheibub, and Fernando Limongi. 1997. "What Makes Democracies Endure?" In Larry Diamond, Marc F. Plattner, Yun-han Chu, and Hung-mao Tien, eds., *Consolidating the Third Wave Democracies*. Baltimore: Johns Hopkins University Press.

———. 2000. *Democracy and Development: Political Institutions and Well-Being in the World, 1950–1990*. Cambridge: Cambridge University Press.

Puls, Detlev, ed. 1979. *Wahrnehmungsformen und Protestverhalten: Studien zur Lage der Unterschichten im 18. und 19. Jahrhundert*. Frankfurt/Main: Suhrkamp.

Putnam, Robert D. 2000. *Bowling Alone: The Collapse and Revival of American Community*. New York: Simon & Schuster.

Raeff, Marc. 1983. *The Well-Ordered Police State: Social and Institutional Change through Law in the Germanies and Russia, 1600–1800*. New Haven: Yale University Press.

Rakowska-Harmstone, Teresa. 2000. "Post-Communist East-Central Europe: Dilemmas of Democratization." In John Garrard, Vera Tolz, and Ralph White, eds., *European Democratization since 1800*. New York: St. Martin's.

Ranum, Orest. 1993. *The Fronde: A French Revolution 1648–1652*. New York: Norton.

Ray, James Lee. 1998. "Does Democracy Cause Peace?" *Annual Review of Political Science* 1: 26–46.

Reed, John. 1977. *Ten Days That Shook the World*. London: Penguin. First published in 1919.

Remak, Joachim. 1993. *A Very Civil War: The Swiss Sonderbund War of 1847*. Boulder, Colo.: Westview.

Riall, Lucy. 1998. *Sicily and the Unification of Italy: Liberal Policy and Local Power 1859–1866*. Oxford: Clarendon.

Ringrose, David. 1996. *Spain, Europe and the "Spanish Miracle" 1700–1900*. Cambridge: Cambridge University Press.

Rokkan, Stein, and Derek W. Urwin. 1982. "Introduction: Centres and Peripheries in Western Europe." In Stein Rokkan and Derek W. Urwin, eds., *The Politics of Territorial Identity: Studies in European Regionalism*. London: Sage.

Rosanvallon, Pierre. 1992. *Le Sacre du citoyen: Histoire du suffrage universel en France*. Paris: Gallimard.

Rosenband, Leonard N. 1999. "Social Capital in the Early Industrial Revolution." *Journal of Interdisciplinary History* 29: 435–58.

Rosenberg, Harriet G. 1988. *A Negotiated World: Three Centuries of Change in a French Alpine Community*. Toronto: University of Toronto Press.

References

Rougerie, Jacques. 1964. *Procès des Communards.* Paris: Julliard.

_____. 1971. *Paris libre 1871.* Paris: Seuil.

Rubin, Jeffrey W. 1997. *Decentering the Regime: Ethnicity, Radicalism, and Democracy in Juchitán, Mexico.* Durham: Duke University Press.

Rucht, Dieter, and Ruud Koopmans, eds. 1999. "Protest Event Analysis." *Mobilization* 4, no. 2, entire issue.

Rucht, Dieter, Ruud Koopmans, and Friedhelm Neidhardt, eds. 1998. *Acts of Dissent: New Developments in the Study of Protest.* Berlin: Sigma.

Rueschemeyer, Dietrich, Evelyne Huber Stephens, and John D. Stephens. 1992. *Capitalist Development and Democracy.* Chicago: University of Chicago Press.

Ruff, Julius R. 2001. *Violence in Early Modern Europe, 1500–1800.* Cambridge: Cambridge University Press.

Ruffieux, Roland. 1986. "La Suisse des Radicaux, 1848–1914." In Jean-Claude Fayez, ed., *Nouvelle Histoire de la Suisse et des Suisses.* Lausanne: Payot.

Rule, James B., and Charles Tilly. 1972. "1830 and the Un-Natural History of Revolution." *Journal of Social Issues* 28: 49–76.

Russell, Conrad. 1971. *The Crisis of Parliaments: English History 1509–1660.* Oxford: Oxford University Press.

Sauter, Beat Walter. 1972. *Herkunft und Entstehung der Tessiner Kantonsverfassung von 1830.* Zurich: Schulthess.

Schultz, Patrick. 1982. *La Décentralisation administrative dans le département du Nord (1790–1793).* Lille: Presses Universitaires de Lille.

Schumpeter, Joseph A. 1942. *Capitalism, Socialism, and Democracy.* New York: Harper & Brothers.

Scott, Jonathan. 2000. *England's Troubles: Seventeenth-Century English Political Instability in European Context.* Cambridge: Cambridge University Press.

Scott, William. 1973. *Terror and Repression in Revolutionary Marseilles.* New York: Barnes & Noble.

Shapiro, Gilbert, and John Markoff. 1998. *Revolutionary Demands: A Content Analysis of the Cahiers de Doléances of 1789.* Stanford, Calif.: Stanford University Press.

_____. 2001. "Officially Solicited Petitions: The *Cahiers de Doléances* as a Historical Source." In Lex Heerma van Voss, ed., "Petitions in Social History." *International Review of Social History,* Supplement 9: 79–106.

Sheller, Mimi. 2000. *Democracy after Slavery: Black Publics and Peasant Radicalism in Haiti and Jamaica,* Warwick University Caribbean Studies. London: Macmillan.

Shorter, Edward, and Charles Tilly. 1973. "Les Vagues de grèves en France." *Annales; Economies, Sociétés, Civilisations* 28: 857–87.

_____. 1974. *Strikes in France, 1830–1968.* Cambridge: Cambridge University Press.

Smith, Angel. 2000. "The Corporatist Threat and the Overthrow of the Spanish Second Republic." In John Garrard, Vera Tolz, and Ralph White, eds., *European Democratization since 1800.* New York: St. Martin's.

Solnick, Steven L. 1998. *Stealing the State: Control and Collapse in Soviet Institutions.* Cambridge, Mass.: Harvard University Press.

Sørensen, Georg. 1998. *Democracy and Democratization: Processes and Prospects in a Changing World.* Boulder, Colo.: Westview.

275

Steinberg, Jonathan. 1996. *Why Switzerland?*, 2nd ed. Cambridge: Cambridge University Press.

Stone, Bailey. 1981. *The Parlement of Paris, 1774–1789*. Chapel Hill: University of North Carolina Press.

Stone, Lawrence, ed. 1994. *An Imperial State at War: Britain from 1689 to 1815*. London: Routledge.

Suny, Ronald Grigor. 1993. *The Revenge of the Past: Nationalism, Revolution, and the Collapse of the Soviet Union*. Stanford, Calif.: Stanford University Press.

———. 1995. "Ambiguous Categories: States, Empires, and Nations." *Post-Soviet Affairs* 11: 185–96.

Suter, Andreas. 1997. *Der Schweizerische Bauernkrieg von 1653: Politische Sozialgeschichte – Sozialgeschichte eines politischen Erieignisses*. Tübingen: Bibliothetca Academica Verlag.

Sutherland, D. M. G. 1982. *The Chouans: The Social Origins of Popular Counter-Revolution in Upper Brittany, 1770–1796*. Oxford: Clarendon.

Tanner, Albert. 1982. *Spulen – Weben – Sticken: Die Industrialisierung in Appenzell Ausserrhoden*. Zurich: Juris Druck.

Tarrow, Sidney. 1998. *Power in Movement*, 2nd ed. Cambridge: Cambridge University Press.

Tilly, Charles. 1982. "Britain Creates the Social Movement." In James Cronin and Jonathan Schneer, eds., *Social Conflict and the Political Order in Modern Britain*. London: CroomHelm.

———. 1986. *The Contentious French*. Cambridge, Mass.: Harvard University Press.

———. 1995. *Popular Contention in Great Britain, 1758–1834*. Cambridge, Mass.: Harvard University Press.

———. 1997. "Parliamentarization of Popular Contention in Great Britain, 1758–1834." *Theory and Society* 26: 245–73.

———. 1998. *Durable Inequality*. Berkeley: University of California Press.

———. 2001a. "Historical Analysis of Political Processes." In Jonathan H. Turner, ed., *Handbook of Sociological Theory*. New York: Kluwer/Plenum.

———. 2001b. "Mechanisms in Political Processes." *Annual Review of Political Science* 4: 21–41.

———. 2002a. "Event Catalogs as Theories." *Sociological Theory* 20: 248–54.

———. 2002b. *Stories, Identities, and Political Change*. Lanham, Md.: Rowman & Littlefield.

———. 2003a. "Changing Forms of Inequality." *Sociological Theory* 21: 31–36.

———. 2003b. "Inequality, Democratization, and De-Democratization." *Sociological Theory* 21: 37–43.

———. 2003c. *The Politics of Collective Violence*. Cambridge: Cambridge University Press.

———. 2003d. "When Do (and Don't) Social Movements Promote Democratization?" In Pedro Ibarra, ed., *Social Movements and Democracy*. New York: Palgrave.

Tilly, Charles, and Lesley Wood. 2003. "Contentious Connections in Great Britain, 1828–1834." In Mario Diani and Doug McAdam, eds., *Social Movements and Networks: Relational Approaches to Collective Action*. New York: Oxford University Press.

References

Tilly, Charles, Louise A. Tilly, and Richard Tilly. 1975. *The Rebellious Century, 1830–1930*. Cambridge, Mass.: Harvard University Press.

Tishkov, Valery. 1997. *Ethnicity, Nationalism and Conflict in and after the Soviet Union: The Mind Aflame*. London: Sage.

———. 1999. "Ethnic Conflicts in the Former USSR: The Use and Misuse of Typologies and Data." *Journal of Peace Research* 36: 571–91.

Tocqueville, Alexis de. 1983. *Correspondance d'Alexis de Tocqueville et de Francisque de Corcelle*, vol. 15. Paris: Gallimard. Oeuvres Complètes.

———. 1991. *Oeuvres*, vol. 1, André Jardin, ed. Paris: Gallimard.

Tolz, Vera. 2000. "Russia's Democratic Transition and Its Challenges." In John Garrard, Vera Tolz, and Ralph White, eds., *European Democratization since 1800*. New York: St. Martin's.

Townshend, Charles. 1995. "The Culture of Paramilitarism in Ireland." In Martha Crenshaw, ed., *Terrorism in Context*. University Park: Pennsylvania State University Press.

Traugott, Mark, ed. 1995. *Repertoires and Cycles of Collective Action*. Durham, N.C.: Duke University Press.

Trechsel, Alexander. 2000. *Feuerwerk Volksrechte: Die Volksabstimmungen in den scheizerischen Kantonen 1970–1996*. Basel: Helbing & Lichtenhahn.

Trotsky, Leon. 1965. *The History of the Russian Revolution*. London: Victor Gollancz.

Vanhanen, Tatu. 2000. "A New Dataset for Measuring Democracy, 1810–1998." *Journal of Peace Research* 37: 251–65.

Varese, Federico. 2000. "Pervasive Corruption." In Alena Ledeneva and Marina Kurkchiyan, eds., *Economic Crime in Russia*. The Hague: Kluwer Law International.

———. 2001. *The Russian Mafia: Private Protection in a New Market Economy*. Oxford: Oxford University Press.

Vernon, James. 1993. *Politics and the People: A Study in English Political Culture c. 1815–1867*. Cambridge: Cambridge University Press.

Volkov, Vadim. 2002. *Violent Entrepreneurs: The Use of Force in the Making of Russian Capitalism*. Ithaca, N.Y.: Cornell University Press.

Vovelle, Michel, ed. 1987. *Bourgeoisies de province et Révolution*. Grenoble: Presses Universitaires de Grenoble.

de Vries, Jan. 1976. *The Economy of Europe in an Age of Crisis, 1600–1750*. Cambridge: Cambridge University Press.

———. 1984. *European Urbanization, 1500–1800*. Cambridge, Mass.: Harvard University Press.

de, Vries, Jan, and Ad van der Woude. 1997. *The First Modern Economy: Success, Failure, and Perseverance of the Dutch Economy, 1500–1815*. Cambridge: Cambridge University Press.

Watkins, Susan Cotts. 1990. *From Provinces into Nations*. Princeton: Princeton University Press.

Wells, Charlotte C. 1995. *Law and Citizenship in Early Modern France*. Baltimore: Johns Hopkins University Press.

Westrich, Sal Alexander. 1972. *The Ormée of Bordeaux: A Revolution during the Fronde*. Baltimore: Johns Hopkins University Press.

Whitehead, Laurence. 2001. "Three International Dimensions of Democratization." In Laurence Whitehead, ed., *The International Dimensions of Democratization*, expanded ed. Oxford: Oxford University Press.

Wiegandt, Ellen. 1992. "The Jura Question: A Challenge to Swiss Ethnic Peace." In David Howell, Gert von Pistohlkors, and Ellen Wiegandt, eds., *Roots of Rural Ethnic Mobilisation*. New York: New York University Press.

Wirtschafter, Elise Kimerling. 1997. *Social Identity in Imperial Russia*. DeKalb: Northern Illinois University Press.

Woloch, Isser. 1970. *Jacobin Legacy: The Democratic Movement under the Directory*. Princeton: Princeton University Press.

———. 1994. *The New Regime. Transformations of the French Civic Order, 1789–1820s*. New York: Norton.

Woodruff, David. 1999. *Money Unmade: Barter and the Fate of Russian Capitalism*. Ithaca, N.Y.: Cornell University Press.

Wylie, Laurence, ed. 1966. *Chanzeaux: A Village in Anjou*. Cambridge, Mass.: Harvard University Press.

Wyrsch, Paul. 1983. *Der Kanton Schwyz äusseres Land 1831–1833*. Lachen: Gutenberg. Schwyzer Hefte, vol. 28.

Yashar, Deborah J. 1997. *Demanding Democracy: Reform and Reaction in Costa Rica and Guatemala, 1870s–1950s*. Stanford, Calif.: Stanford University Press.

Zaret, David. 2000. *Origins of Democratic Culture: Printing, Petitions, and the Public Sphere in Early-Modern England*. Princeton: Princeton University Press.

Index

Index

House of Lords, 151; forestalling of Catholic Emancipation by, 151; Irish home rule and, 160; passing of Catholic Emancipation by, 152

Hundred Days, 100

Hungary: discrimination against, by Romania, 232; Freedom House analysis of, 209, 210; internal conflict in, 216

Hunt, Lynn, 106

Huntington, Samuel P., 11, 12

Iberia: Carlist wars of 1833–39, 88; Catalonia and, 89; centralization of, 82–83; claim making in, 87; coercion power in, 82; colonization efforts of, 82; contention in, 89; de-democratization in, 240; democratic viability of, 250; 1850–2000, 232, 236; expulsion of Muslims in, 82; farming in, 83; forbidden contention in, 87–88; government capacity of, 82–83, 238; history of, 70; internal conflicts of, 83–84; local struggles in, 89–90; local vengeance in, 84; low-capacity government of, 167; military in, 83, 89, 91–92; military intervention in, 236; performances in, 84; political history of, 81; popular contention in, 86–87; post-1793, 83; pre-1793, 83; protected consultation in, 87; rebellions in, 88; revolution of 1848, 84; revolution of 1820–23, 88; revolutionary situations in, 88; revolutionary situations of, 85–86, 89; royalist rising of 1922–23, 88; in 17th century, 81–82; state path of, 54; tolerated contention in, 87–88; transition in, 82; U.S. military presence as external party, 237; violence in, 88; vs. Eastern Europe, 81; vs. Low Countries, 47–48; vs. Russia and Balkans, 217

Iceland, Freedom House analysis of, 209

ideal-case reasoning, 39

identities: in Brabant, 77; citizenship and, 61; contention and, 60; contentious, 63; democratization and, 60; detached, 59, 68; embedded, 59, 63; embedded vs. detached, 59–60; government capacity and, 63; movement, 61; political, 59, 65; religious, 200–201; in undemocratic politics, 61

income, governmental stability and, 250

India, 6; activism in, 244; colonization of, 243; religious exclusion in, 256

Indian National Congress, 244

indigenous populations: enslavement of, 243; extermination of, 243; extermination of American, 244; ghettoization of, 243

indirect rule, 49; in Africa, 49; origin of, 49–50; popular associations and, 127; war and, 109

industrialization: in France, 2; in France and England, 28; 19th-century, 78; rural, 188; in Switzerland, 187

Inglis, R. H., anti-Catholic petition of, 153–154

intermediaries, 107; elimination of, 120

international relations, 256–257

Iraq, Freedom House analysis of, 209

Ireland, 28; in 1650, 42; agricultural workers in, 166; agriculture in, 137; casualties in, 160; civil war in, 138, 161; conscription in, 161; democratization of, 34, 164; disease in, 135; dissidents of, 6; dissolution of parliament in, 149; emigration from, 136; Freedom House analysis of, 209; German support of, 160; in House of Commons, 143;

291

Index